LIBRARY/NEW ENGLAND INST. OF TECHNOLOGY
P9-DGX-904

Death, Bereavement, and Mourning

Samuel Heilman
editor

Death, Bereavement, and Mourning

Transaction Publishers
New Brunswick (U.S.A.) and London (U.K.)

This book is printed on acid-free paper that meets the American National Standard for Permanence of Paper for Printed Library Materials.

Library of Congress Catalog Number: 2004058009
ISBN: 0-7658-0278-3
Printed in the United States of America

Library of Congress Cataloging-in-Publication Data

Death, bereavement, and mourning / Samuel Heilman, editor.
p. cm.
Includes bibliographical references.
ISBN 0-7658-0278-3
1. Death—Psychological aspects—Congresses. 2. Bereavement—Psychological aspect—Congresses. I. Heilman, Samuel C.

BF789.D4D348 2005
155.9'37—dc22 2004058009

To the memory of all those who died in the 9/11/2001 attacks

Contents

1

Introduction

Samuel Heilman

Faith, as anthropologist Clifford Geertz has written, "sustains, cures, comforts, redresses wrongs, improves fortune, secures rewards, explains, obligates, blesses, clarifies, reconciles, regenerates, redeems, or saves," when it manages to work for those who have it.[1] The human encounter with death is often precisely the occasion when the bereaved need to be sustained in their loss, cured of the anxiety that the meeting with death engenders, and comforted in their grief. It is a time when they often seek to redress wrongs in themselves or in the relationships that death has shaken and upset. In both the collective and individual responses to the trauma of encountering death, we discover efforts to counter the misfortune and to explain the meaning of the loss, to turn memory into blessing, to reconcile life with death, to regenerate life, and redeem or save both the bereaved, and in some ways, the dead. And often, it is the brush with death that moves those who are bereaved but have survived to take on new and often solemn obligations.

Sometimes these obligations transform the bereaved and mourning in ways that lead to growth and maturity; other times they lead to unremitting anger or melancholia. The repercussions of either of these reactions are significant for they largely shape the life for those who have survived, either for good or for bad. But in either event, the starting point is death and bereavement. This is no less true for individuals as for groups.

Given these parallels between the elements of faith and the response to death and bereavement, it is therefore no surprise that even those who have no or little contact with matters spiritual often find themselves turning to faith or something that they often call "the spiritual" when confronted by death that has touched them personally. Nor is it surprising to find that some scholars argue that concern with and response to death is among the primordial elements and core concerns of the spirit, and a kind of deep wellspring of religion. Religion or spiritual notions often emerge as powerful influences in the life after death. They play a part in constructing meaning out of grief, human suffering, and ultimately death. This too can lead to maturity and growth or, it can lead to obsession and a desire to fantasize. The bereaved and grief stricken look to religion to somehow solve the problem of death, to "cure" its cause, to defeat it. Faith can accomplish this when it leads to a belief in an afterlife or sees meaning in a life lived but lost. Yet religion can also lead to what Robert Lifton in this volume has called an "apocalyptic face-off," the fear of vulnerability that a brush with death engenders and that leads to a desire to purify life by hastening the end, heaven on earth.

To be sure, there are a variety of religious or spiritual expressions—some steeped in tradition, others unique and new—that the bereaved and mourning experience in their time of loss, but there appear to be some common elements in all of them. Among these are an intensified self-awareness, a fear of or at least an anxiety about the propinquity of death and dead bodies (at its most rudimentary, a feeling that death is somehow contagious and rapacious, still hungry for more) and a sense of vulnerability. In time, these feelings, once their chaotic overtones have been stilled, also may become transformed into a growing exploration of the spiritual, a profound sense of rebirth, newfound feelings of self-mastery or confidence, and a deeply held conviction that "life goes on." At the personal level, the aftermath of death often brings as well that religious experience that William James called "the individual pinch of destiny," which moves the bereaved to ask the most existential of questions: "Who am I? What am I supposed to do? What is to become of me? Where does finality lie?"[2]

While the answers to these questions are by no means simple or unequivocal, the asking of them is in fact an expression of and often the stimulus for even more spiritual reflection, which may in time expand and grow increasingly complex. Indeed, one often finds that the close encounter with death, the feelings of bereavement, and the process of mourning lead for some to an intensified devotion toward their own religious traditions (ironically, even among many who have otherwise become alienated from or remained ignorant of those traditions). For others, it may be expressed by a shift from no spiritual commitment to a devout spiritual life.

Most often, although surely not always, I have found that established religious traditions are the receptacles for the spiritual transformations engendered by death, bereavement, and mourning. This should not come as a surprise to students of religion; for both in so-called "primitive" and "modern" cultures, among the most widespread occasions for turning to traditional religion and ritual are the encounters with death. The way the body is disposed of, the processes of separation from the dead, and the practices of mourning to which the bereaved turn are frequently those that are time-honored, wrapped in mystery and tradition. The comfort or at the very least the spiritual and practical shelter these offer is often in their capacity to transform the chaos of death into the order of continuity. The fear of death subsides as the anxiety of bereavement gives way to the relative calm of mourning, which turns in time to a sense of renewal.

While what I have described here operates at the personal level—an area that is certainly worthy of more investigation—the aftermath of the events of September 11 demonstrated that this turn to the spiritual functioned at the collective level as well. It did not matter who those who lost family members or loved ones in the disasters of that day were, the entire nation (and certainly the people of New York) were devastated. All felt bereaved; all were grief stricken. And the collective response stimulated an outpouring of spiritual expression—or at the very least a public display of a turn toward spirituality. It was as if the occasion of the death and bereavement of so many at once created a mirror that forced all of those who had survived—and everyone who felt touched by the loss felt like a survivor—to reflect not only on the lives lived and lost but also on essential existential questions of what is most meaningful in life. Perhaps nothing more vividly articulated this than the featured obituaries in the *New York Times* or the memorial service held at New York's Yankee Stadium. This service, a collective expression of a multiplex spirituality in which a variety of religious traditions of mourning were played out, was held in a "temple" of the physical. As such it transformed that place from a location where baseball is played into an outdoor cathedral where the dead had the power to raise the living to a new consciousness of the sanctity of life. Imams, rabbis, ministers, priests, public officials, celebrities, and the bereaved shared in a spiritual experience that was at once rooted in traditional expressions of particularistic religion while also expressing a kind of universalistic civil religion—and the place of peanuts and Cracker Jack became the place of prayer and memorializations. Spirit triumphed over flesh; spirituality trumped physicality.

This gathering was unusual but by no means unique. The practice of public reflection and memorialization, the lighting of candles, the sanctification of space and time has occurred in many places where death touches the collective. Thus at the site of assassination of public leaders or figures, where mass death has occurred, or even at the place where an accident has resulted in sudden death, one repeatedly discovers signs of monuments and memorials that are nothing less than exercises in spiritual symbolization, markers left behind to not only note a death but also remind all who see them of the spiritual experience of bereavement in which they may thereby share. Whether at bombed cafes in Jerusalem, at Ground Zero in Manhattan, at Dealy Plaza in Dallas where John Kennedy was killed, or Central Park in New York near John Lennon's murder or the renamed Yitzhak Rabin Square in Tel Aviv or even along the interstates where car fatalities have occurred, we have all seen the often spontaneous memorials, the candles, the offerings, the signs that remind us that the spiritual overwhelmed the mundane here. In a sense one might argue that these sorts of spiritual transformation constitute the beginning of the healing and regeneration that begins within the mourning experience.

But the events of 9/11 and their reminder of our vulnerability as well as the ever-lurking presence of death and destruction that can intrude upon life even from a blue, cloudless sky on a glorious autumn day may also lead to (and have) a descent into the culture of death. Death can beget more death if its does not lead to reconciliation, regeneration, and rebirth. In the aftermath of 9/11, we have seen healing but also war, comfort but also increased insecurity and terror, enhanced collective memory but also a sense of collective dread. We have looked forward to a sense of peace, but we have also seen intimations of Armageddon. And we have seen expressions of unending bereavement, of dead and death that cannot be laid to rest, at least not yet.

Geertz tells us that "the communal dimensions of religious change, the ones you can (sometimes) read about in the newspapers are underresearched, the personal ones, those you have (usually) to talk to living people in order to encounter, are barely researched at all."[3]

This volume, and the conference out of which it grew, makes an effort to see what we can learn in the aftermath of those devastating events of September 11, 2001 about both the personal and the collective response.

Our approach is interdisciplinary because we know there is no single view that can provide understanding of so complex a set of experiences. Some of the chapters here are by psychiatrists and psychologists—both those who are clinicians and those who deal with collective experience. The papers draw as well from the disciplinary perspectives of the historian, sociologist, literary critic, folklorist, anthropologist, social worker, theologian, poet, and undertaker. Each has something essential to teach us about what we can learn as we reflect on 9/11, and its death and bereavement. Death, bereavement, and mourning have multiple meanings.

Thomas Lynch, poet and undertaker, tells how much we need to take our leave of a body; no matter how broken and devastated, for, as he puts it, "we cannot let go of what we do not hold." That lesson is central to the pain that so many of those who lost loved ones in the disaster but were never able to take leave of their bodies, and accordingly who may not yet have been able to let go. These are people who are still trapped with their missing others, waiting for the disaster to end. Those who have lost control over their dead in some sense, he shows us, have likewise lost control over their lives.

There is an irony in this, Lynch tells us, since so many Americans have become so uncomfortable with the funerary caskets and dispatch the dead with a minimum of contact with the remains. Hence an understanding of this lesson from the missing bodies of 9/11 tells us, perhaps, that we have needs in mourning that we have allowed to remain unfulfilled for too long. We need to learn how to make the missing dead and stop allowing the dead to go missing. That, Lynch tells us, is what will allow us "to grieve in meaningful and manageable ways."

Peter Metcalf asks a more fundamental question, comparing our response to death of the Nyakyusa of Tanzania, for whom the encounter is fraught not only with sorrow but a fear "that unquiet ghosts will bring more deaths." That, however, Metcalf asserts is not our fear in the wake of 9/11. Ours is a fear, he suggests, born of incomprehension—"we understood that the attack had deep political significance, but we did not, and do not, understand what that significance is." Accordingly, we do not know how to respond, and that "exasperates" us. Yet that exasperation is precisely what Metcalf finds valuable for it forces us to maintain the search for meaning.

Folklorist Ilana Harlow, in her consideration of the shrines and memorials following the attacks, shows us the popular expression of the quest for meaning and remembrance. She reminds us as well that, "bodies are important components of rites of passage. The presence of a corpse at funerary rites is necessary not only for the psychological purpose of making death real to the bereaved, but is also necessary for transition rites to be performed, for the dead to be incorporated into the hereafter. Without a body there are no funerals, only memorial services." But she also tells us how so much of what the shrines that emerged—including even the anthropomorphization of the twin towers themselves—were an effort on the part of the living to avoid the natural tendency to forget, telling us that, "creativity counters the destructiveness of death." The creations include everything from tattoos to shrines. In effect, her description and analysis of the various mementos and reminders of the dead and the disaster show how the living go on living and the dead go on living with them. This is particularly striking when she describes how certain mourners chose "to be inscribed with names or portraits of loved ones," thereby "incorporating their dead (or their sweethearts) into themselves." Beyond this, she shows us how the mementoes and shrines became the enduring expressions of how the dead go on living with the living. This is particularly important since in the aftermath of 9/11, as Harlow explains, "the plurality of Death was so overwhelming as to threaten awareness of its singularity." That was why, she argues, the New York City fire department abandoned the idea of doing a single memorial service for all the dead and chose instead to arrange individual funerals and memorials.

There are mementoes of grief itself, something extraordinarily important perhaps because there remain so many missing victims. Here the process of collective memorialization becomes especially important, but there is always a risk of these becoming fetishistic images or, what some might argue are even worse, expressions that verge on kitsch. This does not require only massive monuments; small items have served in some cases as touching mementi mori—and anyone who has seen the pile of shoes in the Holocaust memorial in Washington, D.C. and felt its power to recall the murdered millions cannot deny this. Yet the question of what makes an effective monument—particularly for an event of the social and cultural proportions of 9/11—is an enormous challenge, as Harlow's descriptions show us. Moreover, it is a challenge whose aim is to make the dead alive again, an expression of mourning's mental and imaginative labor. But, there is no less a risk that in the dissemination of this memory, indifference may overtake even the impetus to memorialize. Hence, the ultimate challenge of 9/11 memorializing is to provoke thoughts of revitalization and metamorphosis rather than indifference.

Psychiatrist and anthropologist Henry Abramovitch suggests that ironically it is the many missing, and the inability of those whom they have bereaved to fully mourn them, that insures that 9/11 memorialization will not devolve into indifference. The memorials have the capacity, he argues, to transform the "bad death" of 9/11—with its brutality and unexpectedness—into something closer to a "good death." He sees much that has transpired since 9/11, and that will likely emerge as the space called Ground Zero is restored, as being something like the end of the provisional and liminal period in which the bereaved nation (and the many who have not completed or even begun their mourning) now find themselves, more than two years after the disaster. He crafts his argument by looking at a wide variety of rites of mourning, and demonstrates that we who still grieve after 9/11 are repeating some fundamental archetypes of culture.

Carrying on with this perspective, Eliezer Witztum, Ruth Malkinson, and Shalom Rubin explain why some of these objects and memorials—as described by Harlow—can serve as essential aids to the psychology of dealing with the trauma and pain of bereavement. Via these objects and memorials, the bereaved find a way of holding on to the missing and the dead, and of reconstructing their lives and making sense out of them. And that is something that each family and each person who felt the grief and pain of loss needed to do by themselves.

This, however, had unintended consequences, some of which we discover in reading Warren Spielberg's personally revealing piece. Spielberg, working as a therapist and counselor in a Brooklyn firehouse, shows us the way in which these new American heroes were often overcome with survivor guilt. Not only the various memorials for the firefighters, but no less the realization of their absence created ripples of grief. He provides an insider's look, coupled with the insights of a working psychologist who has provided the survivors with therapy, at how much the absent firefighters still constitute a presence—"ghosts" he calls them—in the lives of their fellows. He too, like Thomas Lynch, informs how the absence of the dead bodies of their fallen comrades plays upon the hearts and minds of those left behind, and how the absent dead can be a far harder burden to carry than anyone else that these firefighters have had to hold in their arms. As Ilana Harlow poetically captures it: "Death is an embodiment of the philosophical problem of the one and the many."

Paul C. Rosenblatt reminds us that grief is not simply an individual experience, although in the individualism that is so much a part of the American experience it sometimes seems that is all it is. But, Rosenblatt shows us how we can look at the events in the aftermath of 9/11 and discover how much grief and bereavement mean to the family. The destinies and behaviors of people linked together in the family are so interwoven that the loss of one has repercussions for all the others, often in ways that are unexpected and not always realized for those who become bereaved. His argument that "if one loses a co-worker who nobody else in the family knew, can still become a family grief," is particularly relevant to the realities following 9/11/2001. So many of the survivors of that day who lost co-workers, or even who felt the loss of people who shared the building with them, experienced a bereavement that often changed the nature of what went on in the survivors' families. The sadness and sense of loss—often inexplicable in the quotidian logic—nevertheless played a role in unexpected ways, as Rosenblatt hints, when families either tried to "ignore the individual's grief, try to suppress it, or try to connect with it." In fact, Rosenblatt provides a key for seeing the nearly endless ripples of reaction to bereavement and felt grief in so many aspects of family life that it enables us all to see why the disaster continued to reverberate in the seemingly protected environment of the family. He shows us how it was possible for an attack on the American nation and people to be felt as a wound in the family life of Americans. As such he offers us information that may not cure the pain of the loss but by explaining where it comes from mitigate some of its anguish. Now we know why we felt what we did in situations and settings so far from "Ground Zero."

Rosenblatt tells us as well how important it is to articulate the various meanings that such losses have for the family. Talking about what the attacks and the consequent losses represent to us as a family—nationally and in our individual families—is clearly not just therapeutic; it is essential to what we often call "closure." In a sense, this volume and the conference on which it is based, is part of that process. One of the most remarkable things about what began as an academic effort to use the first anniversary of the 9/11 disaster as an opportunity to reflect upon and understand what we could learn about death, bereavement, and mourning is that participants at the conference drew more than simply academic knowledge from the papers and the sessions. In fact, in a way far beyond any other academic conference in which I had ever participated, the gathering took on characteristics of a therapeutic assembly. People came not only to learn but also to articulate the meaning of the event for themselves and for the New York family. Set against the backdrop of a plethora of commemorative happenings throughout the New York area, and indeed the nation, the conference became symbolic and significant not only for its content but also for its expression. It was a family gathering of mourners and their consolers during what was both informative and therapeutic, an educational and socially healing experience among survivors. This volume then continues that dual character; it provides understanding and "family meanings." But, as Rosenblatt reminds us, "the family process of meaning making is not necessarily easy or comfortable. People may disagree strongly." Moreover, he tells us there are often "tensions over who is most bereaved, who most deserves sympathy, whose needs, beliefs, feelings, and memories should take precedence, who should have the primary role in speaking about the loss for the family or in making decisions about rituals and memorials." No less in these papers, not all of which look at the meaning of the events in the same way, will we find that to be true.

That is certainly an underlying theme of the chapter written by Witztum, Malkinson, and Rubin who remind us of the very important cultural differences in how people relate to death and bereavement. Drawing on their understanding of the Israeli experience, they raise the both the wider context and the specific American framework within which we need to consider the events of 9/11 and what they have taught us about death, bereavement, and mourning. They also suggest that the grief, bereavement and mourning that have emerged since then have many of the same characteristics as post-traumatic stress syndrome. As they argue, "the grief in the face of a catastrophic and unexpected event is not simply grief that can resolve itself into mourning; it is trauma that abides or at least lasts longer." Moreover, as they suggest, the trauma, like the sense of loss, is not limited to those who have actually lost a family member or loved one but in effect touches the entire society of those they call "passive participants," people who feel bonded to the grief by sharing in a national trauma from which it resulted (the clinical elements of this are actually provided).

What Witztum, Malkinson, and Rubin are telling us is that in events of such massive national proportions as the attacks of 9/11 or the Israeli experiences of terror during the Intifada, grief, loss, and trauma become intertwined in ways that have complex psychological dimensions that researchers will have to examine in new ways and that therapists may have to deal with in novel approaches—something that Robert Niemayer and Warren Spielberg demonstrate has already begun. Moreover, as Witztum, Malkinson, and Rubin tell us, they have forced us to reassess the psychological truism that those bereaved who are "endlessly" attached to the dead are pathological in their grieving. After all, much of this is really part of the national expression of vengeance and mourning, abetted by the fact that so many were killed and so many remain missing.

In his consideration of the trauma of 9/11 in the case of one grieving relative who experienced much of this, psychologist and therapist Robert Neimeyer frames an account, both abundant in detail and analysis, which allows the reader to enter into the tragedy and feel the transformation it has wreaked. This is an instance of what he and others call "complicated grief." He shows the reader how even such grief that is connected to horror and helplessness ultimately can allow for transformations that lead to "hope and healing."

Neimeyer tells us that part of this process requires people to construct and reconstruct themselves in the framework of a narrative of healing. These narratives suggest that there is some moral sense to life, something that leads beyond random acts of violence. For some people religion may help shape this narrative, but as Neimeyer shows us, the narrative is not limited only to those whose lives are guided by traditional faith. There is more than one way to arrive at some teleological conclusion. But, as he explains, the events of 9/11 have presented a powerful challenge to this need to construct a moral and teleological narrative. At the national level, the president has tried to offer a narrative in which the American people emerge stronger and unbowed when the time for grief has past. At the individual and familial level, however, each of the bereaved needs to construct that story for him or her self and place themselves in its triumphant, transformative, high moral ending. That is not always easy, particularly when the death one mourns was the result of events or actions that undermine a view of the world that was part of one's narrative of how the world is.

Those who lost loved ones in the 9/11 events and who until then believed in tolerance, beneficence, justice, and a benevolent divinity or moral universe, for example, were—as "Sara" the mourner whose experience Neimeyer describes—doubly bereaved. They lost not only their loved one, but also an accepted order or "assumptive world." Both consequences required transformation and "meaning-making" of prodigious proportions. How survivors reconstructed life with a "decimated system of meaning" that had heretofore provided them with orientation is what concerns Neimeyer. And what he finds and describes is "growth through grief."

Neimeyer sees in 9/11 and its aftermath the capacity of the bereaved, no matter what their background or beliefs, to "harness" the considerable power of ritual to help them reconstruct the narrative of their lives. Like so many of the others in this volume, he enlarges the reader's respect for the great importance of ritual helping us to come to terms with death—no matter how devastating its presence or form. It is the order of life that responds to the chaos of death.

Chaos also concerns Neil Gillman, who is disturbed by the difficulty that the suffering of 9/11 and its aftermath engendered in the capacity of his theology to reassert the order of his faith. It is not the presence of evil in the world that surprises him, but it is its growing weight in the balance of power that causes his despair in the capacity of theology to help reassert a moral order in the face of the chaos of death brought about by evil intentions. Reminding us that "the data of experience are never perceived in a totally objective way; we see what we want to see, what we are prepared to see, what we have been educated to see, what we already believe we are going to see," Gillman argues that often the theologies that frame or even define what we see as chaos and establish an order are inextricably tied up with who we are or understand ourselves to be. For moderns, the old answers and traditional ways of looking at the world may be insufficient for dealing with the evils that have befallen humanity in the last few generations. The events of 9/11 have reminded us, once again, and quite insistently that this is the case.

He shows us as well how ritual helps us in this process of regaining order out of chaos, giving us a better understanding of the religious and theological motivations behind the plethora of ritual-like activities that were no less ubiquitous than the memorials that marked the aftermath of 9/11.

For Charles Strozier, the aftermath of 9/11 turns our thoughts to the apocalyptic violence that is so much a part of what he calls "the new terrorism" that is part of the new twenty-first century. We are not bystanders to this because given the scale of the destruction and the target of the attacks, we in the United States—and perhaps all of those who share in Western civilization—have shared in a collective trauma. In articulating his "thoughts on apocalyptic violence," Strozier takes issue with those who do not recognize that the disaster of 9/11/2001 "changed everything." The import of the impact of that day, its events and aftermath, he argues, comes "in part because of the scale of the death that occurred, in part due to the form of the dying, and in part due to the psychological shock of it all."

Strozier takes us into what he calls the "zones of sadness" and allows us to hear that shock as he shares the accounts of survivors, whose descriptions still echo with the trauma and confusion that the death and destruction engendered. These are voices that are striking not for their articulate metaphors or poetic accounts, but instead for the inarticulateness of their astonishment, so real and unvarnished. They remind us of how death and bereavement may begin as little more than a cry from heart, a scream in the dark.

He shows us that the affects of death are related to how close one is to it, arguing that New Yorkers had a different experience. But of course, as Strozier's paper makes clear, "closeness" is an ambiguous concept—for it conflates the physical and the emotional. The zones of sadness he has described are not just places on the ground; they are also areas in consciousness. As such bereavement and mourning are also subject to the same ambiguities and those who experience them are in a variety places. Indeed, his paper allows readers who were not there to get closer. He explains how the attacks on the twin towers, New York, and one should add the Pentagon, "rocked the ground of our being," and undermined our sense of invincibility. This of course is precisely what death always does to life, and it is an important and anxiety-provoking element of bereavement. As Strozier tells us that the terrorism that attacked America has "been everywhere in the world," so he is in a way reminding us that so too have death, bereavement, and mourning. The events of 9/11 and their aftermath have only reminded us of this existential truth, albeit in a profoundly disturbing and traumatic way.

Strozier connects all this with the idea of apocalypticism, and what he calls the "great questions of beginnings and endings." Because of the new terrorism, death in the form of apocalypticism has become an abiding threat, and is also "everywhere in the world"—or at least it feels that way for many people since 9/11. The previously unimaginable and unbelievable have become a part of the contemporary din of death. These echoes continue to fill the air, a lingering reverberation of the explosions of that fateful and world-shattering day. Nuclear, biological, and chemical threats, terror, the apocalypse, and death are now all in the air—or at the very least in the imagination. What once only God could do—the death of all—man can, and might, accomplish. That thought, so much on the mind in the 1950s and again during the darkest days of the Cold War, has risen again from the ashes of 9/11. This, Strozier tells us, instills in us all some of the anxiety of paranoia. Death is perceived paranoically to be around every corner. "A paranoid style takes shape that merges self and world."

In my own concluding chapter, I draw upon the Jewish perspective on death in order to provide a template for understanding how we all can be repaired from the breach that the events of 9/11 and its aftermath have engendered. My argument is that if we are to emerge from all this with confidence and a feeling of increased energy, with a sense that chaos has been vanquished and order restored, bad death turned into good, and collective consciousness healed, we would do well to follow the guidelines provided by Jewish tradition. Judaism reminds us that there *is* something to be done in the face of death, and even in the aftermath of a death like that of 9/11. In this tradition is not only the recognition that we are none of us alone but tied to a collective whole, that when we are bereaved we are not alone in our bereavement, and that death—and particularly mass death such as we experienced on 9/11—has the paradoxical ability to intensify our collective consciousness, our attachments to our community, and our appreciation of life. As Raymond Firth once put it: "The death of every person must be followed by a reaffirmation of the social character of human existence."[4]

These chapters, each in its own voice but in an extraordinary harmony when read together, provide us with an understanding that 9/11 was not simply a day of disaster but also a lesson in death, bereavement, mourning, and memorialization. The brutality, horror, and trauma, which seemed to mark the day and its immediate aftermath, have given way, as these pages observe, to complexity and wonder—even to that sort of affirmation of which Firth writes.

* * *

I want to thank all those who made the conference out of which these reworked papers came: The Graduate Center and the Harold Proshansky Chair in Jewish Studies, generously endowed by the Weiler and Arnow families, James P. Nolan, Jr., Bonnie Tippy, and the New York State Funeral Directors Association, Project Liberty at Ohel, and the Museum of Jewish Heritage. Without their concerted support and encouragement, this all would not be possible. I also want to thank all those in the offices of Public Affairs, Continuing Education, and Special Events who helped in the preparations, including Nan Shaw, Jane House, Barry Disman, Joan Piper Harden, David Levine, David Manning, and their staffs. The president of the Graduate Center at CUNY, Frances Degen Horowitz, has been particularly supportive of the conference and the Proshansky Chair projects. I especially want to offer my gratitude to my assistant Thomas Soehl who has been invaluable in helping me put this all together.

"There are two parties to the suffering that death inflicts," Arnold Toynbee once noted, "and in the apportionment of this suffering, the survivor takes the brunt."[5] I hope this volume will demonstrate that while Toynbee may have been correct about the suffering, he may have missed the point in that the suffering can bring with it growth and understanding. That may be the true consolation.

Notes

1. Clifford Geertz, *Available Light: Anthropological Reflections on Philosophical Topics* (Princeton: Princeton University Press, 2000), p. 178.
2. Ibid., p. 182.
3. Ibid., p. 179.
4. Raymond Firth, *Elements of Social Organization* (London: Henry E. Walter Ltd, 1951), p. 64. See also David G. Mandelbaum, "Social Uses of Funeral Rites," in Herman Feifel, ed., *The Meaning of Death* (New York: McGraw Hill, 1959), p. 189.
5. Arnold Toynbee, *Man's Concern with Death* (London: Hoddard & Stoughton, 1968), p. 271.

2

Local Heroes

Thomas Lynch

Some days the worst that can happen happens.
The sky falls or evil overwhelms or
The world as we have come to know it turns
Towards its eventual apocalypse
Long prefigured in all the holy books.
The end-times of old grudge and grievances
That bring us each to our oblivions.
Still, maybe this is not the end at all,
Nor even the beginning of the end,
Rather, one more in a long list of sorrows
To be added to the ones thus far endured
Through what we have come to call our history—
Another in that bitter litany
That we will, if we survive it, have survived.
God help us who must live through this, alive
To the terror and open wounds: the heart
Torn, the shaken faith, the violent, vengeful soul,
The nerve exposed, the broken body so
Mingled with its breaking that it's lost forever.
Lord, send us in our peril local heroes.
Someone to listen, someone to watch,
Someone to search and wait and keep the careful count
Of the dead and missing, the dead and gone
But not forgotten. Some days all that can be done
Is to salvage one sadness from the mass
Of sadnesses, to bear one body home,
To lay the dead out among their people
Organize the flowers and casseroles

Write the obits, meet the mourners at the door,
Drive the dark procession down through town
Toll the bell, dig the hole, tend the pyre.
It's what we do. The daylong news is dire,
Full of true believers and politicos—
Bold talk of holy war and photo-ops.
But here, brave men and women pick the pieces up
They serve the living tending to the dead.
Here the distant battle is waged in homes.
Like politics, all funerals are local.

That poem was written in the aftermath of September 11, 2001 at the request of John Eirkson and Wilson Beebe and Bonnie Tippy—executive directors of the Pennsylvania, New Jersey, and New York State Funeral Directors Associations—who had asked for something by which to honor the men and women in funeral service in their respective states who volunteered to work at Ground Zero and at that field in Pennsylvania retrieving and returning the dead to their people; and to honor the funeral directors who stayed home and helped to organize and direct the thousands of services that marked the human toll of September 11 almost four years ago.

At about the same time, Wilson Beebe of the New Jersey Funeral Director's Association was fielding a question from some eager journalist about what the cub reporter called the "windfall profits" about to be realized by the funeral industry from the events of September 11. While doctors, nurses, contractors and clergy, mayors and municipal workers, pundits and politicos all worked overtime because of what happened here, it was assumed, at least by this nameless reporter, that everyone but the funeral directors worked long hours for the purest of motives. In September 2002, in an editorial remarkable for its wasted words and precious space in the *New York Times*, Adam Cohen opined that prior to World Com, the "funeral industry had set the standard for venality"—demonstrating yet again that funeral directors, like this writer, are what my wife calls an easy target.

Accustomed as we have become to the cheap shot and sucker punch, I was honored as a funeral director to be asked by Professor Heilman to examine what we have learned about grief and bereavement since those terrible events; and I do so to honor the work that my father did, my sisters and brothers do, and my colleagues and fellow professionals around the country do. It is always good to be among people who, like funeral directors, spend a fair portion of their waking hours and working lives among the sick and suffering, the dying and the dead, the brokenhearted and the ones on the mend because in a way that selling Buicks or Batesville caskets maybe doesn't, the care of our fellow human beings in times of trouble brings us face to face with the existential dilemmas for which there are no easy answers, no ready cures, no sound bites or certain outcomes; face to face with our recognizable but often inexplicable humanity. Such people play in the deep end of the pool where we must sink, swim, or remain afloat on faith, on hope, on the love of family and friends, or the kindness of strangers. It seems our humanity is most engaged at just such times, when the power of our presence, our witness, our willingness to listen to the most difficult and inexplicable facts of life—we love, we grieve, we breed, we disappear—is better medicine than any easy answer.

* * *

Connecting the dots between cause and effect, between expectation and experience, between what we know and what we feel, between what we've heard and what we see makes the ancient and difficult business of bereavement somehow more manageable.

I know this from what I have read and reasoned, from what I have myself experienced and from what I've seen among the saddened and heart-sore, the widowed and bereft with whom I've worked and from whom I've learned so many lessons over the last three decades of my life as a funeral director in Milford, Michigan.

I remember a boy—a man, I suppose, in his twenties—who was killed in a plane crash in 1974 in Alaska. If he had lived he'd be my age now. Everyone knew the casket would have to be closed. The twin-engine aircraft had smashed into a mountain and burned and it was sometime before the body could be recovered. He was in a black pouch, treated with topical chemicals to prevent further putrefaction. The pouch was put into a Ziegler case—a kind of metal box that fit inside the wooden casket. The casket was covered with a spray of carnations with a ribbon that read "Our Beloved Son." Everything was going as it should go. But early in the morning, the day of his funeral, his father came to the funeral home and insisted I show him his son's burnt and broken body. He was not going to bury a body he hadn't seen. And while the odor was offensive and the sight horrendous, the man reacted like the fathers of dead boys

I've seen down the years—with a kind of gratitude that I had returned his son—his darling boy, he called him—who was somehow still lovely to his father even in death. And I remember the mother of a girl kidnapped from the car in my town's Central Park where she was parked necking with her boyfriend on an autumn evening. It was six months later that her body was found, buried in a shallow grave to which the authorities were lead by the aberrant man who tied her boyfriend to a tree and took her away and after he'd had his way with her, pitched her in the little trench he dug out in a field not a mile from her home. "Are you going to tell me I can't see my daughter?" this broken woman asked me. She'd been advised by her pastor, by her parents, by her former spouse, by anyone and everyone to "remember her the way she was." Truth told I was hoping their counsel would prevail. But she was insisting. And I was equivocating, hoping that cooler heads would prevail. But in the end I told her that if that was the only way she could be certain, if seeing meant believing for her, I'd be with her when she looked. What I saw was a mess—a badly decomposed approximation of something only remotely human. What the girl's mother saw was a girl, gone these long months, badly mistreated and now returned. She did not smell rotten flesh or see the skull beneath the skin but saw enough of her daughters hair, and enough of her ankle tattoo and enough of the shape and size of it all to be sure that the body was hers. And being sure, she covered her in her own bed clothes, had us put her in a wood box and, after the prayers and lamentations, had the body burned and the ashes buried with her great grandparents in the family plot.

We cannot let go of what we do not hold. We cannot take leave of what we do not have. And with the massive sadness of 2001, the following years of mourning are made all the more sad by the fact that, like the Famine dead in Ireland in the nineteenth century and the Holocaust dead of the twentieth century, so many of the families of the dead of September 11 in the twenty-first century lost not only their lives but any small measure of control over their deaths. Their lives and their bodies were lost to them.

Not only did they die, they disappeared. There's the terrible fact of the matter. *We will not get them back to let them go again*, to wake and weep over them, to look upon their ordinary loveliness once more, to focus all uncertainties on the awful certainty of a body in a box in a familiar room, borne on shoulders, processed through towns, as if the borderless country of grief could be handled and contained, as if it had a manageable size and shape and weight and matter, as if it could be mapped or measured.

Humankind consigns its dead to oblivions we choose—the grave, or flames, or tomb, or sea, or open air. And the doing of it is the way we deal with it. These hard duties have their comforts. The recitation of rosaries and Kaddish, processions and committals, the living's confrontation with the dead, difficult as it is, is a comfort. So the further hurt of that late-summer Tuesday's dead is that it will not be kin that scatters them, or friends who carry them or family ground that covers them, or their beloved who last whispers soft goodbyes. They are the lost—too vastly buried, too furiously burned, too utterly commingled with the horror that killed them to get them back, to let them go again. We could not rescue very many. We recovered all too few. There are hundreds, thousands dead and gone, Godhelpus.

We know this the way we know the weather and the date and dull math of happenstance we are helpless to undo.

I've been a funeral director for thirty years. I've waited with the families of abducted children, foreign missionaries, tornado victims, drowned toddlers, Peace Corps volunteers, firefighters overcome by flames, passengers in fallen planes, Vietnam and Gulf War casualties—waiting for their dead to be found and counted, identified and returned to them from whatever damage or disaster claimed them. And I've heard no few well-meaning ignoramuses suggest that the body in the box, there among the gladioli and hushed respects, was "just a shell" or "only the tent" or some other metaphor to minimize the loss. They meant, of course, to say that our souls outlive us, that we are more than blood and bone and corporality. But the bodies of the dead are not "just" anything or "only" anything else. They are precious to the living who have lost them. They are the seeing—hard as it is—that is believing, the certainty against which our senses rail and to which our senses cling. They are the singular, particular sadness that must be subtracted from the tally of sadness. So the cruelty is real, the pain of it unspeakable. It is as if, until they are returned, their deaths belong to their murderers, the media, the demographics or the larger history of the world at large. But if they are victims of terrorism, casualties of a widespread war, part of a national tragedy, they are no less spouses and parents, daughters and sons, dear to friends, neighbors and fellow workers who are not only missed in the general sense, but missed as surely in the flesh—in beds, at desks and dinner tables, over drinks and talk and intimacies—the one and only face and voice and touch and being that has ceased to be. And their deaths, like their lives, belong to the precious few before they belong to the many who care.

Forty years ago the great muckraker Jessica Mitford wrote *The American Way of Death.* She quite properly and quite profitably lampooned the undertakerly mistake of concentrating on selling the box rather than serving the bereaved. On the math of caskets there was probably no one better. On the meaning of death, the dynamics of grief and mourning, there was probably no one worse. Her own experiences with "a death in the family" were never quite "discussed," either in the original or revised version of *The American Way of Death* or in two volumes of her autobiography. When her first daughter, Julia, died of measles and pneumonia in a London clinic at age four months, she wrote: we "fled…to Corsica" where she lived "in the welcome unreality of a foreign town, shielded by distance from the sympathy of friends." When her first husband died—his plane disappeared over the North Sea in November of '41, it got a one-sentence mention in the Introduction of the second volume of her autobiography. And when her first son was run down by a bus at age ten in Oakland, California in 1954, she wrote nothing, never mentioning his name, which was Nicholas, and discouraged conversation about him between her daughter, Constancia, and her other son, Benjamin. When I dined with her surviving children four years ago, in the East Village, they told me "Mother was a very private person." If we were on Oprah, we'd connect the dots between her heartbreaks and her muckraking, between her anger and her denial, but let's just leave it at this: she could do the math, but not the mourning; she could do the numbers but not the meaning; she could do the bottom line but not the bigger picture. She was good at the fashions but not the fundamentals.

Still, ever since Mitford, we've been throwing the body out with the box. In an effort to avoid caskets, inconvenience, and expense, we've been avoiding the fundamental obligation of the living to confront their dead and dispose of their dead with honor and ceremony and that pause that distinguishes human kind from the other species—to participate not only in the memory of the dead but the disposition of their bodies. We have treated the dead human body like an accessory to, rather than an essential of, the difficult business of grief and mourning. For most of a generation now we have happily dismissed the dead from their obsequies—dispatching them by cell phone and gold card to their hasty and unwitnessed burials or cremations—whilst we plan the "events" heavy on finger food, warm fuzzies, some Hallmark sentiments and new age music, and, needless to mention, "life-affirming" talk during which someone will almost always declare a "closure."

When do the missing become the dead? When do the lost become the lost forever? When does hope give way entirely to grief? When will searching no longer serve the living or the living that have died? How will each family's lamentation be heard above the nation's keening? Where is God in all of this?

The dead of course, do not much care. They are predictably indifferent to such details. Perhaps it is the first gift of paradise. The dead don't care. Only the living do. Whether faith furnishes our heavens, or doubt leaves the decor up for grabs, or wonder keeps the particulars ever changing, Whomever Is In Charge There must take care of them. God is good to them, wherever God is these days. The dead who occupy these places know our hearts, our hurts, and how we have searched and watched and waited for them.

We do what we do for the living's sake. The living must decide when the time has come to cease looking and begin to mourn, to organize the liturgies of thanks and praise and affliction, to shake a fist in God's face and say the ancient prayers. All the dead require is witness and remembrance—to say they lived, they died, they matter to us.

What the living need, of course, is to grieve in meaningful and manageable ways.

So if we must leave them to a burial we did not choose, a fire we did not want for them, is that place not hallowed by the common pyre and grave it has become?

There has been talk and will be more, of course, of what to build there. Build witness and remembrance, high into the sky. Name the dead, keep the count and record of what happened there. Don't forget. Build what says that while the dead don't care, their deaths mattered to the living who watched and waited and searched among the ruins and prayed and hoped and only let go grudgingly, when they were sure that God, Whomever God is these days, was there.

Like any good wake or shiva well sat, the time since the disaster has given us pause—time for all the high energy, labor intensive, often untidy rubrics of grief that must be conducted when there has been a death in the family. As a nation we've behaved much like any large and sorely damaged, close-knit if occasionally dysfunctional group of relations dealing with heartache and permanent loss.

* * *

We act out things we cannot put in words. We put into words those things we cannot do.

So we have wept and processed, eulogized and elegized, searched and watched, marched behind pipers, stood silently among our ruins. We have made war and rumors of war. We've done the candles, gladioli, shrines, and casseroles. We've done our best for the living and the dead and still sadness comes and goes in waves. We have filled the sorry days with hyperbole and understatement, open arms and fingers pointed, excess and shortfall, barbarity and humanity, love and hate. As with any funeral there've been moments of the ridiculous and the sublime, the shameful and humane. We have affirmed our faiths, our fears, ranted and prayed, accused and comforted.

And like any good funeral those who needed to look have had the chance to while those who couldn't bear it could look away and busy themselves with less discomforting realities. Like a body in a box at the end of a room, that sixteen-acre gaping wound at the south end of the Manhattan has become the corpse to which our countrymen have come to gaze upon the facts of life and death. It is the seeing that is believing, the godawful witness—from which we recoil and to which we are drawn—that we nonetheless must bear if we are to honor the dead and heal our hearts. Twenty-five thousand people a day have stood in line to pay their respects. Like good funeral directors, our leaders have stood with us there so we could view the "remains"—the unbearable truth, surrounded by flags and floral wreaths and memorials, with the worst of the ravages removed: the nearly twenty-thousand body parts, the fewer than three hundred bodies, the horrid mountain of disaster.

Nonetheless, that pit we look into from the vantage on Church Street is the remnant of a former reality in which we were safe within our own borders, snug in our super power, a boomtown and a boom nation in which peace and prosperity seemed unassailable.

At Ground Zero on the one year anniversary of that horror, while the litany of the dead and gone was read, achieving the cadence of lamentations, all I could hear were the lines of a poem written years ago by Michael Heffernan, in the midst of a sickness—a mortal peril that threatened his son, his household, his family's future.

"Merciless Beauty"

Look to the blue above the neighborhood,
and nothing there gives any help at all.
We have seen the fuchsia, and it doesn't work.
Time flows away. The mystery it fills
with our undoing moves aside awhile
and brings a new reality into play,
apparently—and here is the main idea:
the wind of time appears to blow through here,
the periwinkle and the mayapple
trembling in wind that is of their own kind,
a gorgeous color of a clarity
that fills our eyes with brightness to see through,
for all the good it does us, and to tell
the morning glory from the glory of God.*

"Closure"—whatever it means to the pop-psyche crowd—cannot be proclaimed, and may never really be achieved. So no one can say when all this will be done. Certainly it is not now. All we can do is a day at a time. Like good funeral directors—a little obsequious and eager to please—our well-intentioned leaders are gently urging us along. The mayor wants us to cut it in stone and call it a day and not to forget that we have a cash flow problem. Our president wants to fan the grief into a foreign policy. There are, not surprisingly, quibbles over the money and the monuments. There has been an abundance of what we funeral directors call "the helpful Hannah's"—neighbors or in-laws or distant cousins who want to run the show but not to pay for it.

Still something about returning home from these anniversary observances has the feeling of returning from a graveside or a pyre—our shoes dusty with the digging, our faces hot from the fires, our hearts heavy with fellow feeling and resolve. We return to our lives both broken and ennobled. Like every family come home from these duties, we find the space still full of absences.

* Grateful acknowledgment is made for permission to reprint: "Merciless Beauty" from Love's Answer, by Michael Heffernan, University of Iowa Press, 1994.

The facts are still the facts: they're gone. Our people, our towers, our cities, our nation, our lives and times, all changed forever. And the enduring sadness waiting there—a weariness, a wariness, a catch in the breath, a sigh—hope bristling underneath the fear that things will never be the same.

The nation returns to its life and times like a widow come home from her dead husband's grave, clutching the folded flag to her breast, the patriotic consolation prize. I have seen the look in such survivor's eyes—it is proud and bitter, angry and fatigued. After the sympathies and shovel work, after the high talk and comforts, she is still alone. The house is full of reminders; the bed is empty. She plans for a monument, worries over the mortgage payments, the well being of her children, the future of her household and the world. Her heart is torn between the opposites: love and grief, faith and fear, hope and despair, rage and peace. Every morning brings fresh peril and possibility. All she can do is a day at a time.

The mystery it fills with our undoing moves aside awhile and brings a new reality into play—God help us.

3

"A Passion of Grief and Fear Exasperates Us": Death, Bereavement, and Mourning—What We Have Learned a Year after 9/11

Peter Metcalf

My title is a phrase taken from one of the best-known ethnographic accounts of emotional reactions to death. In Godfrey Wilson's (1939) description of a funeral among the Nyakyusa of Tanzania, a helpless grief is rapidly displaced by displays of aggression. One might conclude from his data, coming as it does from a culture so remote from our own, that there is something universally human, something "natural," about the horror of the events of 9/11 hardening into military resolve. Nothing could be further from the truth. On the contrary, it serves only to show the hazards of facile ethnographic analogy. I am in fact not interested in making 9/11 look familiar or acceptable in any way—just the reverse.

It is of course easy enough to identify with Nyakyusa reactions, particularly their first reactions. People appeared dumbfounded by their loss, "stumbling about as though blind with grief," and muttering incoherently. Even after the corpse was buried, they sat down on the newly-filled grave "with their arms on one another's shoulders rocking to and fro' and weeping." Slowly, however, the mood changed. Two half brothers of the deceased took up spears and ran back and forth wailing the man's name. "Then," Wilson continues, "at last, the drums begin in earnest and the young men start to dance...the insistent vital rhythm of the drums and the sight of the leaping dance fall on the sensibilities gratefully, bringing relief from the almost unbearable tension." Now conversation bubbles up as men arrive from other villages to join the dance, and the mourners brandish their spears and hurl them into the ground "fighting invisible enemies." One of the half-brothers "who appeared to be so greatly affected seven or eight hours before, is laughing gaily as he dances" (Wilson 1939: 24-7).

It is this transition that Nyakyusa explained to Wilson in the phrase that now seems so eerily relevant: "a passion of grief and fear exasperates us." It captures neatly the mood of the nation in the immediate wake of 9/11. But what exactly were our griefs and fears? The greatest fear of the Nyakyusa is of the dead themselves—hence the rapid burial. They have a very explicit fear: that unquiet ghosts will bring more deaths. But surely that is not what we fear. It must be something else, something entirely different, and that is the value of borrowing the Nyakyusa phrase: it forces us to *contrast* our situation and theirs.

One might argue that the origin of our grief is obvious enough at least, but even here there is a problem. The proposition is undeniably true for those who lost friends and family. For them, there is nothing but shock, disorientation, and blank incomprehension. They must have been as distraught as the Nyakyusa that Wilson observed—and may well still be, almost four years after the events. For them, I think, no mere ritual will provide relief, except perhaps those they devise for themselves.[1]

Such was the scale of the disaster that there are many thousands of the bereaved. There are however literally millions—and not only in America—who felt a real sense of personal loss and uncertainty despite knowing nobody who died in the World Trade Center. In contrast to most of the authors in this volume, it is the latter that I am concerned with. In his paper, Charles Strozier describes the psychic impact of 9/11 in terms of three zones of exposure to shock, radiating out from "Ground Zero" to the limits of Manhattan. Extending his model, I was I suppose in about zone 12, in central Virginia. What I have to report is that the University of Virginia came to a halt. Most teachers spontaneously cancelled classes or turned them over to group discussion. Teach-ins and vigils were organized by impromptu action groups of both students and faculty.

From friends in London, I learned that the public reaction there had been more remarkably intense, probably more so than in some American cities. It is not hard to find the reasons for that. In the last century, London has seen its share of bombings and terrorist attacks. More importantly, London is second only to New York as a center of international trade. London is perhaps zone 4 in Strozier's model. Though I have never seen the statistics on this, it is entirely possible that there were more Londoners killed in the Twin Towers than there were, say, Los Angelinos.

Nevertheless, it is necessary to put the disaster in context. The human carnage of 9/11, grievous as it was, is far less than that which occurs annually on our roads. For what exactly then are the majority of us grieving? What exactly do we fear? To me it seems obvious that we understood that the attack had deep political significance, but we did not, and do not, understand what that significance is. What we are experiencing is a passion of *political* grief and fear.

* * *

What struck us all is that the events of 9/11 are unprecedented. Consequently, we all set about looking for precedents. There are parallels with natural disasters. The widespread outpouring of sympathy for New Yorkers was similar to that which occurs when storms wreak havoc on the Atlantic coast or floods inundate the Mississippi valley. But no one wanted to draw this parallel. That left only one real alternative: war. This classification has its advantages. As we learned in the bombing campaigns of the Second World War, and again in Vietnam, attacks on civilian populations invariably stiffen the national resolve. So journalists reached for the Battle of Britain analogy. For one rare moment Americans everywhere identified with New Yorkers, attributing to them that indomitable spirit of survival that might usefully have been acknowledged decades earlier when New York's financial and social problems brought only callous indifference from the rest of the nation.

The even more popular analogy to Pearl Harbor had the additional rhetorical advantage of suggesting a proper reaction: a vast national mobilization against the enemy. But at the same moment it posed the most difficult question: who was the enemy? Thankfully, government spokesmen were quick to point out that an attack by terrorists acting *in the name* of Islam did not mean that America was at war with Moslems. At the time they were given credit for learning from the mistakes of the Second World War, when loyal Japanese Americans were persecuted. There was, however, a more visceral reason for their reaction. The United States cannot possibly afford to have hostile relations with an Islamic world whose oil is vital to the national economy. The terrorists would have been only too pleased to bring down, not only the World Trade Center, but also the whole world economy. At least our government did not fall into that trap, and even briefly tried to draw Moslem nations into dialogue—although that phase seems to be well and truly over.

In the meantime, the seemingly unavoidable analogy with war left the government fighting shadows, like the Nyakyusa warrior waving his spear. The invasion of Afghanistan, like Nyakyusa drums, brought "welcome relief from the almost unbearable tension," but when the excitement was over we were left with the same uncertainties. Perhaps the passion is fading, but the grief and fear continue to exasperate us.

* * *

Shortly after 9/11, I read a commentary on it by Marshall Berman, whose most famous book takes its title from a phrase coined by Karl Marx. The condition of modernity, he argued, is such that, *All That Is Solid Melts Into Air* (1988). The endless quest for development means that all edifices, however grandiose and impressive they seem to be, are fated eventually to be swept away by the same processes that created them. How ironic, Berman remarks, that this phrase should be so literally born out. In the global economy that now rules our lives, what institution could possibly have seemed more solid than the World Trade Center, and yet it disappears before our very eyes, into thin air. (In parenthesis, let me make it clear that there was no element of gloating in Berman's article; he was not pleased about being born out. He was just as distressed as everyone else by the events, and only struggling to make sense of them.)

As someone who has written about death rituals in different places and epochs, drawing on the ideas of Robert Hertz (1906), what strikes me most forcefully is not the obliteration of the building, but of those inside it. I am told that the temperatures inside the towers reached such heights that droplets of melted metal were dispersed into the atmosphere. So violent were the forces released in the collapse of the towers that debris was distributed over a large area of Manhattan. Everyone in the world knows about the enormous pall of dust that enveloped Manhattan like some alien monster, and how it settled inches deep on the ground, and made its way inside everything. We now know that it contained all kinds of toxic and carcinogenic elements, but what many people outside New York do not realize is the appalling charnel stench that accompanied the dust. As Charles

Strozier's paper describes it, this is a kind of dreadful secret shared only by those who lived and worked close to the disaster. The ghastly overtones of endo- cannibalism make it a dramatic example of what Geoffrey Gorer (1955) called the "modern pornography of death." But even outside New York, everyone knew that the medical facilities alerted to receive the dead and injured stood idle because there were no dead and injured to be found. Instead the victims of the attack had simply melted into air.

We are left with a kind of macabre satire on Berman's portrayal of modernity as consuming itself. Here it is the moderns themselves that are consumed. Has anthropology anything to say about this?

* * *

In my previous writing, I have followed Hertz's cue, and focused on culturally prescribed modes of disposal of the dead. What is surprising about this is the enormous variety of techniques employed. In different times and places, corpses have been burned or buried, immediately or years later. They have been preserved by smoking, pickling, or embalming, or ritually butchered and fed to vultures or hyenas. They are eaten, raw or cooked, or simply abandoned, along with the entire encampment. Often a variety of techniques is used in sequence. In short, there is virtually no imaginable way of disposing of corpses that has not been the norm somewhere, sometime. Hertz's insight was that these different techniques, wrapped in rituals lasting anything from hours or years, express different attitudes to what it is not only to die, but also to live. The massive emotional impact of death gives drama and force to mortuary rites, in all their diversity.

To the extent that I have come habitually to pay attention to modes of disposal as a way of gaining entry into whole cultural understandings of the meaning of life itself, I am disoriented in yet another way by 9/11, as if there were not already quite enough ways. I have never before set out to discover corpse-less death rites, although they must always have existed. I am not thinking here of memorial rites after disposal of the corpse—there are any number of those. I am thinking of occasions when people simply went missing. In the twentieth century, this was made only too familiar in both World Wars, when civilians at home were left holding nothing more than a black-edged envelope to tell them that they had lost a husband or a son. How did they deal with such a thing? Certainly, their accumulated suffering weighed heavily on all the familiar understandings of the meaning of life and death. No one is ever likely to quote again, except in bitter irony, the old maxim that Horace gave us: *dulce et decorum est pro patria mori*—it is sweet and proper to die for one's country.

What is additionally appalling about 9/11 is that husbands and wives posted off their loved ones that morning without any presentiment that they would simply vanish into thin air. No one joined up, or put on uniforms, or marched off to waiting troop trains. The only apt comparison I can find for this is those unsettling cases where a murder has occurred, but the corpse cannot be found. There are cases, I understand, where murder convictions have been obtained even lacking a corpse, but the legal ambiguities are immense, to say nothing of the emotional ones. And, of course, this is no mere analogy. The victims of 9/11 *were* murdered: a totally unprecedented mass murder of thousands of people in an area that we all took to be as secure as anywhere in the world and in manner none us had ever dreamed possible. Reason enough for a societal sense of insecurity!

Unfortunately, however, mass murders are not exactly unknown in the USA. Will it do any good to describe them as some kind of ritual? Think, for instance, of the black humor involved in the expression "to go postal." Did the invention of the phrase mean that we had learned to accept that every once in a while workers would suddenly start spraying bullets at their current or former workmates? Note also that these men (it is almost never women who commit mass murders) often evidently planned from the outset to take their own lives. So there is nothing unprecedented about the act of suicide/murder in the events of 9/11. In fact, there was a spooky parallel that emerged as police uncovered letters and diaries of the supposed radical fundamentalist attackers. Like the men who "went postal," they turned out simply to be misfits, and not at all the kind of strict observers of Islamic law that we expected. (You remember the FBI discovered journals of the hijackers, with details of visits to strip joints and so on.)

Again, consider the recent string of lethal and suicidal attacks by schoolchildren on their teachers and fellow students. Were they not as shocking in their way as the events of 9/11, even if the body counts were not as high? At the time, they provoked cover stories in *Time* and *Newsweek*, with all kinds of socio-psychological punditry. At first, Europeans were inclined to attribute the killings to some violent streak in the American psyche, but then similar attacks occurred there too, and it became obvious that they were part of a general malaise. Eventually, however, the stories disappeared off the front pages, displaced by financial scandals and the like. The tendency is to say, "that's the kind of world we live in now," and then forget it.

What I would like to say—and what I took Marshall Berman to be saying—is that the events of 9/11 do indeed show what kind of world we live in now. *But what kind of world is that exactly*? It worries me that the many events that were planned for the anniversary of 9/11 had the effect of ritualizing our reaction to 9/11. In writing this, I may have done just that. (I take Paul Rosenblatt to be saying the same thing in his remarks elsewhere in this volume.) So let me say plainly, as an anthropologist: do not look to ethnographic analogy for a formula that will make 9/11 somehow acceptable or digestible. Nor are you going to find a way out (with all respect to my learned colleagues) through theology, or psychology, or poetry. Our job is not to find relief in a war dance, or to find relief at all, but to continue being "exasperated" by a "passion of grief and fear." We have to go on asking, and really asking, what kind of world it is we live in now, and how do we feel about that, and what shall we do about it? We have to confront unflinchingly the social and political realities of our world. That is what we owe to the victims of 9/11; that and nothing less.

Note

1. Ilana Harlow provides some moving examples in her paper, elsewhere in this volume.

References

Berman, Marshall (1982), *All That Is Solid Melts Into Air: The Experience of Modernity*. New York: Simon and Schuster.

Gorer, Geoffrey (1955), "The Pornography of Death," reprinted in Geoffrey Gorer, *Death, Grief and Mourning*. Garden City, NY: Doubleday, 1965.

Hertz, Robert (1906), "Contribution a une étude sur la représentation collective de la mort." *L'Année sociologique* 10: 48-137.

Wilson, Godfrey (1939), *The Constitution of Ngonde*. Livingstone, Northern Rhodesia: Rhodes-Livingstone Institute.

4

Shaping Sorrow: Creative Aspects of Public and Private Mourning

Ilana Harlow

Many traditional responses to death involve the creative impulse through art, music, and rituals connected to funerary rites. These include improvised poetic lamentations, gravestone design and adornment, stories about the dead that capture their essence and thus seem to conjure them up, and mourning quilts pieced out of the clothing of the deceased. In our time, in addition to such traditions and sometimes in lieu of them, there is an increased tendency among mourners to craft personal rituals and memorial art in response to death.[1] Commemorative art and ritual provide "structured opportunities for the expression of grief"[2] and also serve as testaments to enduring relationships between the living and the dead. Creativity can counter the destructiveness of death. Creative acts not only give those encountering death a project to focus on, but also provide them with a way to physically enact their grief—to give shape to sorrow, and to evoke the presence of the dead among the living.

Rituals of September 11

On September 11, 2001, New York filled with such overwhelming sorrow that rituals of grief spilled out of private homes and lives into public spaces. Feelings of loss were inscribed on the City itself. People used every medium at their disposal to express themselves; some even scrawled messages in the dust from the explosions that coated vehicles and windows in the area. All available public surfaces—brick walls, phone booths, bus stop shelters, and subway stations—were plastered with Missing Person posters. Public parks, fire stations, traffic islands, building stoops, and even curbsides throughout the City became the sites of continually evolving shrines of ritual objects, candles, flowers, poems, and artworks. The city was awash in a creative expression of grief that was of a magnitude that approached the enormity of loss.

Candlelight vigils pierced the darkness of City nights after the devastation. At many of the shrines around the City, red, white, and blue candles flickered alongside Christian votive candles, Jewish memorial *yahrtzeit* candles, and offertory candles petitioning a range of intercessors from St. Anthony, to the Virgin of Guadalupe—patron of Mexico—to San Elias, the Baron of Cemeteries, to the Siete Potencias de Africa of the Afro-Cuban religion of Santeria. The vision of many small candles burning *en masse* seemed to convey the unity felt by the diversity of people who lit them. These candles that represented the souls of the dead, prayers for the peaceful repose of their souls, prayers for the welfare of the injured, and prayers for peace, also represented solidarity. The waxes from the various candles dripped onto each other on the sidewalk and flowed together, recalling the usually inaccurate metaphor of America as a melting pot. New Yorkers came together in a public ritual that in its transcendence of any single belief system represented all of them.

The shrines were not only *representations* of the diverse yet united New York community of mourners; they functioned to *foster* a sense of community and *communitas* as well. People rallied around them. Although they were sites of ritual, their character was "eminently social," as Emile Durkheim might have phrased it. Even though (or perhaps specifically because) they were venues for the simultaneous display of a *range* of spiritual and political sentiments, the shrines symbolized a sense of "us-ness." As Durkheim has noted, "An emblem is useful as a rallying point for any sort of group by expressing social unity in material form; thus making it more obvious to all... The emblem is not merely a convenient process for clarifying the sentiment society has of itself: it also serves to create this sentiment..."[3]

Usually, the power of ritual stems from its basis in a particular social group and in shared psychological associations and memories. On September 11, members of diverse groups spontaneously joined together—and the power of ritual stemmed from the fact that each individual was performing his or her own rituals of loss and remembrance in a communal venue. Rituals ranging from Tibetan

Buddhist chanting to Jewish *shmira* (watching over the dead while reciting Psalms for them) were all enacted in the public sphere, in what were shared ritual spaces.[4] Most of the rituals performed, and objects left, at a shrine near a housing project on the Lower East Side were in the Latino Catholic tradition, but community members there said that on several nights, their Asian Buddhist neighbors came to light incense at that same shrine. At other shrines, strings of origami cranes made by both Japanese and American students (some folded out of red, white, and blue paper), expressing the makers' wishes for healing and peace, hung side by side with portraits of the Catholic saint Padre Pio, Jewish stars, and Native American dream catchers. (The origami cranes found all over the city, intended to express sympathy, are associated with an earlier episode of great suffering.[5] In Japan, such cranes are sometimes left in the Peace Park in Hiroshima, which commemorates the devastation and the victims of the atomic bomb dropped there in 1945.)

Massive shrines, such as the one at Union Square Park, presented us with a vast mixing of Eastern and Western, Old World and New Age. It seems that the carpeting of Union Square with flowers and candles might not have been possible without our collective experience of the 1960s and the search for spirituality that took place in those times. Candles and flowers—objects, whose public display was at one time associated with hippies and flower children who were intrigued by Buddhism and experienced life on ashrams, and adopted and adapted Eastern traditions as part of their lives—have become mainstream symbols of peace and hope.

Many Americans today feel free to adopt appealing rituals and symbols from religions to which they do not necessarily belong.[6] Indeed, the September 11 shrines themselves were an adaptation of the custom of marking the place where a person has been killed with roadside or sidewalk shrines. This increasingly popular practice in the United States, adopted by people of many faiths, is an updated version of simple roadside crosses often erected at sites of sudden death in predominantly Catholic countries such as Ireland, Mexico, and Puerto Rico. As folklorist Joe Sciorra, among others, has pointed out, the crosses "manifest the belief that the souls of those who die unexpectedly and fail to receive the Last Rites of the Catholic Church are suffering in Purgatory…the marker serves then, as a lasting reminder for passersby to pray for the person's soul and thus speed its eventual arrival to Heaven."[7]

Death is an embodiment of the philosophical problem of the one and the many. Jacques Derrida has written on both the plurality of Death and of each death as a singular event.[8] It seems particularly appropriate to keep this in mind when thinking about a disaster such as September 11 when the plurality of Death was so overwhelming as to threaten awareness of its singularity. The Fire Department, overwhelmed by loss, considered holding one large memorial service for the fallen but ultimately decided to arrange individual services.[9] Posters depicting or listing the missing, tributes to individual dead, and the *New York Times*' thousands of "Portraits of Grief"—its democratic, anecdotal obituaries of the victims—helped make us more aware of the singular. In fact, we cannot understand "the big story" and its impact without knowing the thousands of individual stories that comprise it. Still, September 11 is very much about the plurality of Death witnessed by so many, and about *public* mourning.

Personal losses were citywide and national losses as well. Traditional death rituals separate mourners from the rest of society for a set period of time requiring that they dress and conduct themselves according to their changed status. But what happens when all of society is in mourning? On September 11, it seems, many people felt the need not only to express their grief outwardly among family and friends but also to do so *publicly*. Because the grief was so great, it could not be contained in individual homes and it became physically enacted and represented in *community* living rooms like Union Square Park and Washington Square Park where people gathered to be with their greater New York family.

New Yorkers looked towards past encounters with grief to help form their responses to the tragedy. In my synagogue, for example, on the Friday after September 11, a joyous prayer welcoming the Sabbath, *L'chah Dodi*, was sung to the tune of *Eli Zion*, a dirge that recalls destruction in another city—Jerusalem—in ancient times. Another instance of responding to the tragedy by adapting existing traditions occurred in the New York Police Department. When a police officer is killed, his or her colleagues wear a black elastic mourning band over their badges. With so many rescue workers dead, the black band became part of police officers' daily uniform. Many New York officers wore those bands for more than a year. Eventually, black bands with 9-11-01 written on them were manufactured and some officers chose to wear these across their badges.

Other officers chose to wear a black bar pin with the date of the tragedy inscribed on it.

In Florida, mourning bands raised an intriguing issue regarding private and public mourning, as well as regarding civically enforced ritual. In Tampa, Florida police officer Ernie Hedges arrived at roll call on September 12 with a black band across his badge to honor fallen officers. A supervisor told him to remove the band since the police chief had not approved it. He refused and was cited for insubordination. By that time, the police chief, unaware of this incident, had issued a memo stating that the department would remain in a state of mourning for seven days and that officers in uniform should wear black bands over their badges for this period. The memo was too late for Hedges who was disciplined.[10]

A final example of looking to the past to form responses to the September 11 tragedy: In many New York neighborhoods, memorial murals, painted by graffiti artists on city walls, are a familiar part of the urban landscape.[11] These vibrant splashes of color amidst the gray of the city, celebrate those who used to enliven the streets with their presence. Memorial walls generally include portraits of the deceased, dates of birth and death, and images that convey something about who they were. The walls, often memorializing those who died young, sometimes violently, on the city streets, keep the dead in the community and also are constant reminders of community loss. Drawing on this familiar idiom, on the afternoon of September 11, graffiti artist Chico painted a memorial wall dominated by images of the smoking towers and inscribed "In memory of family and friends, RIP Sept. 11, 2001." In the next few weeks, dozens of memorial murals honoring the dead of September 11 were created all around the City. In the tradition of memorial walls, these soon became sites of community gathering. Missing posters were affixed to the walls; candles, flowers, and teddy bears were left on the sidewalk below. The City's public spaces became sites of intimate expressions of sorrow.

Missing posters, first made in the hopes of finding the missing, ultimately serving as tributes to the dead, were miniature, ephemeral forms of memorial walls. Some posters were hastily scrawled but others demonstrated much thoughtfulness and creativity. In addition to the practical function of trying to locate the missing, the project of making the posters often gave mourners a focus at a difficult time. As journalist Marshall Sella put it, "Desperation and empty time conspired to create other customs."[12]

In another public ritual, those who did not suffer a personal loss made pilgrimages to sites where Missing posters were hung in greatest concentration. The pilgrimages were seemingly spurred by a sense of obligation to witness our dead and pay them last respects. People studied the photos, read the names, learned about lives that are no more. Some of the missing had been recently married; some had tattoos in private places; some had small children; some had Caesarean scars; many of them were in their twenties—at the beginning of promising careers. People in this so-called "anonymous city," where everyone is always on the run, took the time to learn the faces and stories of the dead. This was particularly striking in the Times Square subway station and in Grand Central Station, crossroads of the subterranean pathways of the city, where shrines developed around these posters. People clearly on their way to somewhere else simply stopped. It reminded me of a definition I once heard of sacred space as a place where moving bodies are rendered still.

The Transformative Power of Ritual

Ritual is a creative act and often a transformative one. It effects change in the world. Many speak of Ground Zero as hallowed ground, as sacred space. Yet it was defiled space as well. The vast outpouring of humanity that we witnessed in acts of heroism at Ground Zero, and the ritual shrines that were created around its perimeter to honor the dead, functioned to *transform* defiled space into sacred space. Also, rescue workers sacralized a piece of the destruction itself. Ironworker Frank Silecchia came upon a twenty-foot tall beam that had fallen from one of the towers and landed upright in the form of a perfectly symmetrical cross. The discovery was made on the morning of the third day after the attacks. This made it all the more meaningful as a symbol of faith since, according to Christian tradition, Jesus was resurrected on the third day after his crucifixion. In addition, on the right arm of the cross was attached a piece of insulation thought by some to resemble Jesus' shroud.[13]

The creative transformation of the destroyed girder into something sacred began symbolically with Silecchia's interpretation of it as such. The consecration continued at a physical level when names of some of the dead and the phrase "God Bless our Fallen Brothers" were etched into it. (Also, in a show of the patriotism that was intertwined with almost all September 11 rituals, a welder attached newly minted state quarters to the foot of the cross.)[14] These additions to the cross were not considered a desecration of it but ways of dedicating it to a cause and thus enhancing its sacredness. The transformation was completed at a metaphysical level when, in October 2001, a priest blessed the cross with holy water. The cross is now mounted like a saintly relic on a cement block above Ground Zero. A jewelry maker has crafted its likeness in the form of a crucifix pendant. These necklaces were being sold at St. Paul's Chapel, which served as a refuge for rescue workers and volunteers.

The Anthropomorphization of the Towers

In addition to this sacralization of a piece of the World Trade Center, there was a widespread metaphoric anthropomorphization or personification of the towers.[15] Postcards depicting the towers were left at shrines just as photographs of the dead were. Included among Missing posters of victims of the attack were several variants of Missing posters listing the towers as victims. One which bore magic marker renditions of the towers read: "Missing: two handsome twins, Age 28." A postcard of the towers was inscribed with the handwritten message, "They are missing. I am looking for these two great brothers of New York." A child's drawing of the towers set against a night sky studded by a lone, frowning star, gave each tower a face and a broken purple heart. Their eyes were closed and each was swaddled in an American flag.

Several images portrayed the towers as angels. One hand-drawn picture posted at the shrines showed the towers against the clouds, bedecked with wings and halos hovering over the New York City skyline. At the annual Greenwich Village Halloween Parade a costume was worn by a man and a woman each standing inside a cardboard construction of one of the towers. Each tower was outfitted with wings and a halo and the couple held hands as they marched. At some shrines there was a letter signed by Towers One and Two apologizing for not staying up long enough for everyone to evacuate. In another letter one tower recalls to the other that the pain was unbearable and "you fell at my feet."[16] Less reverent than images of the towers as angels and victims was a widely circulated image on the Internet that purported to be a proposal for the rebuilding of the World Trade Center. It consisted of a complex of buildings of different heights that were in the configuration of a hand giving the viewer the finger.

At the May 30, 2002 ceremony that marked the end of the recovery effort at Ground Zero, the last World Trade Center beam was carried out of the pit with the respect usually accorded a human body. The ceremony was very much about making absence present, about saluting absence. A stretcher bearing no body, symbolizing all those who have not been found, held an American flag. The flag was folded up in a triangle, the way flags are when presented to families of soldiers or policemen killed in the line of duty. The stretcher was carried up the ramp out of the pit and placed in a Fire Department ambulance. A truck that slowly made its way up the ramp out of the pit followed the stretcher. Lying atop this flatbed truck was a fifty-eight ton steel column from the World Trade Center that was wrapped in black muslin, and covered by an American flag and a wreath of flowers. Thus, the column looked like an appropriately huge coffin in what seemed like a funeral procession for the fallen skyscrapers. Of course, this vast symbolic coffin also represented the vast number of *human* victims who were *not* laid to rest in coffins. Underneath the muslin, the steel column was adorned with spray painted farewells and with the numbers lost by the Fire Department (343), the Port Authority Police Dept (37) and the Police Department (23). When the truck carrying the beam reached the ambulance it paused and Taps were sounded.[17]

The anthropomorphization of the towers indicates that the World Trade Center was mourned both for the loss of the buildings themselves and for their symbolic representation of all the people inside them and below them who were killed. This confluence and equivalence of the towers and the human victims was seen in artworks around the city. For example, at the Union Square shrine a miniature version of the towers made of novelty license plates each imprinted with a first name—David, Ann, Guillermo—commemorated both the buildings and the people who filled them, who were torn from our midst. A poster hung both at the fence near St. Paul's chapel and in Grand Central terminal conveyed this same feeling. It was a graphic of the twin towers made out of thousands of tiny photographs of the faces of the victims.[18]

Even before the attacks, the Word Trade Center had been assigned a personality that caused people to relate to the buildings in a social manner. It seems that if thousands of people had been killed in a building that was not as distinctive—that building might not have been anthropomorphized as the towers were (or the way the Chrysler building or Empire State Building might have been) because of their status as social beings.[19] When first built, the towers were nicknamed "David" and "Nelson," after the Rockefeller brothers, the banker and the governor, who were largely responsible for their construction. In common parlance, the towers were sometimes known as "the twins." Additionally, the towers' architecture had a "personality"—representative of the striving towards great achievement and power. For some they represented the arrogance that is sometimes necessary to attain these goals. Still, it seems that if the buildings had come down but no people had been killed, there would not have been the kind of "angel" and "missing victim" imagery that was seen. This imagery seems to have resulted from the fact that the towers came down and the people died simultaneously, their ashes commingled.[20]

Inscription

Inscription was the dominant form of creative expression in response to September 11. Messages of grief, compassion, love, and hate were written in the dust from the attacks; on rolls and rolls of butcher block paper spread out on the ground at Union Square Park; on the statues there and at Washington Square Park; on stickers stuck onto storefronts; and on plywood boards set up against Nino's restaurant on Canal Street, who also provided pens and blank stickers for this purpose.[21] T-shirts of fire departments and police departments sent in a show of support from around the country and hung at shrines bore not only the names and logos of the departments but also messages written in marker. As mentioned above, the last steel column was spray painted with names (and the body count) of the dead; and the cross set up at Ground Zero was similarly etched with names of the dead and messages to them.

Since the attacks, some fire engines have been painted with the names of the men their firehouses lost on September 11; some also have been painted with decorative crosses and phrases like "Always with us" or "In memory of our fallen brothers."[22] One firehouse that lost many men even enlisted museum conservators to help preserve a kind of inscription that is usually ephemeral. The work assignment board from September 11 listing, in chalk, the names of men who were sent to Ground Zero and did not return, was framed behind glass as a memorial to them.

Perhaps most striking were the layers upon layers of inscription at the shrines. Passersby appropriated any available surface to add their own inscriptions to the mix even if it was on someone else's poster or drawing. Missing Person posters had messages to the dead written on them, both by friends and strangers. When room ran out on the posters at "New York's Wall of Mourning" at Grand Central Terminal, people wrote messages on the foam core that served as backing for the posters. On a poster depicting the towers set against a sky made out of tiny blue letters spelling out the names of the deceased, people circled the names of people they knew and wrote messages to them or about them in the margins. It was not considered a vandalization of the artwork or of the Missing posters to write on them. The shrines were considered communal creations in response to communal loss and therefore all additions were considered valid ones.

Perhaps the ultimate form of inscription is the self-inscription of tattooing. Not surprisingly, tattoo parlors saw a big increase in clientele in response to September 11. Some tattooists actually saw this as an opportunity to do their part for "the cause" and offered September 11 tattoos either free of charge or at a considerable discount.[23] Although tattoos are a phenomenon among a relatively small segment of the American population, they record and reflect national sentiment and experience. One can infer from the standard flash of skulls, daggers, ships, military insignia, and In Memoriam crosses for fallen comrades, national emblems like the American eagle or the American flag, and patriotic slogans like "Death Before Dishonor" that many designs were developed in the context of death and war. The fact that a tattoo is indelibly injected into one's skin suggests the opportunity to powerfully display one's lasting devotion to individuals, groups, or ideologies. In response to September 11, many people chose to be inscribed with permanent displays of patriotism with designs like American flags or eagles and the date 9-11-01. Others got an image of a crying Statue of Liberty, or the twin towers in flames, or full back tattoos of the entire World Trade Center scene. Many requested firefighter helmets or police officer shields, some with the words "Gone but not forgotten" or "Never to be forgotten." One tattoo read "In Memory of the Brothers" and included an FDNY shield with 5555 as the shield number since that is the code signal for the bells tolled at the funeral of a firefighter who dies in the line of duty.[24] Some memorial tattoos were of portraits of victims. When people choose to be inscribed with names or portraits of loved ones, they transform themselves by incorporating their dead (or their sweethearts) into themselves.

It is important to incorporate our dead. We can achieve this not only physically through tattoo, but also metaphorically through ritual, and most basically by telling stories about them. Our memories of them are internal, invisible inscriptions within us. "Stories capture the essence of a life and make it portable," notes Steve Zeitlin. These stories are "a way of carrying our loved ones with us wherever we go."[25]

Jacques Derrida, who has studied what he calls "the work of mourning," suggests that for mourning to be successful, mourners must "interiorize" the Other, must make them a harmonious part of themselves since, as he puts it, our friends "can no longer *be* but *in us*."[26] This is the same sentiment expressed in a Ted Berrigan poem posted at a shrine near City Hall that begins:

The heart stops briefly when someone dies
a quick pain as you hear the news and someone passes
from your outside life to inside. Slowly the heart adjusts
to its new weight...

Narrative

Following the September 11 tragedy, the media became involved in the public performance of what are usually private rituals of grief. Radio and television broadcasters, many of whom were at a loss for words, read poetic elegies to the City during the news hour.[27] Again and again on September 11, the networks broadcast footage of United Airlines flight 175 slicing diagonally into the South tower and erupting in a fireball. Repeatedly, we heard the details of flight numbers and moment of impact. Yet, as folklorist Steve Zeitlin commented, this was not just the usual sensationalism of the media. This was, rather, the beginning of the public telling of the story of our loss. In our personal lives, when loved ones die, often their last days, hours, and moments are recounted again and again. Similarly, the recurring broadcasts addressed our need to hear and retell the story of any death, to help make it real. Undertaker and poet Thomas Lynch has noted that such images and details are the first step in assimilating the unfathomable—what he calls, "the round and witless horror of someone who / one dry night ceases measurably to be."[28]

The narratives we repeat after someone we know dies help the living to assimilate the unfathomable in more ways than one. In addition to the repetition of the story making it more real, we sometimes craft a narrative of death in a way that offers a measure of comfort. This was the case in a story that emerged after the death of Fire Department chaplain Mychal Judge. The well-liked "Father Mike," as he was known, rushed to the scene of the World Trade Center tragedy where he was killed by the collapsing buildings. In a story that is a testament to the high regard for Father Mike both as a dedicated chaplain and as a devoted man of faith, at first it was reported that he was struck in the head by falling debris when he removed his helmet to administer last rites to a firefighter who had been struck by a falling person. Later this report was revised since his body had been found in the lobby of Tower One where he probably took refuge after giving last rites but then was killed in a collapse of rubble.[29] Within minutes of Father Mike's death, over 250 firefighters, who were climbing a stairway in an effort to rescue victims trapped on the higher floors, were killed when the tower fell in on itself.

The close temporal proximity of the two tragedies—the death of Father Mike and the deaths of hundreds of his charges—suggested a narrative, and perhaps a cosmic, connection between the two. A firefighter on the news that night said that Father Mike was taken first so that this man, who had been an integral part of the firefighters' lives, baptizing their children and performing their marriages, could continue to tend to them in their deaths, on their journey to heaven.

At Father Mike's wake, firefighter Brian Thomas said, "God was taking 250 firefighters up to heaven and he needed someone there to help him. That's the only way you can rationalize what happened to Father Mike."[30] This poignant image, an *incipient* story about Father Mike's role in heaven, was later elaborated upon and crafted into an entertaining narrative in which the purview of his chaplaincy was expanded to include not only firefighters but also all of the victims. At his "month's mind," a traditional Irish memorial service, "…one of the speakers suggested Father Mike may have been 'working the door' at heaven in the moments after his death. In this scenario Father [Mychal] Judge, holding St. Peter's ear, put in a good word for each of the thousands that sought entry after the terrorists struck. 'He's OK!' 'Yea, I know her,' 'Good man, there' Judge would nudge the celestial bouncer till the horde somehow all entered into paradise. The image drew smiles from those who experienced Judge's legendary ability to affirm others."[31]

Another victim of September 11 was Harry Ramos, who was in the World Trade Center when it was attacked. He stopped to help a stranger and did not survive. His wife Migdalia Ramos, who missed him dearly, was angry with him. His concern for a stranger cost her family a husband and a father. A month after the attacks, she was unexpectedly in her mother's apartment building when a fire broke out. After escorting her children to safety, she went back into the building to save an elderly blind woman whom she knew lived alone. The story she tells about the fire is not a story of a recently bereft family, suffering through yet another calamity or put in a situation where more family members might have been lost. Rather, the story she tells about the fire and her response to it, interprets the incident as a message from Harry—helping her to see why he did what he did.[32]

Many of the stories we tell about coincidences interpret them as a medium of communication—from the dead, from God, or from the universe. Coincidences are woven into stories designed to demonstrate that the unusual coalescence of events makes sense within a larger scheme of things. "Tales like plays, demonstrate a full interdependence of human action and fate—a meaningfulness—that is…not necessarily characteristic of life," writes sociologist Erving Goffman.[33] Telling tales about our lives is a way of making them seem crafted, even as they unfold. Such narratives were a common response to the devastation of September 11.

Narratives told in response to tragedy seem to function in ways similar to redressive rituals devised to address social rupture. Some aspects of such stories can be understood quite nicely within Victor Turner's model of the social drama. In his scheme, social breach leads to crisis—a phase in which latent social tensions come to the surface. This is followed by a self-reflexive and creative phase that often prompts the performance of redressive rituals that result in either reintegration or recognition of schism. Analogously, people whose lives are breached or ruptured by the tragic death of a loved one can enter into a state of crisis, such as a crisis of faith, in which latent existential questions often become overt. The creative formulation and telling of a narrative about the rupture is thus a redressive act. Some stories convey an immitigable schism in the scheme of things; others, such as the ones told about Father Mike and Harry Ramos, encourage the integration of the disruptive event into a larger scheme, into a master narrative.[34]

One Year Later

When a family member dies, the memory of that person often is acknowledged at festive family gatherings such as weddings and baby namings. September 11 was an occasion of public loss and mourning and so it seemed any public gathering must somehow acknowledge the memory of those who perished. Indeed, an Italian *giglio* festival in July 2002 began with the sounding of a fire engine siren in memory of the fallen; the 2002 New York Lincoln Center Out-of-Doors festival in August was dedicated to the local firehouse and to the American Spirit; And the 2002 U.S. Open Tennis Tournament held in Queens, New York was presided over by a tattered American flag from Ground Zero.

While the memory of the tragedy and the dead remains with many of us, for some it lost much of its emotional charge after only one year. An August 2002 trip to Ground Zero, which is now a construction site, illustrated that many visitors had no sense of the place as sacred. They were laughing, snacking, videotaping, drinking, and posing for photos in front of the site, as they would at any other tourist attraction. Earlier visitors had littered the place with bottles and paper cups. Nearby, vendors were hawking mawkish wares to consumers who wanted a part of it all. These included souvenir booklets with the words "Terror" and "Tragedy" emblazoned in red letters across the tops; Ground Zero t-shirts and baseball caps; and postcards of the devastation such as a crumpled fire engine. One woman looking through the postcards commented excitedly, "Oh good, you have lots of different ones!" Some might view all this as "a return to normalcy."

One avenue away, at the shrine near St. Paul's chapel, the same solemnity and hushed tones that have been there since September 2001 could still be found. Even though the visitors to Ground Zero were closer to the actual site of death, without any remnants of the *physical* devastation and without shrines bearing witness to *emotional* devastation, they did not respond to the tragedy of the site. As noted above, the shrines were not only creative and emotional outlets; they also created a sense of unity among mourners and transformed the ground they sat upon into sacred space.

The shrines were among the first and the most enduring public responses to the tragedy. The keepers of many shrines around the City decided to take them down on December 31, 2001, choosing the end of the year to bring one stage of mourning to a close. In

September 2002, however, shrines near Ground Zero, at Grand Central, and near St. Vincent's Hospital, were still being visited and added to. At Grand Central Station, someone added a poster of Daniel Pearl, the Wall Street Journal reporter abducted and slain in Pakistan, as another victim of terrorism. Also added was a newspaper article about the widow of a September 11 victim who ultimately committed suicide. These additions at the shrines conveyed that the tragedy of September 11 was ongoing.

In November 2002, a decision was made to gradually dismantle the shrine in front of St. Paul's chapel with the goal of having it all removed by the end of December 2002. Local residents complained both that it had become unsightly and that it was simply something that they did not wish to be reminded of every day. The church complied yet set a slow schedule for the shrine's dismantling to allow Christmas-time tourists to see the memorial.[35] On September 11, 2002 many of the places that had been the sites of shrines after September 11, 2001, such as firehouses and Union Square Park, were revisited. New shrines were created. These "anniversary shrines" were markedly more contained and orderly than the massive shrines that had evolved directly after the attack. It seems that the shrines were external indicators of their creators' moods. Directly after the attack, people were overwhelmed, and there was a sense of the chaotic. And, *so many* of the city's residents wanted to *do* something. This was reflected in the early, overflowing shrines. The smaller, anniversary shrines illustrated that a year after the attacks, a semblance of order was restored to city life.

Shrines can serve as points of contact, places of communication with the dead, as portals to the otherworld. Although Union Square was not an officially designated site for public grieving in September 2001, it did not randomly emerge as the site of a huge communal shrine and vigil either. At first, the public was not allowed down below 14th Street. Union Square, which borders on 14th St., was as close as many people could get to the devastation. Later, as more and more of the City opened up, shrines could be seen further and further down—and almost every police barricade, every traffic cone, every outer limit to the site of death had flowers left at it. Many people wanted to get as close as they could to the sanctified place where it seemed the souls of the dead must hover.

When someone dies, survivors are left with the responsibility of maintaining the relationship with the deceased. At many shrines mourners have written notes to the dead, just as they sometimes do at cemeteries. Many families will never get the bodies of their loved ones back. They do not, and will not, have cemetery plots to visit. This recalls the scene in Melville's *Moby Dick* when Ishmael enters a seaside chapel in which there are markers for those lost at sea—people who have "placelessly perished without a grave." He appreciates that the desolation of mourners for these dead is much greater than mourners whose dead lie buried beneath the green grass who can say "Here, here lies my beloved." Families of those who perished in the Holocaust and do not know where the bodies of their loved ones lie, have devised surrogate gravesites. Tombstones of family members who died after the war often also list the names of all family members who were murdered during the Holocaust and had no tombstone. Perhaps the families of the victims of September 11 will adopt this practice. Bodies are important components of rites of passage. The presence of a corpse at funerary rites is necessary not only for the psychological purpose of making death real to the bereaved, but is also necessary for transition rites to be performed, for the dead to be incorporated into the hereafter. Without a body there are no funerals, only memorial services.[36] This ritual importance of the body was seen in a period of public mourning that New York experienced in the summer of 1999, when a plane piloted by John F. Kennedy, Jr. crashed into the sea. Much effort was expended searching for his body and retrieving it from the water. Once this was accomplished, it was returned to the water in a sea burial.

Shrines have become a traditional and expected response to tragedy in the past few decades—they were prominently seen after the bombing in Oklahoma City, the shooting at Columbine, and after the death of Princess Diana in an automobile accident. Usually, once funerals begin, services and gravesites replace shrines as sites of pilgrimage to leave flowers and other mementos.[37] In the absence of bodies buried in cemetery plots, some people who suffered personal losses are using the shrines in the same way that mourners use the cemetery—visiting and leaving adornments on special occasions such as Christmas or birthdays. "Happy 24th Birthday Jimmy Quinn" proclaimed a big green poster on the gate of St. Paul's Chapel. This sign was hung next to a newspaper article about this gregarious go-getter written by his brother, recounting how a group of his buddies went out to eat on his birthday, and commenting that even dead, "he can still fill a place with friends." Usually shrines are ephemeral, flowers wilt and notes get damaged by rain and faded by sun. When people became aware of this, they started laminating their notes and putting photos in plastic sleeves. Missing Posters, turned into tributes to the dead not only through the passage of time but because a new genre of poster was created, *intended* as tributes. A flyer with a photo of a young man on it read "Missed," instead of "Missing." At first, most messages at shrines were addressed to the public—"Have you seen this person?" or "Look at who this person was" but they increasingly became places to leave messages addressing the dead, "We miss you," "You will never be forgotten." Near the shrine at St. Paul's chapel there was a bicycle chained to a bus stop pole in memory of delivery boys who were killed. Also attached were a Mexican flag with the image of the Virgin of Guadalupe and a note in Spanish and in English: "If we looked for you and didn't find you, we will understand that you arc in heaven." "*Si te buscamo y no te hallamas comprendemos que ya llegaste al cielo.*"

Usually the kind of memorialization seen at shrines honoring victims of violent deaths does not replace traditional funerary rites; rather, it "emerges as adjunct ritual which extends the opportunity for mourning to individuals not conventionally included in traditional rites."[38] And indeed, notes were written not only by mourners who had suffered a personal loss but by the general public as well. The public shrines were designated places where people who would not officially be considered mourners but who were experiencing feelings of sorrow and loss could define themselves as mourners and participate in the mourning process. At Grand Central Terminal, for example, a note was attached by an anonymous commuter to the Missing poster of a man with a beaming smile. It read, "Every morning I see you smiling. I miss you. We never met."

By expressing our grief physically, creating memorials throughout the city, we were left with physical representations of our grief. These memorials, which gave mourners a focus, helping them to shape their sorrow, were also constant reminders to keep the memories of the dead present in our lives. In November 2001, two months after the attacks, I finally decided to go out for a bit of enjoyment. I went for a bike ride in Central Park. Every few yards along the bike path there are utility poles, and every single pole had a red, white, and blue ribbon wrapped around it, topped by a white bow. They seemed to say, "You are having fun on a Sunday in the park, but don't forget...don't forget...don't forget."

Notes

1. Steve Zeitlin and I explore this phenomenon in *Giving a Voice to Sorrow: Personal Responses to Death and Mourning* (Perigee Press, 2001).
2. This phrase is from the last page of Patricia Lysaght's article "Caoineadh Os Cionn Coirp: The Lament for the Dead In Ireland," *Folklore* 1997.
3. Emile Durkheim, *The Elementary Forms of the Religious Life* [1915] (The Free Press, 1965), p. 262.
4. According to Jewish tradition, the body of a person awaiting burial should never be left alone. Even through the night, community members sit by the casket, usually reading Psalms. At Ground Zero there were many unrecovered bodies; and at the Medical Examiner's office and makeshift morgues, many bodies and body parts were awaiting identification. It was likely that some of these were the bodies of Jews. Therefore, members of the Jewish community took shifts sitting near the bodies and reciting Psalms, performing their own tradition in public places.
5. Traditionally 1000 cranes are made for healing. The well-known story of "Sadako and the Thousand Paper Cranes" tells of a Japanese girl stricken with leukemia caused by the atomic bomb in WWII. Sadako learns of a Japanese fable that states that the maker of one thousand origami paper cranes will be granted a wish and unsuccessfully attempts to regain her health in this way.
6. *Giving A Voice to Sorrow*, p. 5.
7. Martha Cooper and Joseph Sciorra, *RIP: Memorial Wall Art* (Henry Holt and Company, 1994), p. 10
8. Jacque Derrida, *The Work of Mourning* (University of Chicago Press, 2001).
9. Kevin Flynn "An Attention to Detail, an Emphasis on Dignity," *New York Times*, October 5, 2001.
10. *St Petersburg Times*, Sept. 21, 2001
11. Memorial walls are discussed in *Giving a Voice to Sorrow*, pp. 192-200.
12. Marshall Sella, "Missing: How a Grief Ritual is Born," *New York Times Magazine*, Oct. 7, 2001. Sella traces the origin of Missing posters to the family of Mark Rasweiler—his poster was the first of its kind. His family had created and posted it on the afternoon of the attack. Caryn Wiley, one of his daughters, worked in an advertising firm. She and her husband ran off 800 copies of a Missing placard with the basic information of photo, height, weight, and phone numbers to call. They posted flyers at hospitals and shelters. Once the Missing posters caught on, they spread swiftly. Creators of posters started adding additional details such as the clothing the missing were wearing and any identifying marks.
13. Although the shrines reflected diverse religious belief, traditions connected to rescue workers were primarily Christian. This makes sense since the occupations of firefighter and police officer are traditional in many Irish and Italian Catholic families. In at least two memorial services, the self-sacrifice of firefighters who were killed "going up the down staircase" attempting to rescue victims still inside the tower were compared to Jesus ascending the hill of Calvary for his crucifixion.
14. "A Symbol of Faith Marks a City's Hallowed Ground," *New York Times*, Oct 5, 2001, p. B12.
15. "The myriad forms of anthropomorphism range from literal to metaphoric." Steward Guthrie, *Faces in the Clouds: A New Theory of Religion* (Oxford University Press, 1993), p. 92.
16. The letters were written by a man named Martin Hopkins.
17. Dan Barry, "Where Twin Towers Stood, a Silent Goodbye," *New York Times*, May 31, 2002.

18. The towers, in this poster, stand against a sky made out of tiny blue letters spelling out the names of the deceased.
19. People think they have social relations with things. "It is possible for inanimate objects, no less than for human organisms to form parts of the generalized social [other] for any human individual in so far as he responds to such objects socially or in a social manner... Thus no objective humanlike traits are necessary for something to strike us as humanlike." Guthrie, p. 96. Figure 5-1 in Guthrie's book shows the Empire State building and Chrysler Building (two other buildings with distinct personalities that are located quite near each other) as a male and a female passenger on a cruise around Manhattan who eye each other flirtatiously on deck near the rail. He comments: "We imagine social relations even among buildings." And the Chrysler Building and Empire State Building are shown in bed together in two paintings in Rem Koolhaas' *Delirious New York.*
20. Guthrie observes that anthropomorphization happens when there is an equivalence of people and non-human objects. Guthrie, p. 134.
21. Nino's also dedicated itself to feeding rescue workers free of charge.
22. The practice of memorializing firefighters on the rigs of the firehouses to which they belonged is not new. An example of this is displayed in the Friendship Firehouse Museum in Alexandria, Virginia where a nineteenth-century hose reel bears memorial photos of two firemen who died in 1855.
23. Shaila Dewan , "Tattooed Badge of Courage," *New York Times*, Sept. 30, 2001.
24. A photograph of this tattoo was printed to accompany the story by Kevin Flynn, "An Attention to Detail, an Emphasis on Dignity," *New York Times*, Oct. 5, 2001.
25. *Giving a Voice to Sorrow*, p. 106.
26. *The Work of Mourning*, p. 159. Derrida writes, "Not to recognize the intractable reality that the dead are now only 'in us' would be not only a form of denial but a betrayal of the dead friend, a failure to accede to the unique event that the friend has undergone."
27. Many broadcasters chose to read segments of W. H. Auden's "September 1, 1939" or E. B. White's *Here is New York.*
28. Excerpted from Thomas Lynch's poem, "A Death," in *Skating with Heather Grace* (Knopf 1986), p. 5.
29. Jennifer Senior, "The Fireman's Friar," *New York Magazine*, Nov. 12, 2001.
30. Reported by Beth Harpaz for the Associated Press, "Beleaguered NY Firefighters Mourn," Sept. 17, 2001.
31. This description of Father Mike's month's mind, which took place on October 11, 2001, was written by Gerry Regan for *The Wild Geese Today—Erin's Far Flung Exiles* (thewildgeese.com).
32. Mary Williams Walsh, "Impulse to Help Allows a Wife to Understand," *New York Times,* December 10, 2001, p. B1
33. Erving Goffman, *Frame Analysis: An Essay on the Organization of Experience* (Harper and Row, 1974), p. 559.
34. Ilana Harlow "Unravelling Stories: Exploring the Juncture of Ghost Story and Local Tragedy," *Journal of Folklore Research* 1993, Vol. 30, No. 2/3, p. 196 note 3.
35. Michael Wilson, "St. Paul's Chapel Slowly Dismantles 9/11 Memorial," *New York Times*, November 8, 2002.
36. In the absence of a body, the family of one firefighter conducted a funeral service for him incorporating a flag-wrapped casket holding a vial of his blood. Michael Ragusa, the last of the 343 fallen firefighters to be memorialized, had once donated a blood sample to a bone-marrow clinic. His family retrieved the vial and placed it in a casket, which they buried on September 8, 2003.

37. Sylvia Grider, "Spontaneous Shrines: A Modern Response to Tragedy and Disaster," *New Directions In Folklore*, October 2001, p. 1. *http://www.temple.edu/isllc/newfolk/shrines.html*
38. C. Allen Haney, Christina Leimer, and Julina Lomerey, "Spontaneous Memorialization: Violent Death and Emerging Mourning Ritual," *Omega* 35: 159-71, 1997, p. 16.

5

Where are the Dead? Bad Death, the Missing, and the Inability to Mourn

Henry Abramovitch

The events of September 11, 2001 carry indelible images, seared into the collective consciousness of all those who watched the events, either in person or on TV. Watching these images created an "imagined community of mourners" (Abramovitch 2001a; 2001b) who participated in these events via these images of ultimate horror (Lifton 1978). Each observer became a symbolic participant in these events. The images begin with the planes deliberately crashing into the twin towers of the World Trade Center. They continue with the subsequent fire and smoke, and the horrendous spectacle of people leaping from the upper stories. They conclude with the systematic collapse of the buildings at "Ground Zero" crushing nearly all those left inside. This sequence of images continues to circle like looping videotape, not only on television screens, but also in the collective memory, like the "rerun" nightmares of victims of posttraumatic stress disorder (PTSD).

These repeating images and nightmares are indications that the trauma is not "safely" in the past but continues to occur in the psychological tense of "present continuous." That is to say that the events have not happened in the past, but are, in a psychological sense, still continuing to happen. A *New York Times* poll, published exactly two years after September 11, 2001, revealed that two thirds of New Yorkers were worried about another attack, an increase from the year before. Under such circumstances any mourning is difficult, if not impossible, since mourning is based on the ontological assumption that the loss is in the past. It is only once the loss is experienced as "over" and with a certain amount of psychic distance, that the work of mourning can begin. Instead of mourning in America, we find continuing anxiety and grief as the predominant affect.

There is, however, another set of images that impedes the work of mourning. It is the image of the missing dead. It may be paradoxical to speak of the "image" of the missing dead, since one cannot see what is missing. Yet when one looks at a photograph taken at a family celebration, one immediately notices the key family member who is missing from the picture. So many people disappeared without a trace. Almost half of the bodies of those who died on September 11, 2001 were never found. The search to come to terms with the missing bodies of the dead remains a central concern, not only for those directly involved, but also for collective mourning.

The voices of the relatives of the missing continue to play an important role in the ongoing debate and controversy about what to do with the site of the disaster. The unease with how to treat the place where these missing people were last seen is reflected in the fact that after two years, the New York State legislature has still failed to set up a Commission to oversee commemoration of the event.[1] Joseph Maurer, one of a group of surviving relatives who engaged in civil disobedience protests against the rebuilding at Ground Zero as "a sacred burial ground," claimed: "Office space can be put anywhere. This is a graveyard, it can only be in one spot here on hallowed ground."[2]

In this chapter, I will discuss why the missing present such a challenge to the work of mourning in terms of good/bad death distinction using comparative ethnographic material.

Good versus Bad Death

In many societies, the occurrence of a death severely disrupts social life so that "it is stricken in the very principle of its life in the faith it has in itself" (Hertz 1960:78). The functionalist perspective stresses how in order to transform all deaths into good ones, mortuary rites served to resolve the disruptive tendencies that operate at times of social crisis. Malinowski demonstrated how ceremonies counteract the centrifugal forces of fear, dismay, and demoralization associated with death and provide powerful means of reintegration of the group's shaken morale (Palgi and Abramovitch 1984). These funerary rituals that concern both the dead and the bereaved must provide an answer to the meaning of life for the community at a time when it is most threatened. The ceremonies in which they are played out provide an occasion for reasserting the vitality of the core values of the society.

While there are many culture specific elements attached to how to characterize a particular kind of death, there is a universal cultural distinction and between a good death and a bad death.[3] A good death represents a cultural ideal that reenacts a symbolic victory over death, provides meaning, and allows for the regeneration of life (Bloch and Parry 1982). It involves, first and foremost, not sudden, bloody, or unexpected or meaningless dying trajectories. Ideally, it is a death without brutality, nor punctuated by anger.

A bad death does the opposite. It leaves survivors despairing and helpless in the face of meaninglessness, evil, or nothingness. Unpredictability, violence, or intentional harm are widespread attributes of a bad death. Archetypal examples of bad death include suicide, homicide, and death in a traffic accident. In addition, among the "bad" are violent deaths, especially when sudden, unexpected, bloody, intentional, committed in anger (murder, suicide, reckless teenage driving), or resulting in painful agony, as well as the death of young people. Other proposed universal aspects of bad death include non-performance of the required mortuary rituals or non-performance of other obligations toward the dead person (Abramovitch 1999).

Traditionally, the image of good or bad death played a central role in the collective imagination of a society. It often played a key role in the "defining moment" in a person's life of "how to die." Often the actual circumstances surrounding the death, or even the very moment of death, provided the cultural definition of good and bad death. A good death also has culture-specific "positive attributes" beyond being a mirror of bad death. A good death must enact symbolic victory over death by reasserting the core values of the society. Since core values do vary considerably from culture to culture so too the specifics of good death vary.

My survey of good death reveals that the key aspects of a good death include such things as:

- Dying at a preferred or auspicious time: Hindus prefer to die during a specific festival (Parry 1994); Jews prefer to die on a Tuesday or before Yom Kippur; and so on.

- The setting and posture at time of death: Navaho elect to die outside their hogan since a death inside will permanently pollute the structure; the Gusii of East Africa die in front of hearth on right side for males, left side for females; Tibetan Monks should perish sitting in lotus position; and so on.

- Preferred cause of death: Homeric heroes yearn for death in battle; Hindus to die in such a way that the soul leaves from the Brahamanic aperture in the top of the skull and not through some lesser orifice (Parry 1994); and so on.

- Thoughts and actions at time of dying: Jews are supposed to call out *sh'ma Yisroel*: "Hear O Israel, the Lord Our God, the Lord is One" and have concluded a special confessional; Hindus and many Buddhists know that one's last thoughts help determine the nature of one's next reincarnation; and so on.

- Performance of often extremely elaborate rituals as a means of good death: The inability to perform these rituals in proper sequence automatically converts a "good death" into a "bad" one. An orthodox Jew who cannot be present to say Kaddish at a parent's grave; a Hindu who is not present at the funeral pyre; and so on.

A good death provides closure. The loss can be mourned and placed in the past. In contrast, the impact of bad death lingers dangerously and rarely leads to closure; it extends the liminality of grief and bereavement. As such, a bad death is akin to an uncompleted task that remains incomplete and therefore establishes an endless sense of obligation. A bad death is much harder to "put behind us" with a feeling of obligations fulfilled than a good death. Whether we use the experience-near language of wandering ghosts or the experience-distant language of depth psychology of disturbing "internal objects," we are haunted by a bad death.

The dying person and the survivors may experience the death in different ways; what may be a good death for one may not be such for the other. Kubler-Ross (1974) demonstrated that dying individuals may come suddenly to a final acceptance of their demise only moments before death and they therefore experience a good moment of death. Relatives, however, are not always prepared for the end and may experience the death as bad and even traumatic, as in the case of a young daughter traumatized by her mother's calm and peaceful death (Abramovitch 1999). In a similar way, victims who were able to express feelings of love by cell phone and say goodbye just before the moment of their death conceivably might have allowed those to whom they spoke to experience more closure than those left behind without such messages. Alternatively, the caller may have felt ready to die after the conversation and the goodbye, while the recipient who survived may not have shared the aftermath of goodness in the goodbye.

The fate of the missing dead may be understood in terms of this good/bad death distinction and elaborated by using comparative ethnographic illustrations, including my own fieldwork among the Betsimisaraka of Nosy Boraha, in Eastern Madagascar (Malagasy Republic). Among the Betsimisaraka of Eastern Madagascar, death rituals stand in the center of social life (Bloch and Parry 1982; Abramovitch 1974). Similar to many societies, the Betsimisaraka use expensive and elaborate mortuary ritual as a way of demonstrating status and power so that the expense incurred by a funeral is often an enormous financial burden (Abramovitch 2001a; 2001b). The atmosphere is not always sad or somber but may even take on a festive atmosphere so that one may speak of "celebrations of death" (Huntingdon and Metcalf 1991).

One such celebration of death is the "second funeral" or secondary treatment of the remains ("fahamadihana"), which may be said to be the final rite of passage. (Hertz 1960; Bloch 1971; Abramovitch 1975). The second funeral occurs some years after the burial, once all the flesh has decomposed. The bones of the deceased are dug up from the earth. In a complex ritual, the bones are placed on a woven reed mat. The elder male of the lineage, bending down on one knee addresses the spirit of the deceased, saying how she or he has not been forgotten, how so many people have come to honor them, how much goods and spirits have been prepared in their honor and so on. He then goes on to "make peace" with the deceased and call on all the Great Ancestors ("razabe") from all the sacred spots in the area to accept this new candidate into their midst as a new Ancestor. Acceptance into the ancestral realm completes the lifecycle ritual and is a cause for great celebration. Once this has been accomplished, the audience, organized according to gender and seniority, begins to drink the ancestral brew, fermented rice beer, and to dance in a joyous "end of mourning" ritual. Bloch (1971) reports that some even dance with the bones of their loved one. Eventually the bones are wrapped in white linen on other mats and placed with various ritual objects, old coins, and a bottle of spirits in "shade houses," small wooden or cement sarcophagi shaped like miniature versions of their regular houses. In times of illness or misfortune, family members will come to the shade house to ask for intervention from these ancestors. As one informant put it: “As a parent punishes an unruly child, so too, the ancestors care for us by sending us illness.” If a Malagasy dies and is buried abroad, say in the former colonial power France, the extended family will save up for generations in order to send someone to France to bring his bones back to the earth of the ancestors (“tanindraza”).

My informants among the Betsimisaraka were very explicit about their image of the very worst type of bad death. It was when the body of the deceased was never found. In practical terms, it occurred when the deceased was lost at sea, without the body ever being recovered. The “badness” of this death revolves around the ritual importance of the second funeral. If the body is unavailable, then the ritual cannot be performed and the soul can never become an ancestor. If the person has drowned at sea and the body is not found, initially, a large stone is paced in graveyard. Eventually, a small carved wooden statue, called *tsangaolona*, literally a “standing man,” is set up in place of the sarcophagi. This statue both looks like a standing man but also symbolically stands for the lost bones of the deceased, which are thereby retrieved. This standing man statue becomes the focus of all future ritual activity. In other Malagasy or African societies, the spirit of the deceased is said to enter and reside within the statue. It takes on many of the qualities of sacred space that a gravesite monument may in contemporary civilization. But the memorial unlike the gravesite remains more ambiguous. Because the body is not there, there remains doubt as to whether the spirit truly entered it. Since there is no formal ritual that reassures relatives, there remains a cultural anxiety: Did the spirit of the dead person truly become assimilated into the statue or does it remain a dangerous wandering ghost? The Malagasy bad death clearly involves many culture-specific aspects. But it nevertheless contains elements that seem widespread if not actually universal.

The Victims of 9/11

With this background, we can now assess the victims of September 11, 2001 in terms of the good/bad death distinction. The victims of 9/11 whose bodies are still missing include most of the attributes that make up a “bad death.” They are sudden, unexpected (literally out of the blue sky), bloody, carried out with intentional brutality, committed in angry vengeance upon individuals, many of whom were in their prime, at the start of a day of activity, who often died in painful agony. These were not people ready or expecting to die that day. Finally, the absence of a body means that in practice the necessary mortuary rituals could not be performed.

Mental health professionals believe that the lack of remains makes it harder for survivors to overcome grief and move on. The use of corpse-less memorial services remains problematic for many: "We had a memorial service, but basically we just had a picture, and we got a headstone. My wife visits the headstone periodically, but I don't find it particularly helpful because I know there's just nothing there."[5] Such memorials may provide some partial closure but they do not relieve the cultural anxiety.

At the time of the recovery phase, there was controversy concerning the recovery of these bodies. "Wasn't it better," some argued, "to leave the corpses undisturbed in a spontaneous mass grave?" Behind this question is the supposition that if everything remained buried, no one would know who among the victims were corpse-less. All would somehow be equally dead and buried, ready to be mourned. But of course this would deny the uniqueness of the victims and the cultural or religious traditions to which they were tied; the religious traditions of Christians, Muslims, Jews, and Hindus are all based on knowing the time of the death and performing specific rites on the corpse.

Any skyscraper that will literally encase the dead in the building foundations cannot serve as a place for the souls of the unburied, nor a mass grave. In Hebrew such mass graves are called *kever achim*, a "grave of brothers-and-sisters" who are made siblings by sharing a common end. In one sense, the shared death does create a sense of kinship between those who died; but in another sense such collectivization denies the very individuality of the deceased, which the families so wish to celebrate. In either case, building over this sacred ground entombs the dead without giving them a tomb so that the dead are felt to be trapped underground. They are not only permanently embedded in their liminality but can never make their literal journey to the family mortuary grounds nor their symbolic journey to their rightful place in the next world. Hertz (1960) and others have argued that there are profound parallels between the soul's journey in the afterlife and the status of mourners. The stages along the soul's journey parallel the stages in the return of the mourners to their normal social status. When the dead are unincorporated, the mourners are also permanently stuck in their roles of mourners. In psychiatric framework, such "stuckness" can be easily pathologized as "pathological grief reaction" or "interminable mourning." It remains pathological insofar as the mourners remain engaged with the fate of their dead instead of readjusting to their new social roles (to use a sociological metaphor) or to withdraw and reinvest their emotional energy or libido, to use a psychoanalytic metaphor.

The missing body, however, has a more general significance, which transcends any specific religious practice. Death, like birth, marriage, initiation, and other lifecycle events, can be understood, following Van Gennep, as a rite of passage. All such rites of passage have three phases: separation, liminality, re-incorporation. The missing dead have a problematic status at each phase. The moment of separation between life and death is blurred.

For Hindus, who believe in cremating the dead, there can be no prayers for the departing soul until a death has been declared. Similarly, for Jews, the practice of sitting *shiva* is supposed to follow the burial, but if there is no funeral, when does the *shiva* begin? And without the Hindu cremation and the Jewish *shiva*, the grief of bereavement cannot be ritually and culturally surmounted. Important leave-taking rituals remain incomplete. Since no body is found and rituals remain undone, the soul of the loved one remains permanently in a liminal state and may be referred to as "the unincorporated dead." The unincorporated dead do not have a fixed conceptual location but are akin to souls that wander restlessly from place to place. The collective concern for their re-incorporation is expressed in phrases like "Rest in Peace"; or to use the Hebrew phrase "May you be bound up in the bond of life." Instead, the unincorporated dead remain trapped between the realms of the living and the dead.

Many African societies conceptualize such wandering souls as dangerous, "hungry ghosts." These unincorporated dead are seen as lonely and seeking incorporation in the world of the ancestors, where they will receive their due offerings. These ghosts are therefore perceived as "hungry" in the sense that they do not receive their due of ancestral offering and as a result they may injure or even kill close kin. At times of illness, death, or misfortune, much effort will be spent in trying to appease and accommodate such wandering hungry souls. The attitude toward these wandering ghosts is therefore ambivalent. On the one hand, they are feared, since they are seen as a main source of illness and misfortune, but on the other hand, they are objects of pity, since they are close kin who have not found their proper resting place but wander endlessly looking for their "home."

Nor can these ancestors be called upon as a "cultural resource" to intercede on their behalf in time of need, since the communication between the living and these dead is disturbed and dangerous. The ghosts desperately still need the living to lay them to rest, but the living find they cannot accomplish this; they lack the necessary remains. In a sociological/psychodynamic sense, these ghosts can also be seen as representing the "unfinished business" between the current and the former generation. Every generation has tensions with its predecessors but in the contemporary period of tremendous modernization and "culture loss," the inter-generational strain may be great indeed. Even secular individuals may experience these wandering ghosts in a phenomenological way, when they appear in troubling dreams, via intrusive memories or a nagging sense of unease.

From another point of view, these ghosts represent unconscious aspects of the personality of the mourners. These repressed feelings are easily projected onto culturally appropriate supernatural objects, such as these unincorporated dead. The ritual activity designed to appease these ghosts at the same time serves a therapeutic function to help integrate these formerly projected aspects. For example, grief is widely thought to include anger toward to departed loved one for their very act of abandonment (Freud 1959; Rosenblatt, Walsh, and Jackson 1976). That is, when the remains are missing, both the dead are abandoned by the living and the living feel even more abandoned by the dead. When this anger over abandonment is unconscious, it may at times be projected outward onto the deceased spirit who is subsequently perceived as "angry" or "hostile" to its living survivors. Rites that pacify the angry spirit also serve as a culturally appropriate catharsis toward the survivors' original survivor anger. The relatives of the missing dead have no clear cultural repertoire for dealing with this anomalous situation, as the Betsimisaraka do.

In one sense, they resemble the relatives of those warriors who are "missing in action." They may privately suspect that their loved ones are indeed dead but to publicly admit to this possibility is to abandon them again, to be complicit in their demise. To give up hope is, in a symbolic sense, to murder them again, since it is their very hope that is keeping them alive. Families of those missing in action are permanently stuck in the liminal phase—unable to separate and unable to reincorporate into society in a new status. They often feel guilty about continuing their lives without their missing relative.

Relatives of those killed in the twin towers almost certainly know that their loved ones are dead, never to return. Yet, like families of MIAs, some have a latent, irrational fantasy (more common in the immediate aftermath) that somehow, improbably, "hoping against hope" that they will return home, a hope that paralyzes their forward movement, that prevents them form mourning. Sometimes the state or some other social institution can end this by declaring the missing to be dead and by creating a memorial to affirm this reality. This has of course been an important part played by the institutions and authorities of America in the wake of 9/11. They have sought with these memorials to lay the missing to rest, to undo some of the badness of their predicament.

The task is, then, how to renegotiate the demise of the missing from a terribly bad, lingering death into one that is, if not good, then at least a better death that provides improved opportunities for closure.

The response to mass casualty situation often leads to creative responses. After World War I, the unidentified dead were symbolically entombed in the Tomb of Unknown Soldier, which in England included a single unknown warrior from each of the different branches of the military (Gregory 1994). The Tomb of the Unknown can be seen as analogous to the Malagasy *tsanganolona* designed to contain the wandering spirit of the unincorporated dead. Similarly, the Vietnam War memorial provided a locus of sentiments and a source of healing for that entire generation (Scruggs and Swerdlow 1985; Harrison 2003). Contemporary use of the Internet as a medium for mourning may represent another unique solution (Abramovitch 2001a; 2001b).[6] The memorial at Ground Zero is still unfolding as a medium for personal and collective memory.[7]

In a traditional society, people knew how to behave when faced with death and dying. In many modern societies, individuals no longer have such clear social rules to guide their behavior. They often feel confused or uneasy in these circumstances. Although the roots of this change are complex, it appears related to a fundamental change in the traditional nature of society as composed of *both* the living and the dead. "If the structure of African cultures is that of a dialogue (between the living and the dead), then the structure of Western society is that of a monologue—but the monologue of the dead" (Bastide 1968:104). Lifton (1978) proposed the term "the broken connection" to describe how the link between the living and the dead has been severed in contemporary society. Conceptually, the issue can be put in terms of a question: Where are the dead? The literal and symbolic responses to this question, therefore, continue to provide key insights into the deep structure of society.

Although Bastide was making a point about the absence of ancestral presence in modern Western life, his metaphor could well be used in connection with the missing dead of September 11, 2001. So long as their bodies are not found, nor their souls "contained" in some symbolic or ritual container, then the structure of interaction between the dead and the living is that of a monologue of the dead. The survivors and society at large are still searching for a way to restart the dialogue.

Conclusion

Psychotherapists who work with the bereaved typically emphasize the importance of the relationship with the deceased as the key factor in the work of mourning (Abramovitch 1999). They emphasize the importance of working through ambivalent feelings of rage, survivor guilt, and abandonment toward the departed. The inability to work through these feelings is believed to be associated with pathological grief. "The central task of the therapy is to resolve the disturbed object relations with the introject of the deceased which has interfered with the normal work of mourning" (Parkes, Laungani, and Young 1996; Stroebe, Stroebe, and Hansson 1993; Volkan 1982; Abramovitch 1999:256).

The events of September 11, 2001 highlight how this object-relations perspective fails to take into account the importance of how the death itself occurred and the cultural performance of appropriate mortuary ritual. Events surrounding the moment of death, the absence of a body, and the funeral lend "badness" to the death. For relatives of those who perished in the twin tower attacks, the badness of the death included three phases of the dying process: the events immediately preceding death, the moment of death, and the rituals after death. The circumstances surrounding the loss itself, even more than the ambivalent relation with the deceased, distinguishes a traumatic loss from a less traumatic one.

From a sociological perspective, the missing represents a permanent challenge to closure and putting these events safely in the past.

Instead, the missing remain ambiguous, liminal figures hovering at the boundaries of the living and dead. They are unable to return to the living but at the same time, they cannot cross over to the land of the dead. Virgil, in the sixth book of the *Aeneid*, gives an evocative picture of the fate of the unburied. Aeneas has ventured down to the underworld guided by a Sybil. He comes to the River Styx and there observes the souls of the dead waiting to be taken across by Charon:

> They stand; each pleads to be the first to cross
> the stream; their hands reach out in longing for
> the farther shore. But Charon, sullen boatman,
> now takes these souls, now those; the rest he leaves;
> thrusting them back, he keeps them from the beach.
>
> That disarray dismays and moves Aeneas:
> "O virgin, what does all this swarming mean?
> What do these spirits plead? And by what rule
> must some keep off the bank while others sweep
> the blue-black waters with their oars?"

The priestess answers:

> "...All those you see are helpless and unburied.
> That ferryman is Charon. And the waves
> will only carry souls that have a tomb.
> Before his bones have found their rest, no one
> May cross the horrid shores and the hoarse waters.
> They wander for a hundred years and hover
> About these banks until they gain their entry
> To visit once more the pools they long for."[8]

The image of the souls of the unburied yearning to cross over but unable to do so is a poignant one, crystallizing their liminal status. However much these souls try to find their place on the other side, they cannot do so. A few lines later in the epic, Aeneas meets his faithful pilot, Palinurus, who fell off their boat and disappeared without a trace. Palinurus begs Aeneas to carry him across so that at least in death he can find a place of rest. The Sybil confirms the hopelessness of the pilot's fate. He, too, must wait on the beach unable to cross over to the other shore. The priestess, however, does prophecy that in the future a plague will reawaken interest in his miserable fate and neighboring cities will band together "o make peace with your bones; and they will build a tomb and send solemn sacrifices; the place will always be named Palinurus." For Virgil, the unprocessed dead represent a danger. In terms of Mary Douglas' well-known analysis, these missing fall between categories and hence are dangerous and impure. In collective memory, they attract attention to themselves. Until the society has made peace with their bones and builds a solemn memorial, the dead will continue to disturb the peace of the living. One hopes that the missing of 9/11 and those who long to mourn for them will not have to wait for one hundred years in order to find peace.

Notes

1. *New York Times*, Sept. 11, 2003.
2. *New York Times,www.nynewsday.com/news/sept* Sept. 3, 2003.
3. I am aware of only a single ethnographic challenge to the claim that a good/bad death distinction represents a human universal. Woodburn in his important essay "Social dimensions of death in four African hunting and gathering societies" claims that in "immediate-return" hunting-gathering societies, "There is no clearly defined distinction between a good death and a bad death involving different procedures and different consequences for the dead man and the mourners" (Woodburn 1982:203). In general disposal of the body is simple, there is no search for a cause of death, little concern with an afterlife, no ritual experts, and no clearly defined restrictions on mourning. His conclusions, as he himself admits, are open to doubt since they are not based on any direct observation of a death: "I should say at once that in some respects my knowledge is limited. During the entire period of nearly four years that I have spent living among the Hadza (of northern Tanzania) no one, apart from one child who died two days after birth, ever died in a nomadic camp in which I was at the time living, nor was I ever informed of a death at a nearby camp in time to be able to witness the procedures followed. My knowledge of what actually happens when somebody dies is based not on observation but on a mixture of accounts, often somewhat contradictory, about what does and does not happen. The Hadza are not keen to talk about what happens at death partly because it is an obviously distasteful subject but, even more important, because they know it is a subject about which outsiders are sensitive and which can lead to the Hadza being treated with scorn and labeled as primitive" (Woodburn 1982:188-9). Likewise, the accounts of Baka pygmies of Cameroon were not based on observation but only on accounts of death in Bantu villages. His two other examples from !Kung and Mbutoi pygmies rely on older ethnographies that did not have death as their prime focus.

   I believe that further fieldwork would reveal an informal good/bad death distinction in the collective recollection of specific deaths, even if there is little ritual marking the distinction.
4. Much of the contemporary discussion of "good death" is medical and concerns dealing with lingering death from cancer. A recent editorial in the *British Medical Journal* 320(7228):129 lists the following principles of a good death:

- To know when death is coming and to understand what can be expected
- To be able to retain control of what happens
- To be afforded dignity and privacy
- To have control over pain relief and other symptom control
- To have choice and control over where death occurs (at home or elsewhere)
- To have access to information and expertise of whatever kind is necessary
- To have access to any spiritual or emotional support required
- To have access to hospice care in any location, not only in hospital
- To have control over who is present and who shares the end
- To be able to issue advance directives that ensure wishes are respected
- To have time to say goodbye, and control over other aspects of timing
- To be able to leave when it is time to go, and not to have life prolonged pointlessly.

Hospices have emerged as new institutions that are designed to provide a good death for everyone (Abramovitch 2001a; 2001b), although this approach has been criticized. See Hart, Sainsbury, and Short (1998), "Whose dying? A sociological critique of the 'good death,'" *Mortality* 3(1): 65-78.

A more recent view argues that although a good death may exist as an ideal, in practice many are satisfied with a "good enough death." See J. D. Mason (2002), "Non-professional perceptions of 'good death': a study of views of hospice care patients and relatives of deceased hospice care patients," *Mortality* 7(2): 191-209.

5. "For families of unidentified, what remains is grief," Associated Press, Sept. 6, 2003; www.stamfordadvocate.com.
6. Many new sites were created for the victims of 9/11 and their families. These websites show photos and provide information and personal obituaries for all the dead, found or missing. There are hundreds of such sites: www.cnn.com/specials/2001/memorial; www.cantcryenough.com; www.legacy.com/nytimes/sept11.asp; for a complete listing of September 11-related websites, see "How America uses the web" at www.archive.org/web/web.php, which lists 417,000 sites; for a definitive review of all web-based news stories, see www.researchbuzz.com/911/mtype. These sites act as "an evolving record of those who died and a place for readers to build a living memorial for them." One can locate victims according to name, age, employer, residence, nationality, crash site, and so forth. There are specialty sites, for example, for gays (www.angelfire.com/f13/uraniamanuscripts/Septs 11.html) and various ethnic groups and nationalities (www. Farsi.com; Farsi.net honors its victims). Other private or public sites, for example, White House Commission on National Moment of Remembrance, include poems, songs, pictures, and tributes (e.g. "Though gone in body, they will never be lost in memory. I will never forget each and every person. Not a day goes by that I don't think of 9/11 and all that we lost. May you find comfort." Sinead O'Donnell, NJ). These virtual registries act as a "surrogate heaven." These websites can be accessed at any time and exist in an otherworldly "virtual" reality. In a practical sense, these websites become a locus of sentiment in the manner described by Malinowski.
7. See the chapter by Ilana Harlow in this volume.
8. Book VI, lines 316-30, *The Aeneid of Virgil: A Verse Translation by Allen Mandelbaum* (New York: Bantam, 1972), p. 143.

References

Abramovitch, H. (1974), "Tromba: A Spirit Possession cult in ile Sainte-Marie de Madagascar." *Taloha* Winter 1975.

Abramovitch, H. (1975), "Report on the Living and the Dead," in J. W. Berry and W. J.

Lonner, eds., *Applied Cross-Cultural Psychology*. Amsterdam: Swets & Zeitlinger, pp. 321-6.

Abramovitch, H. (2001a), "Anthropology of Death," in N. J. Smelser and Paul B. Baltes, eds., *International Encyclopedia of the Social and Behavioral Sciences*. Oxford: Pergamon, Oxford, pp. 3270-3.

Abramovitch, H. (2001b), "Sociology of Death and Dying," in N. J. Smelser and Paul B. Baltes, eds., *International Encyclopedia of the Social and Behavioral Sciences*. Oxford: Pergamon, Oxford, pp. 3267-70.

Ariès, P. (1975), Western Attitudes Toward Death: From the Middle Ages to the Present. London: Marion.

Ariss, R.M. (1997), Against Death: The Practice of Living with AIDS. Amsterdam: Gordon and Breach.

Bastide, R. (1968), "Religions africaines et strutures des civilizations." *Presence Africaine* 66, 82-105.

Becker, E. (1973), *The Denial of Death*. New York: Free Press.

Cline, S. (1996), *Lifting the Taboo: Women, Death and Dying*. London: Abacus.

Elias, N. (1985), *The Loneliness of the Dying*. Oxford: Blackwell.

Freud, S. (1959), *Mourning and Melancholia*, in *Collected Papers of Sigmund Freud*. 4: 152-70. London: Hogarth Press.

Glaser, B. and Strauss, A. (1965), *Awareness of Dying*. Chicago: Aldine.

Glaser, B. and Strauss, A. (1968), *Time for Dying*. Chicago: Aldine.

Gorer, G. (1965), Death, Grief and Mourning in Contemporary Britain. London: Cresset.

Gregory, A. (1994), *The Silence of Memory: Armistice Day 1919-1946*. Oxford/Providence: Berg.

Lifton, R. J. (1978), *The Broken Connection: On Death and the Continuity of Life*. New York: Simon & Schuster.

Kearl, M. (1989), Endings: A Sociology of Death and Dying. Oxford: Oxford University Press.

Kubler-Ross, E. (1969), *On Death and Dying*. New York: Macmillan.

Mitford, J. (1963), *The American Way of Death*. New York: Simon & Schuster.

Nuland, S. (1994), *How We Die*. London: Chatto & Windus.

Parkes, C. M. (1986), *Bereavement: Studies of Grief in Adult Life*. Harmondsworth: Penguin.

Parkes, C., Laugani, P., and Young, B. (1996), *Death and Bereavement Across Cultures*. London: Routledge.

Rosenblatt, P.C., Walsh, P., and Jackson, A. (1976), *Grief and Mourning in Cross Cultural Perspective*. New Haven: Human Relations Area Files Press.

Seale, C. (1998), *Constructing Death: The Sociology of Dying and Bereavement*. Cambridge: Cambridge University Press.

Stroebe, M. S., Stroebe, W., and Hansson, R. O. (1993), *Handbook of Bereavement: Theory, Research and Intervention*. Cambridge: Cambridge University Press.

Volkan, V. (1982), *Linking Objects and Linking Phenomena*. New York: International Universities Press.

Walter, T. (1994), *The Revival of Death*. London: Routledge.

Woodburn, J. (1982), "Social Dimensions of Death in Four African Hunting and Gathering Societies," in M. Block and J. Parry, eds., *Death and the Regeneration of Life*. Cambridge: Cambridge University Press.

Anthropology of Death

Abramovitch, H. (1999), "'Good Death' and 'Bad Death,'" in R. Malkinson, S. Rubin, and E. Witztum, eds., *Traumatic and Non-traumatic Loss and Bereavement*. New York: Psychosocial Press.

Ariès, P. (1974), *L'Homme devant la mort*. Paris: Editions du Seuil, Paris [Aries, P. (1981), *The Hour of our Death*. Trans. H. Weaver. New York: Knopf].

Bloch, M. (1971), *Placing the Death: Tombs, Ancestral Villages, and Kinship Organization in Madagascar*. London and New York: Seminar Press.

Bloch, M. (1988), "Death and the concept of person," in S. Cederroth, C. Corlin, and J. Lindstrom, eds., *On the Meaning of Death: Essays on Mortuary Rituals and Eschatological Beliefs*. Uppsala: Uppsala Studies in Cultural Anthropology 8. Acta Universitatis Upsaliensis.

Bloch, M. and Parry, J. (eds.) (1982), *Death and the Regeneration of Life*. Cambridge: Cambridge University Press.

Danforth, L. (1982), *The Death Rituals of Rural Greece*. Princeton: Princeton University Press.

Hertz, R. (1907), "Contributions a une étude sur la répresentation collective de la mort." *L'Année sociologique* 10: 48-137 [Hertz, R. (1960), *Death and the Right Hand*. Trans. R. Needham and C. Needham. New York: Free Press].

Humphreys, H. and King, H. (eds.) (1981), *Mortality and Immortality: The Anthropology and Archeology of Death*. London: Academic Press.

Huntingdon, R. and Metcalf, P. (1991), *Celebrations of Death: The Anthropology of Mortuary Ritual*. 2nd edition. Cambridge: Cambridge University Press.

Palgi, P. and Abramovitch, H. (1984), "Death: A Cross-Cultural Perspective." *Annual Review of Anthropology* 13: 385-417.

Parkes, C., Laungani, P., and Young, B. (eds.) (1997), *Death and Bereavement Across Cultures*. London and New York: Routledge.

Parry, J. (1994), *Death in Benares*. Cambridge: Cambridge University Press.

Rosenblatt, P., Walsh, R., and Jackson, A. (1976), *Grief and Mourning in Cross Cultural Perspective*. New Haven: Human Relations Area Files Press.

Scheper-Hughes, N. (1992), *Death Without Weeping: The Violence of Everyday Life in Brazil*. Berkeley and Los Angeles: University of California Press.

Recent Writing on the Jewish Perspective of Death

Abramovitch, H. (1993), "The Jerusalem Funeral: An Anthropological Perspective," in R. Malkinson, S. Rubin, and E. Witztum, eds., *Loss and Bereavement in Jewish Society in Israel*. Jerusalem: Kaneh [Hebrew].

Fine, S. (2000), "A Note on Ossuary Burial and the Resurrection of the Dead in First Century Jerusalem." *Journal of Jewish Studies* 51(1): 69-76.

Goldberg, S-A. (1996), *Crossing the Jabbok: Illness and Death in Ashkenazi Judaism in 16th-19th Century Prague*. Trans. C. Cosman. Berkeley and Los Angeles: University of California Press.

Heilman, S. (2001), *When a Jew Dies: The Ethnography of a Bereaved Son*. Berkeley and Los Angeles: University of California Press.

Riemer, J. (ed.) (1995), *Jewish Insights on Death and Mourning*. New York: Schocken.

Wieseltier, L. (1998), *Kaddish*. New York: Knopf.

6

The Firefighter, the Ghost, and the Psychologist: Reflections on "The 9/11 Firehouse Project"*

Warren Spielberg

Introduction

The day after the 9/11 attacks, I went to volunteer in a number of firehouses around my Brooklyn neighborhood, trying to offer assistance to many of the men who were living through the shock of their lives. The stresses that these firefighters would suffer are better known now than they were then. Besides the immediate losses of their three hundred and forty-three "brothers," they faced many other demands.

Many have felt a continuing debt to the widows and families of the fallen. This responsibility has been fraught with conflict and confusion as many men spent more time in the early days with the widows of the fallen than with their own families. Many firefighters, particularly family liaison officers, wished to offer solace and support, but also were fearful of being overwhelmed by the needs of these families. Widows, grateful for this support, still struggled with feelings of loss and anger. As they have tried to sort out their feelings about either the death of their comrades or their husbands, both groups of "survivors" continue to navigate a challenging relationship.

The political and social meaning of the World Trade Center collapse has weighed upon many of the firefighters. A great sacrifice was made by the Fire Department of New York (FDNY), and many members of the department continue to be regarded as heroes. Many brave men and women were lost and recent reports by an outside consultant have suggested that many could have been saved by better

* This paper describes my year as a consulting psychologist attached to a Brooklyn firehouse that had lost seven men in the WTC terrorist attack. It also briefly describes the "Firehouse Project," an FDNY citywide initiative, with which I have been involved.

communications, better command decisions, and by better training and discipline. Many firefighters have felt blamed by these reports.

If the death of so many of their comrades in the disaster of 9/11 was the initial wound in the heart of the firefighters of New York, the inability to achieve full retrieval of the bodies of the men lost at the World Trade Center (WTC) has been like another knife in the heart of many of the men. This is the first time that the FDNY has not retrieved bodies. Only the remains of three out of the seven lost were found from the firehouse where I work as a psychological counselor. Not a week goes by that this issue does not surface during my meetings at the firehouse. The inability to retrieve bodies or to rescue many survivors at the WTC has resulted in a reservoir of feelings of shame and helplessness, particularly acute for people treated as heroes and lifesavers.

Many firefighters remain frightened of a future terrorist incident. Many are urged by their families to quit. Many have already done so. The stresses on families of firefighters have been enormous—overtime, depression, and attendance at a huge number of funerals and memorials (most FDNY members attended close to twenty to thirty funerals in the aftermath of 9/11). Abiding sadness, bereavement, and a wish to get away from the gloom of a formerly enlivened firehouse are also part of these pressures.

The enormous losses of many senior members of the departments have also led to transfers, relocations, and retirements. In a normal year, forty retirement applications are filed per month. During the year following the 9/11 attacks, pension incentives and family pressures to leave pushed that number to forty applications *per week*. As the Fire Department struggles to replace senior men, firefighters must deal with the simultaneous dilemma of having to integrate new members into the life of the firehouse. This can be a challenging and trying experience at all times. But in the face of the all the turmoil post 9/11, many new firefighters ("probies") report that they sense that they are not receiving the level of mentorship and attention that was the norm in the past. Thus even neophytes, no less than the veterans who went through the 9/11 experience, are now experiencing additional stress beyond that which any firefighter feels.

Many of the stresses that the men have reported, however, are not related directly to the specific events of the WTC tragedy. The perceived insensitive actions and words of bystanders—including family members, politicians, and other interested parties—have for a number of firefighters been a source of pain. Unfortunately, in this last category I must include the actions of mental health providers. In general the mental health community has played a crucial role in helping FDNY members. However, at the same time there has been a mass marketing of trauma work, which has turned its treatment into a commodity, a new area for psychological entrepreneurs to ply their trade or a chance for an "experience." This commodity and the initiatives behind its marketing have been too often visited on unprepared firefighters as many untrained and or insensitive clinicians descended upon firehouses in the city. A lot of them did some good, but too many went into the psychological heart of darkness for a good story and then disappeared into the night leaving many individuals exposed and confused. Others have lost personal boundaries and have acted in unprofessional ways, for instance, betraying confidences or handing out false advice.

Despite these considerable stresses, it must be emphasized that the vast majority of the firefighters are coping. Since 9/11, they continue to report to the firehouse, put on gear, and do their jobs. During the year following the attacks, response times actually improved. But the work itself has never been an issue for most firefighters. In fact, having gone on many runs with them over a year, I observed that that is when they are at their best. Away from the tension of the firehouse and the ghosts of the dead, doing something they love, their competence on display, they arrive at some measure of peace.

The Firehouse Project

The first few weeks at firehouses around the city after 9/11 resembled a cacophony of rolling wakes and memorials. Widows and their families sought refuge. Former firefighters appeared at their old houses to offer solace and support. Grieving members of the public appeared en masse with food and tributes. Celebrities also made their appearances. Arnold Schwarzenegger came to one of the houses I have worked with in Brooklyn and handed out cigars. As one firefighter said to me in mid-September, "it's like the FDNY has a broken heart and the public is trying to push both halves back together again." The early support of the neighborhoods was critical in providing solace. Eventually, however, as time wore on the visits of tourists (many of whom would weep uncontrollably) became an added burden. It was as if the firefighters had to offer support for their would-be "supporters." It was not always clear who was helping whom more.

As the fall progressed, I found my volunteer time centered on one particular house off the beaten path in Brooklyn. Firefighters as a group, for a variety of reasons, do not typically utilize psychotherapy services. Counseling and psychotherapy are activities that are both foreign and feared by firefighters. There are many reasons for this. First, many firefighters adhere to the traditional male role model. This model (Spielberg 1993) espouses toughness, independence, and emotional invulnerability. Counseling and therapy require different sensitivities and interests, not normally part of their habits. Firefighters are also fearful of the career ramifications of going for counseling. Historically, those who were referred for counseling in the FDNY were sent to the CSU (counseling service unit) for alcohol or drug abuse issues. Even if they were not, there was a great deal of stigma in being sent for counseling. Finally, although there have been improvements, the mental health field has traditionally fallen short in reaching out to blue collar and working class patients. Practitioners often lack the cultural sensitivity or appreciation of class differences that can make for a successful treatment.

Nevertheless, early on I felt these men would need assistance in coping with their trauma, grief, and rage. As I surveyed the firehouse, I could see men in great pain and under enormous stress. So why not then bring a psychologist to the mountain and assign a psychologist to every firehouse that suffered losses? Through a fortuitous series of events I was able to assist in the development of such a project with Dr. Kerry Kelly, the chief medical officer of the FDNY and with Malachi Corrigan, director of the Counseling Services Unit (CSU). They have worked tirelessly to address the mental health problems that have threatened members since 9/11. From 100 contact hours pre 9/11, the FDNY CSU now provides roughly 3,000 hours a week of direct counseling services to FDNY members.

In December, Dr. Laura Barbanel of Brooklyn College and I, in conjunction with the Fire Department, coordinated a small pilot project with six firehouses—four in Manhattan and two in Brooklyn. The goals of the Firehouse Project were to bring didactic, clinical, and referral services directly to firefighters. How to accomplish these goals was, however, to a large degree, up to each clinician. In March, the FDNY expanded the program to include nearly every house (63) that had lost members. Dr. Barbanel and I have continued to work closely with the FDNY, referring and supervising clinicians as events unfold. Psychologists for this from the program have come mostly from the NYU Postdoctoral Program in Psychoanalysis and from the New York State Psychological Association.

The beginning was difficult. Firehouses are fairly closed systems, with specific codes of relating and traditions of cooperation and subtle hierarchies and politics that are not easy to master. Over the kitchen table reads a sign that says KEEP IT IN THE HOUSE, a testament to the privacy and protection they often give each other. The men had not requested that a psychologist be assigned to their house, nor did they object. Rather looking back on it, they took a wait and see attitude. This was considerably better than other houses where the initial resistance and antipathy was much greater. In some instances, a clinician was not assigned until the members of the firehouse voted to bring one in.

On January 3, 2002, escorted by three peer counselors, I lunched with approximately thirty men in the kitchen of the firehouse. Some listened politely and others with skepticism as I discussed issues of trauma, grief, depression, and alcoholism, but asked no questions. Later that day I met with the officers. They too sat in stony silence as I inquired about the men lost and the circumstances of their demise. Afterward, my mood plummeted. As I was leaving, I asked one of the captains how I did. With a twinkle is his eye he said, "Ah, you sucked." I did not know why but at the time this interaction somehow this made me feel better. Reflecting on it now I am sure that I probably felt better about the hazing I experienced than the deadness and hostility I initially encountered. The captain's comment was also the first example of aliveness I had had all day.

I returned a few days later, but took a different route. My primary goal was to gain acceptance into the system. Without this I would be ineffective. During this period I was aware of both the class and ethnic differences that separated me as a middle class professional and the blue collar men with whom I needed to connect. These class differences are rarely discussed but are often a source of tension between individuals from different backgrounds. In this case many firefighters had fears and animosities towards mental health professionals who they have seen as judgmental and high handed. Accordingly, I downplayed my professional identity and increased my exposure as a novice in a new system that I needed to master.

In order to be accepted, I also felt that the men needed to know of my authentic admiration and respect for their professionalism, skill, and unique dedication to service. Towards this end, I asked for a tour of the house. I received some lessons on the apparatus and the roles and rationales of firefighting. As with new patients, I began an extended detailed inquiry. I researched the types of fires the house gets, the chance of injury, as well as the nature of the men in the house. As best I could, I began to get a picture of the social hierarchy, the stated and unspoken rules of the firehouse, and the actual demands of the job. I am still learning.

Clinical Issues

There were many levels of emotional disturbance and functioning among the forty men. The engine (which is also an EMS service unit and is responsible for setting up the water lines) and the ladder (which is also called a truck, and carries the ladder used to make rescues in tall buildings) companies had both arrived at the WTC before the collapse. The engine and all its men had survived, due to a fortuitous command decision. The men on the engine were sent to the command center across the West Side Highway south of the WTC, where they were able to seek shelter at an underground garage after the first tower fell. Later the officer in charge, decided to move the engine further north so that when the second tower fell, they were away from it. The men on the ladder were, however, immediately sent into the south tower by the command center. All seven men working the ladder perished shortly thereafter.

All the engine men who had survived the collapse of the building were deeply affected. They were living in an altered psychic state. They experienced continuing flashbacks, intrusive thoughts, hyper vigilance, and almost daily nightmares. Most kept replaying in their minds scenes of "jumpers," those individuals who jumped from the top floors of the WTC rather than be burned, or of horrific scenes of carnage that they saw later in the day. None were receiving treatment at the time of my entry into the system. But by the end of the month, they had all gone on extended leave and into counseling. This required extensive discussions with these men and with the officers (some of whom legitimately had worried about manpower shortages). These five eventually returned to active duty.

The remainder of the firefighters was living through various forms of shock, guilt, and impacted grief (Shatan 1973). Consistent with the research on the Oklahoma bombing (Nixon et al. 1999), here too the younger men were in the worst shape. Most had never lost anyone with whom they were close. Many were single and not used to seeking social support. All the men had just completed attending between twenty and thirty ceremonies for the dead. If they missed the service for a friend, due to their work schedules, they often went to another memorial, even if this replacement funeral was of a stranger. All of this often overwhelmed them emotionally, even if they did not realize it.

During this first month of my work with them, I was reminded of the Holocaust memoir *Ruchele*, by Rose Farkas (1988). The author, who had survived the death camps, reported the following event in one of the liberation camps directly after the war. After coming to the camp, she

> ...entered a room where children were shivering and crying softly. The same scene repeated in the next room. I saw a little girl holding the hand of a small boy who was lying on the floor. When I approached, I could see that the child was dead. I told the girl to let go of him. "I can't," she said crying. "My mommy told me never to let go of his hand."

Many of the firefighters too had never learned to let go. In January of 2002, the men's grip on the hands of their comrades was still unyielding. The grip of one of the men of the ladder company was the firmest. He had been off for the day, and missed the WTC collapse. Now he was devoting all his spare time to helping the seven widows and their families. He insisted on making memorial arrangements and would not allow the members of the engine company to help out. In fact, the usual friendly competition between the engine and ladder companies descended into an internecine battle that threatened the cohesiveness of this dual house.

Robert Lifton has brilliantly explicated the psychodynamics of survivors (Lifton 1979). I have found his distinctions between static and animated guilt useful. The person beset by a sense of static guilt is one who is bound and imprisoned by his own feelings of grief, rage, and despair. He lives in two worlds. On one hand he is submerged with the dead and with those he feels he has let down. On another level he is also angry and glad to be alive and free. He is unable to express this duality, because he fears the emotional pain of loss that he feels may undo him. Static guilt also corresponds to Volkan's (1981) notions of complicated mourning, in that there is a clear defense against ambivalent feelings that must be faced in order to free the person from the dead object. Animated guilt is a process that occurs as the loss begins to be recognized and engaged.

When I first arrived at the firehouse, many men were numbed, stuck in rage, and grappling with negative identifications of cowardice and helplessness. These "static" and frozen states coincided with a deep resistance to acknowledging their feelings or sharing them with others. Some were extremely close to the fallen senior men who had raised them as firefighters, and were in "total identification" with their deadness (Smith 1971). This made them act almost like walking dead men, lacking in animation and engagement. Many others were facing reverberations of earlier traumas and losses. However, as I suggested earlier, many problems were also inter-psychic not intra-psychic, arising from specific real world interactions with others. This is true of survivor guilt as well. Many men who felt relieved to be alive were not allowed to voice or even feel such healthy emotions. Some who had done "mutuals" (schedule switches) with the fallen were accused by others of "not doing enough" to help.

In late January 2002, I started doing groups with the men. Trauma, survivor guilt, death imprint, and the dynamics of depression were issues upon which I touched. As the groups proceeded, more and more emotions surfaced. The men began to grieve more openly and also would talk more with one another in between my visits. There were few instances of dramatic catharsis. However slowly, the men moved into a more open and less frozen space where they were able to acknowledge the losses they incurred. This grief eventually opened into a more animated sense of guilt and a reparative stance vis-à-vis the memory of the dead. These reparative actions took many forms, from building a memorial to reaching out further to the families of the dead.

At the same time I worked with the officers. I used the group formats as a way to get to know the men and they to know me. This enabled me to do limited individual work, and to make referrals as needed. During these times, I found it very helpful to share my own experiences during the Yom Kippur War in Israel. My own experiences in a war zone were complex and frightening. On a weekly basis I often remember those who died as well as the traumatic fear of annihilation and the excitation and heightened awareness that such fears of death bring. For the first few weeks after 9/11 I relived my experiences in Israel when as an adolescent as I had volunteered on a kibbutz being shelled on the northern front. During the war I lost friends and saw families shattered. I was able to share with the men these experiences to let them know that it is possible to go through such experiences without becoming psychologically crippled. Unfortunately, many of the men had heard from experts that firefighters in Oklahoma were "psychologically destroyed" by their experiences and that some had committed suicide. Such destructive rumors were rampant during the months after the attack. My own self-revelations were attempts to provide a different model for them to identify with. My message to them was that certainly such experiences shaped one dramatically, but they did not have to cripple. In fact one could eventually make some positive meaning out of them.

During one of the groups I asked the men whether they were having sexual relationships with their spouses or girlfriends and whether the men had begun to do anything pleasurable. Few indicated yes, although some were fearful about indicating they had done so. One man who was close to the men who had died stated that he felt so "driven now, he couldn't even allow himself to laugh." After a few chuckles he felt bad. I asked him how long he allowed himself to laugh. "Not long," he said, grimacing and chuckling at the same time.

The difficulties in mourning were compounded by the absence of the bodies. At this point the remains of only three had been found. As one officer said, "It is important to know that these bodies are not lying around in the garbage somewhere." In general, the men felt that the absence of the bodies was their responsibility and shame. They felt that the men and their families deserved a decent burial with respect and many believed that they would not feel at peace until that occurs. The absence of bodies is unfortunate for other reasons as well. It seems to me that it has contributed to the illusion that the men are not really dead. It has intensified the guilt of survivors ("it's our job to find them, and our fault if we don't") and prolonged their grief reactions. It has also led to unconscious fears of reprisals from the dead in their dreams and reverie. Finally, the absence of a body for burial suggests in fantasy that the fallen may never have been here in the first place. Their sudden disintegration is linked with a "fall into nothingness" that is often unbearable for those left behind.

In February 2002, one of the battalion chiefs began to sit in on my groups. His presence and my growing familiarity with the men increased group participation. I was getting to know the men individually and my capacity to make referrals for individual therapy also increased. In March and April I asked them to write down three things they missed about the fallen. They responded anonymously, which allowed me to bring up things publicly. One wrote, "Bob was my best friend. I transferred to this house to work with him, now he is gone. I talk with his family everyday, I can't stop thinking about him, and his kids—I miss him terribly."

This capacity to admit grief and to feel weakness constituted a breakthrough, even as it demonstrated the depth of the feelings that the firefighter experienced. It was, of course, a direct and unmistakable expression of classic survivor guilt.

These therapy groups took on an eerie and tense silence. The jokes were gone and time stood still. Since 9/11, the men had been living out two lives in double consciousness (Herman 1992). In these groups these lives came together as the dead joined us at the table, to become enlivened by the men's reanimated memories. Preeminent among them were memories of the house leader—John. Even though he was off duty on the morning of 9/11, he had jumped in the truck anyway. John was larger than life—"barreling into the house, teaching the men—putting his arms around new probies and correcting their errors, and basically connecting with everyone," as one of the men put it.

Many in the house had felt John's presence in recent months. One probie, who did not even know him, reported, "I felt his presence—he corrected my mistakes, one day while I was in the basement—moving the water bottles to the right place." Others reported his presence as well. Andy, a close friend of John's, reported looking into his locker everyday as if he was inside—and feeling his love. "I just couldn't move away from his locker."

John was the life of the house. I have been struck by reports from various other firehouses of other ghost sightings. These sightings appear to have been those of similar characters, those who were the leaders and energizing forces. Coming after a very painful series of groups, I felt their emergence as ghosts during this time augured a movement to animation that set the stage for reparations and renewal.

In June, after the closing of the WTC site, group participation and individual needs picked up with a deepening of mourning that have spawned more signs of life in the firehouse. Last month, Ed, a big burly man, tearfully shared a memory of John. "Two weeks before 9/11 we were up all night cooking and talking about our lives. I never felt closer to someone. In the morning we were tired but happy. John looked at me and said, 'You have to do these things you enjoy when you can—you never know when your time is up.'" Ed had brought up the most material about the fallen, particularly John, during this session. This was striking since he had been one of the most silent all year. At the end of the group session, he spontaneously announced that his wife was pregnant. This was new to the others and they congratulated him. Since this time, two other men have announced the pregnancy of their wives in similar fashion. This seemed symbolically to signal a renewed commitment to life, an eye to the future rather than the past.

Fulfilling the Debt

As the mourning process deepened over the winter, the men moved from a numbed frozen guilt to a more "therapeutic depression" (Balint 1953) which featured grief and despair. Many had worked through some of their rage, self-blame, and denial to psychologically inhabit their new world. Many were now ready to move to a more animated position, one from which they could use their guilt in constructive ways.

During this time the men began to work on the building of a memorial wall. The memorial wall was an elaborate construction that featured pictures, uniforms, and personal letters of the families. These materials were encased in two mahogany marble settings that looked as if it belonged in a luxurious hotel. Many firefighters possess advanced construction skills. Nevertheless, the speed with which this memorial was built surprised everyone, the energy driving it enormous. After its completion in April of 2002, the men began to build a warren of cubbies and closet space they said was long overdue. Concurrently, my groups began to turn to questions of meaning, and to the concrete planning of new fundraisers for the families. These discussions were characterized by a more relaxed emotional tone. There was a return of some of the old camaraderie as well. The men began to curtail a tendency to take out their anger and pain on one another.

At the end of one group I asked the following question: How is it possible to take away anything positive from the experience they had undergone? One young firefighter retorted, "I thought you would tell us." I replied that I wished I could—but that it wasn't possible. Another retorted that he thought that perhaps the enormous sacrifices made were required by God in order to save the thousands who lived. Still another countered that having gone to all the funerals and hearing the eulogies about the many fine men, he felt inspired to lead a better life. "Listening to their stories," he recalled, could "teach a man how to live a better life in this world."

The image of a debt is useful here in that its fulfillment can become a harbinger to increased maturity and mental health. Our society is short on paying its debts. Individuals often tend to look at sacrifice and even commitments as neurotic or self-defeating. Yet it is precisely these kinds of acts that assuage survivor guilt. Although it is rarely remembered and understood, our lives are built upon the sacrifices of others. The FDNY has a tradition of paying its debts—through memorials, though actions, and through remembrance. If the horrors of WTC prove to be bearable, it is this close community of commitment and remembrance that will be a factor.

The payment of the debt to the widows is much more complicated. By and large the firefighter community has a tradition of reaching out and supporting widows and their families. Every firehouse assigns family liaison officers who make contact with each family of the fallen, and see to their needs. Liaison officers were among the most psychologically stressed after 9/11. One liaison explained, "I feel like I have a new family to take care of, nothing I seem to do is enough, and my own family is now furious with me."

The needs and the functioning of the widows remained a prime concern for all of the men over the last two years. However, even as many of the widows have made remarkable adjustments, many of the men have continued to feel a sense of burden and guilt with regards to their relationships with them. Often many of the men would say, "I just don't know what to say to them—I feel bad when I see them to know what they have gone through." Despite their efforts, many of the men never seem to feel that they have done enough, and this self-reproach remains a fixture of this complicated relationship.

The Firehouse Project in Perspective

The program here described serves as a unique secondary prevention program in the aftermath of a large-scale trauma or disaster. It utilizes the unique strengths of a service like the firehouse as a fulcrum for the identification and treatment of certain mental and physical disorders recumbent to the disaster. By introducing a clinician into the system itself rather than asking individual members of the fire service to seek treatment on their own, the program was able to bypass resistance and stagnation. Clinicians were drawn into the world of the firefighter, and then placed in roles that required their ingenuity and flexibility. In a real sense, we became part of the "problem." As we lived with the men, we began to more clearly understand how they viewed their losses, their traumas, and their predicaments. We too became part of a tightly knit, often secretive world with its own highly developed system of meaning, symbol, rules, and obligations. Levenson (1983) discusses the idea that the patient gets better only as the analyst himself experiences the same distress and reenacted patterns as the patient and even becomes a co-participant in its formation. For many of us the decision to ride fire engines was not merely the wish of an extended childhood, but rather a sign of our own burgeoning identifications with the fate of the NYC firefighter, post 9/11. As we learned about the unique personalities and histories of the fallen, we too began to mourn them too. As we met the widows, our hearts were filled with both compassion and also something more that felt like the remorse of survivor guilt. As the survivors told their stories, we too began to feel that we had been there with them, seeing jumpers, running for life, and eventually reproachful that we had not been helpful enough. Yet it was through this immersion that we became more useful to the men we were there to help.

The seventy or so clinicians that participated in the program also developed their own ideas about effective trauma treatment and about how to intervene in a system that was unaccustomed to mental health treatment. For my part I have been particularly impressed by what happened to people *after* the event. Traumas in disasters exist in all kinds of venues, all over the world. However, how the traumatized person is dealt with by his family and friends, what kinds of treatments he receives, how the organizational structure and political climate functions to help or impede the individual further—these are the kinds of questions that are of great interest to me. All individuals are traumatized to some degree in their lives. Whether they survive psychologically is dependent on how others recognize the trauma, how they try to help them, and how the system itself copes with the trauma. Since traumas and national disasters (as do family tragedies) always have a political and cultural dimension to the aftermath, this too represents a further area for further study and inquiry.

Debts Owed—Debts Paid

One evening, after I had been working with the FDNY for a while, I returned from work one night to find my street closed off to traffic by nearly ten EMS and FDNY vehicles. I ran down the block to my house to find my babysitter and my two kids sitting in the darkness. An underground electrical fire had blacked out the block. A gas leak in the area had forced an evacuation of many houses. As I resurfaced outside my house I saw the many men of the battalion I had worked with all year.

"Hey Doc," Jim said, "You live here?"

I nodded and asked what was going on. "There's no fire now—just a CO leak. Do you need a flashlight?"

I said yes, since mine was not working. They then checked my house for carbon monoxide gases. The rest of the night I watched them work in 100-degree heat. The chief, the kind of man you would like to have in emergency, directed events and the men played their roles perfectly. People on the street were evacuated from their homes, and the men went house by house checking for noxious gases. An hour later they rescued a pet left in one of the CO houses. The crowd outside cheered. The men looked happy.

The losses of 9/11 remind us of our common links to one another. Yet our personal and cultural tendencies to narcissism, the isolation of our communities, and our refusal to interweave death, bereavement, and mourning into our daily rituals all move us to forget this. The sacrifices of the firefighter community bring us back to this core truth. Our lives are built around small and large connections to one another. Unfortunately this interdependence is often out of awareness. We must therefore consciously strive to remember our own debt to the survivors. We must continue to provide assistance to those who are just beginning to seek treatment or other support services. We must honor the dead by making things right for the living. If we do not, the sacrifices of the fallen will be for naught.

References

Balint, Michael (1953), "The Paranoid and Depressive Syndrome," in *Primary Love and Psychoanalytic Techniques*. New York: Liverlight.

Buber, Martin (1966), "Guilt and Guilt Feelings," in *The Knowledge of Man*. New York: Harper Torchbook, pp. 121-148.

Herman, Judith (1992), *Trauma and Recovery*. New York: Basic Books.

Kardiner, Abram (1953), "Traumatic Neurosis of War," in Silvano Arrieti, ed., *American Handbook of Psychiatry*, vol. 1. New York: Basic Books, pp 245-257.

Levenson, Edgar (1983), *The Ambiguity of Change*. New York: Basic Books.

Lifton, Robert Jay (1969), *Death in Life*. Chapel Hill: University of North Carolina.

Lifton, Robert Jay (1979), *The Broken Connection*. New York: Simon and Shuster, pp 143-146.

Nixon, S., Schorr, J., Boudreaux, A., and Vincent, R. (1999), "Perceived Effects and Recovery in Oklahoma City Firefighters." *Oklahoma State Medical Review* Winter.

North, C., Nixon, S., and Sharrat, S. (1999), "Psychiatric Disorders Among Survivors of the Oklahoma City Bombing." *JAMA* 282(8).

Shatan, Haim (1973), "The Grief of Soldiers: Vietnam Combat Veterans Self-Help Movement." *American Journal of Ortho Psychiatry* 43: 640-653.

Smith, Dan, Christianson, E., Vincent, R., and Hahn, E. (2000), "Population Effects of the Bombing of Oklahoma City." *Oklahoma State Medical Association* 92(4).

Smith, J. (1971), "Identificatory Styles in Depression and Grief." *International Journal of Psychoanalysis* 52: 259-266.

Spielberg, Warren (1993), "Why Men Must be Heroic." *Journal of Men's Studies* 2(2): 173-188.

Sullivan, H.S. (1953), *The Interpersonal Theory of Psychiatry*. New York: Norton.

Thompson, Clara (1988), "The Role of the Analyst's Personality in Therapy," in B. Wolstein, ed., *Essential Papers on Counter Transference*. New York: NYU Press.

Volkan, Vamik (1981), *Linking Objects and Linking Phenomena*. New York: International Universities Press, Inc.

Wolstein, Benjamin (1988), "The Pluralism of Perspectives on Counter Transference," in B. Wolstein, ed., *Essential Papers on Counter Transference*. New York: NYU Press.

7

Grieving Families and the 9/11 Disaster

Paul C. Rosenblatt

Individual Grieving versus Family Grieving

As a person who writes and teaches about grief I constantly live with two realities that are not necessarily compatible: Grief as an individual experience and grief as a family experience. Much of the scholarship about grief deals with the grief of individuals; the English words used to talk about grief are overwhelmingly about individuals; my own experience of grief in my own made-in-the-USA personal psychology often feels individual, even solitary. But I think of grief simultaneously, inextricably, and always as a family phenomenon. I think we cannot understand grief without understanding how it plays out at the family level (Detmer and Lamberti 1991; Kissane and Bloch 1994; Rosenblatt 1993; Shapiro 1994). I know this from a substantial research literature on family bereavement, including my own research—for example, on parents grieving the death of a child (Rosenblatt 2000a, 2000b, 2000c) or on farm families dealing with the death of a family member in a farm accident (Rosenblatt and Karis 1993, 1993-94). I know from my own family life how much we as a family have been impacted, changed, sent spinning, drawn closer, drawn into conflict, made more distant, and learned from family deaths, including deaths of relatives who some of us never knew. So in families that lost someone in the 9/11 disaster I am sure that individual grieving is entangled in family dynamics that have been profoundly impacted by the loss.

Even a death that in a sense is one family member's alone to grieve, for example, if one loses a coworker who nobody else in the family knew, can still become a family grief. How the grieving family member talks or does not talk in the family about the loss and seeks support from the family or avoids it, how the person's grieving changes what ordinarily goes on the family, and how much others in the family ignore the individual's grief, try to suppress it, or try to connect with it makes the grief a family phenomenon.

For deaths of people that more than one family member grieves, family members may turn to one another for emotional support, material help, and help trying to understand what has happened, but often they find that the others who are grieving are unable to offer much (Riches and Dawson 2000; Rosenblatt 2000a, 2000b; Rosenblatt, Spoentgen, Karis, Dahl, Kaiser, and Elde 1991). Grieving people are often not in a good place to help other grieving people. In grief one may struggle to remember things, may struggle to make sense of the death and its aftermath, may struggle not to be overwhelmed by feelings, may be sleep deprived, may have trouble focusing, may turn inward, may be a terrible listener, may have minimal energy, and may be preoccupied by religious issues.

When the family members around one are also struggling, that can make each one's struggle harder. Not only is there the loss due to death, there may be the loss of the full presence, attention, and helpfulness of other family members. One person may want to talk about something another does not want to remember; one person may want to talk about the deceased while another wants to limit pain by avoiding talk; one person cherishes pictures, objects, possessions that are connected with the person who died while for another those things are reminders so painful that they must be put out of sight; one person needs love while the other has nothing to give except her or his own neediness. One person tries to control feelings of being overwhelmed by attending to everyday tasks like mowing the lawn or making a grocery list; for another family member these acts may seem an insensitive denial of the awfulness of the loss. Family members can get into blame battles. Each may blame oneself for what has happened—"if only I had told him to stay home that morning," "if only I hadn't wanted to move away from Los Angeles," "if only I hadn't been a naughty child." In their self-blame they may be less available to others or may feel the others' self-blame denies the validity of their own. They may also blame each other—"It's your fault that he decided to work there." And that kind of blame can be corrosive of relationship and goodwill.

Grieving people often have trouble carrying out the everyday routines of life—getting the laundry done, paying the bills, driving carefully, etc. When everyone in the family is in trouble in such ways, this will multiply the burdens that go along with grieving. They will run short of clean clothes, have problems because bills aren't being paid, have to deal with accidents caused by family member clumsiness or lack of concentration, and so on. Or possibly one person will function to do family tasks and will put aside grief for a while, but that too can make mischief in the family.

For families and individuals grieving a 9/11 loss, as for all who grieve, grief is a journey that cannot be mapped out in advance, and it is not, for major losses, a journey that is likely ever to have an end (Klass, Silverman, and Nickman 1996; Rosenblatt 1996). For anyone in a grieving family, the journey of grieving requires things from other family members. Many people will experience family cooperation in making and retaining individual and shared family meanings about the death and what has happened as a result of the death (Nadeau 1998). One may benefit from family tolerance, if not assistance, if in one's grieving one's spiritual beliefs and practices change or one's economic activities are undermined. One may find the journey so painful or the desire to reunite with the person who died so intense that one will consider ending one's life, and whether or how family members detect suicidal thoughts and what they do or don't do then may have a deciding effect on whether one continues to exist. One may need forbearance, as one is much less of a son, daughter, partner, parent, grandparent, sibling, etc. perhaps for a very long time. For these reasons, and more, grief is a family phenomenon.

Who Counts as "Family" and Who Counts As "Bereaved Family"?

Media stories about the aftermath of the 9/11/2001 disaster give a sense of a struggle to decide who is bereaved. Are we all bereaved? Are New Yorkers and people who live or work around the Pentagon the ones who are bereaved? Is it only people who have lost a close relative? Do we include all who worked at site cleanup? Do we include all New York and Pentagon-area firefighters and police officers? Do gay lovers count? Do secret lovers count? How about ex-spouses, roommates, and best friends? These are questions that the events of 9/11 raise, but they are not questions limited to 9/11 and its aftermath.

When there are economic consequences to being a bereaved family member, the question of who counts as bereaved is partly about money, and particularly in the case of the 9/11 losses those stakes can be high. When there are consequences in terms of who gets to participate in a ceremony or be listed in an obituary, again the stakes can be high. When there are consequences in terms of who receives condolences, offers of help, and sympathetic listening the stakes can be high. Strong feelings of grief do not necessarily translate into recognition in a ceremony or an obituary or recognition by the people around one that one is grieving, will continue to do so for quite a while, and deserves condolences and support. Who is to decide who counts as family? All too often people who grieve quite intensely and who count themselves as bereaved are not counted by others as among the bereaved (Doka 1989; Sklar and Hartley 1990). This is certainly something to keep in mind in the aftermath of 9/11 and its profound impact on the people of New York, the DC area, the United States, and points beyond.

Based on a substantial literature on bereavement, I think we must be open to the possibility that *almost anybody* may grieve a particular death intensely. It does not matter if the person who died was legally a family member, was ever considered a family member by anyone in the family, or was known by anyone now alive to have had a relationship with the person who died. In recent years, people in the United States have come to think about family in ways that defy dictionary definitions (Gubrium and Holstein 1990). Someone who is a blood relative may not be counted as family because of a falling out; someone who is not a blood relative may be counted as family because of the quality of a relationship. People may consciously create what they consider to be a family out of friends and neighbors. Gay or lesbian lovers become committed partners. And on and on. I think the question of who should be counted as family is best answered by saying that the definition of family is subjective and shifting; there are no hard and fast rules. One might say that the way to decide who was family to the deceased is to have had the deceased specify who is family while still alive, but relationship is not necessarily symmetrical. Just as person X can feel that Y is his closest friend, while Y doesn't even count X as a friend (Titus 1978), X may count Y (say, an in-law) as a close relative without Y counting X as even a distant relative. Given all this, it seems appropriate to recognize individuals as bereaved who say, "She or he was family to me," rather than applying a dictionary definition of family.

To put it another way, many people assume that if one didn't have a parent, child, grandchild, spouse, sibling, or other close relative killed, one is not bereaved, or not seriously bereaved. I think that's a mistake. Nobody can decide for someone else who they should grieve and not grieve. Among us are enormous differences in the capacity to feel certain feelings, think certain thoughts, imagine certain things, and relate deeply with people who others would not consider our close family members. Let's not sell people short by assuming that we know what relationships they should or should not grieve intensely. Again, the implications for the aftermath of 9/11 are clear. The intensity of grief is a function of the perception of the bereaved of who and what was lost, and how related the bereaved felt to those who have died.

Another complication in defining family is that, for many bereaved people, family members who have died do not stop being family (Rosenblatt 2000b). One's child may be dead, but one still counts the child in the family when telling others how many children one has; one may still sense the presence of the child who died; one may be doing all one can to reunite with the deceased child; one may talk with the child who died and continue to parent the child who died (for example, by praying for or talking to the child). So the dead may still be alive for many people bereaved after 9/11 and still players in their daily life.

What Goes on in Grieving Families

Newspaper accounts of those bereaved by 9/11 often seem to me to use the word "family" while telling us nothing about families. I have seen many articles that speak of "the 9/11 families," but are actually accounts about individuals who are bereaved. If all we knew about grief is what goes on for individuals, we would miss, I'm making up the number but I don't think I'm exaggerating, 14,500 important family processes that must be understood in order to make sense of grieving families and to understand grieving individuals in the family context. Here I want to talk about eight of the key family processes.

Making Meaning in the Family

One of the most important processes in family bereavement is "family meaning making" (Nadeau 1998). It is about making sense of the death, the many losses associated with the death, what may have caused the death, what has been going on in the family as a result of the death, individual and family grieving, and the future—now that the loss has occurred. Meaning making involves making sense of all these things by naming or articulating them, explaining them, and developing stories about them (Riches and Dawson 1996). Family meaning making involves coming to shared family understandings about these things, framing them in terms that count in one's family and culture—for example, religious terms, medical terms, emotional terms, moral terms.

Bereaved people carry out meaning making as individuals, but their meaning making is usually embedded in family interactions. Family members typically differ in the meanings they give to a death, at least at first, and these differences can be quite challenging (Riches and Dawson 2000). It is also true that family members, perhaps partly through their struggles to push other family members to see things their way, together typically come up with family meanings.

The meanings individuals and families come up with are provisional, fluid, always in revision. The meanings may be situational, with different meanings in different social or physical situations or when different aspects of what has happened are salient.

The family process of meaning making is not necessarily easy or comfortable. People may disagree strongly, and the stakes may be high—for example, in terms of who is to blame for something, or what the fate of the immortal soul of the deceased is, or whether one family member grants another the power to make others give up what they firmly believe to be true, or in terms of personal comfort.

Meaning making when a death has so much visibility as the 9/11 deaths is complicated by the public discourse of government officials, journalists, and everyone else who publicly defines what has happened. It becomes a matter of patriotic loyalty to believe certain things about a death and not others. And meanings that were established yesterday may be altered today by the latest revelation in the news. The news may make a deceased family member a hero (but was he a hero? Was he only a hero? Might he have been known in the family as many other things than a hero?). The news defines the bereaved family members and specific bereaved family members. Is the widow of the deceased/the daughter-in-law/the mother, etc. brave and nobly trying to organize something good for other bereaved? But is she that or only that? Might she be experienced in much different ways by family members? By herself? Perhaps, as with deaths by murder, being in the spotlight and having the death defined by government officials and journalists gets in the way of grieving, makes family processes more challenging, and is a constant threat to disrupt hard-earned provisional family meanings (Peterson 2000).

Dealing with Differences in Grieving

Grieving family members differ often in what they feel and when they feel it; there are often family gender differences in how losses are dealt with. They may often differ in what they say and believe about death, the death, or the person who died. They may differ in how they experienced, think about, and remember the person who died, and they may have different conceptions of what is proper in bereavement. They often differ in where they are in terms of ego development and capacity to understand things (Shapiro 1994), so what some can understand and be able to express others cannot. In a grieving family, these individual differences in how people grieve, when they grieve, and what they grieve can all be challenging (Gilbert 1996; Riches and Dawson 2000; Rosenblatt 2000a). It is a task of grieving family members to somehow coexist with their differences. The differences that exist at a particular time are often not immediately or easily known, and new differences emerge as people reach new feelings, realizations, or capacities to understand or feel, as new needs arise, as people move to new places spiritually, as they learn new things about themselves, and so on (Brabant 1989-90; Johnson and Rosenblatt 1981). So it is a recurrent task in grieving families, a task spread over many years, to deal with the differences. This certainly suggests that the active aftermath of the 9/11 events will be long in their impact.

Families in which more than one culture or religion is represented have additional differences to deal with. The cultural and religious beliefs and practices of one grieving family member may be inconsistent with those of another family member. If, for example, one person's culture and religion calls for minimizing emotional expression and being grateful that God has called the deceased person home, while another family member's culture and religion call for intense emotional expression and a belief that bad things happen only to bad people, the differences can be very challenging. Here too the implications for a culturally diverse population coming to terms with 9/11 are obvious. Assuming that all Americans, or even all those living in America (and certainly in a place as diverse as New York), will mourn in the same ways can only lead to tensions and misunderstandings.

Deciding Who in the Family is Most Bereaved

Not uncommonly in a family somebody is counted by at least some people in or outside of the family as the person who is grieving the most. If a married person has died, it might be the spouse who many consider most bereaved, in contrast to, say, children or parents or siblings. News reports in which someone in a family with a 9/11 bereavement speaks for and about the family appear to reflect the reporter's and the culture's ideas about who is most bereaved.

Yet such news reports may miss a great deal. For example, as we have seen in the case of the 9/11 aftermath, sometimes in families there are tensions over who is most bereaved, who most deserves sympathy, whose needs, beliefs, feelings, and memories should take precedence, who should have the primary role in speaking about the loss for the family or in making decisions about rituals and memorials. Sometimes in families there does not seem to be any conflict about who has the role of primary bereaved, but as time passes problems arise because of the designation of somebody specific as primary bereaved. Some other family member may come to feel that her/his feelings and needs have been discounted, may feel that actually she or he hurts more than the primary bereaved, or may feel that the actions and words of the primary bereaved person have increased his or her pain. Also, the person who is designated by others as the primary bereaved may feel that the grief of someone else in the family—a child, say, or an in-law—is the grief that is most intense and should be of most concern. So sometimes the sense of who is the primary bereaved person is a matter of contention, sometimes the role moves from one person to another, and sometimes carrying the designation feels inappropriate to the person who is designated.

Dealing with Undermined/Lost Relationships in the Family

Often a person who dies had been the link of some family members with others. With the link gone, one may no longer be linked to certain friends and groups (Lofland 1982). Not infrequently, a person who died has been a link among family members (Rosenblatt and Karis 1993-94). For example, their mother may link adult siblings. She may be the switchboard, the family news reporter, and the person who calls the family together for holidays, the peacemaker. What happens when she dies? Nobody may step in to link family members to one another. Nobody may want the job, be good enough at the job, or be accepted by everyone in the job. Or, to take another example, a husband may link his wife with his parents and siblings. When he dies, his widow may find that not only has she lost a husband but also she has lost her in-laws (Rosenblatt and Karis 1993-94). Sometimes parents and siblings of the deceased find that not only have they lost a son and brother they have lost a sister-in-law and access to grandchildren and nephews and nieces.

Family Members Being There Less for Each Other

As was noted above, when people are grieving, for all sorts of reasons, they are often less present for each other. They are less able to do what they usually do. They are likely to be poorer listeners, less able to give of themselves emotionally, less alert, and so on. This means that a family of grieving people, even if driven together by their shared loss, may well find needs not met, may well find that one thing they have in common is disappointment with one another.

Family Economic Losses

Frequently deaths bring substantial economic losses (Rosenblatt 2000b; Rosenblatt and Karis 1993). The person who died was central to the family in providing financially or in other material ways. Also, bereavement may undermine economic activity. Bereaved people who earn their income in sales, for example, may lose the energy, focus, and attitudes necessary for effective selling. Bereaved family members who used to provide needed services for other family members—for example, driving children to school or buying groceries—may no longer do so. Whether needed work is not being done because someone has died and nobody else can or will pick it up or whether the missing work was done by someone who in bereavement cannot do it, the missing work may have to be purchased, an economic cost. And deaths in themselves can be costly —the costs of funerals, lost work days, costs of legal work, and so on. So for many families, not only do they have as a family to deal with the feelings and thoughts concerned with the loss they also have to deal with attendant economic losses.

Family Gaps Left by the Person Who Died

A death in the family can leave gaps of many kinds. The person who died provided a million things, obvious and not obvious, to surviving family members. With the person gone, who will buy the groceries, pick up the child at the daycare center, mow the lawn, keep the tax records, hold me, turn out the light at night, give me someone to come home to, warm my feet on a cold night, etc.? The person who died may well have been central for some family members in defining and maintaining definitions of self and reality (Lofland 1982). With the person gone, who will help me figure out what happened? Who will sustain my reality? Who will support me in being me? Whose life will sustain my assumed future life? Just when this sudden, tragic, unanticipated death has occurred is when one might most need the other who has died to define what is going on, but the other isn't there to do it. The person who died was a "role partner" with others in the family (Lofland 1982). How can one enact roles and maintain identity as, say, parent or spouse, with the role partner who enabled one to be in that role no longer there?

Sexuality

Many couples are linked in powerful, important, valued, and meaningful ways through their mutual sexual relationship. Bereavement can undermine sexuality (Gottlieb, Lang, and Amsel, 1996; Hagemeister and Rosenblatt 1997; Rosenblatt 2000a, 2000b; Schwab 1992). For example, parents who have lost a child typically report that their couple sexuality declines or disappears completely at least for a while. What it does to a couple to lose that central bonding depends on what sexuality means to the partners and what else is going on in the relationship. But it is certainly one of the challenges of a grieving couple that had been sexually involved before a death to come to terms with the change in their sexual relationship.

Bereaved couples may find that other forms of physical contact become more important—touching, hugging, and holding. But for some people, men more often than women, intercourse is crucial for feeling connected, valued, cared about, and comforted. So losing intercourse, even temporarily, can be challenging.

Furthermore, if sexual intercourse resumes it may be quite different than it was before the death. It may be suffused with grief and may be challenging because of all the meanings associated with intercourse (this is how we made her, this is supposed to be a happy time but it's not, this will get in the way of thinking about her but I can't/mustn't stop thinking about her).

Challenges That May be Especially Hard for 9/11 Families

I would not assume that any death is more horrible than any other death for people who are grieving. Still, with sudden deaths in a mass disaster there may be many additional family challenges. I want to speculate about twelve of those challenges that I think are likely to be present and especially difficult for 9/11 families.

No Goodbyes/Bad Goodbyes/Unfinished Business

Sudden deaths are often harder because of goodbyes not said or goodbyes that were angry, nasty, or otherwise unsatisfying. Imagine a child whose last view of his mother was her walking away from him in anger. Imagine a couple whose last interaction was angry and insulting. Bereavement for a sudden death may include a struggle to deal with a goodbye in which one failed to say all one would say if one knew it was a last goodbye or in which one said things one now regrets or in which the person who died said things that continue to hurt because now there can be no subsequent healing interaction with the person. At the family level, these matters may play out in relationship to other family members in ways that complicate family bereavement processes. Imagine, for example, the added pain and guilt of a wife and mother who didn't even bother to say goodbye to her husband at their last parting.

When There aren't Remains

When there are no remains, family members may differ about what to make of what has happened. Some family members will not agree that a death has occurred if there are no remains. For them, the absence of remains means that there is still hope that the person is alive. For other family members, the absence of remains is irrelevant. Other evidence that the person died convinces them. In some families this is an issue of great contention. If some family members think the person may still be alive and others are certain the person has died, it is very challenging to make sense of the situation, to decide what should be done. ("Should we be hunting for the person or grieving his death, disposing of his personal belongings, and carrying out the legal work one carries out when someone has died?")

Even if everyone in the family is in agreement that the person has died, the absence of remains may create family challenges. How can we do ceremonies without remains? If we don't have a burial location, to what place might we go to feel close to the person who died? Can we anticipate a reunion in heaven if there are no remains? What if these are issues about which we cannot agree?

When There are Remains but not an Intact Body

For many family members bereaved by the 9/11 disaster, there are enough remains to establish that their family member is dead, but there is not an intact body. For some family members the absence of an intact body may be a source of great difficulty. The shattering of the body is something additional to grieve, perhaps intensely, perhaps forever. It may mean that there is no intact body with which to communicate in a cemetery, that there is always something missing, that the deceased cannot be intact in heaven, or that the deceased went through extreme pain at death. At the family level, there may be additional areas of meaning making to work out and additional differences that cannot be resolved because of the absence of an intact body. And what is an individual or family to do when they have carried out rituals involving partial remains and then, month later, additional parts of the deceased family member's body become available?

Media Concepts of Grief versus Family Realities

For many people, it is hard enough to grieve without constant reminders from the mass media that experts, editorial writers, and others have ideas about what one should be feeling, doing, and thinking. Family members may differ in how they respond to the media. What if, for example, one person feels a failure because of not grieving the way the media seem to imply about precisely how grieving should be done? What if another is grateful for the media help, while a third is furious at being told what to do, and a fourth is being guided by the media without realizing it? In all these cases, the media clearly plays a part in the grieving.

From another perspective, grieving families invariably bring cultural or even multicultural meanings to a death, invariably have cultural or even multicultural ways of mourning, memorializing, remembering, guiding or expressing or limiting emotions, and so on. Media ideas of what the events of 9/11 will have done to grieving families may reinforce cultural models already operating in some bereaved family members, but they may add a new cultural model that competes with ones already in operation. Adding additional models of how to grieve, what to do, what to feel, what to say, and so on may confuse and undermine the grieving of some individuals. At the family level, the media messages may not get through to everyone or may not get through in the same way, or the diversity of media messages may create a diversity of shoulds and models in family members. So there may be conflict between the cultural models that they were following or were contending over and the new ones acquired from the media.

Societal Narratives versus Family Narratives

As part of the grief process, bereaved people often come to narratives about how the death came about. The 9/11 deaths are challenging to deal with in this regard because almost daily there are new reports about how the 9/11 events came to be or could have been prevented. Although any narrative may be recurrently challenged and revised, the media input may be especially taxing for families bereaved by a 9/11 death. And the problems may be especially difficult if family members deal differently with the daily additions of new information. I can imagine one family member deciding to put narrative on hold until the final story comes out, another family member revises her or his personal narrative everyday, a third deciding to ignore the news, and a fourth sticking to a narrative that seemingly is challenged by some news reports. In a situation like this, family members could feel dissatisfied with or resentful of one another. And they could be long delayed in coming to the kinds of shared narratives that would make it easier to get along with one another and that would move them along in the individual grief process.

The Media Spotlight

Some of those who were bereaved because of the disaster of 9/11 have been in the media spotlight. Their tears, personal stories, efforts to make the world a better place, and criticism of government officials are all in the news. When it is a family in the spotlight, one wonders whether that is helpful. I can imagine that a child who has told millions of TV viewers that there are no problems between her mother and herself connected to the death of her father might find it more difficult to tell her mother later on about problems she is having with her mother. That might not be such a good thing. Also, because the media often use an individual's words and actions to represent a substantial category, often it is one family member speaking for the whole family. While one family member is in the spotlight, others may resent that family member's inviting the media into the interior of the family. In addition, the person in the media spotlight may say things with which other family members disagree strongly, and the fact that what was said was said to millions of others may make for greater resentment and family conflict.

The Money

Private donations, government payments, money raised by the Red Cross, insurance payments, the proceeds of lawsuits—some individuals and families bereaved by 9/11 have received or will receive quite a bit of money—will play a role in the bereavement. Money can help with economic losses associated with the death and can make a better life in various ways for the bereaved. However, money can as well make trouble (Rosenblatt 1983). Family members may differ about who should control the money or for what the money may be used. Friends and relatives, especially others who have experienced heavy economic losses because of the 9/11 or other deaths, may resent that society has deemed the 9/11 losses experienced by selected people deserving of such great financial compensation. Money may make for wealth differences in the extended family or the friendship group, the church or synagogue, the neighborhood, and those differences may be resented.

Is the money necessarily good for a family? Many people in economically well-off families express concern about their children receiving great wealth (Rosenblatt, de Mik, Anderson, and Johnson 1985). They may be concerned that the wealth could make for a life that is meaningless, robbed of purpose, hedonistic in the worst sense of the word, or insensitive to the needs of others. Furthermore, putting a price on the life of someone who was priceless may be experienced by some recipients of the money as cheapening the value of the person who died. In families where some people have more negative feelings about the money than others do, an added burden is dealing with disagreements about the meaning of the money. So while being a solution to some family problems, the money can be a source of other family problems. We have already seen some hints of these conflicts in the distribution of funds to grieving families in

New York. As reported in *Newsday* (December 3, 2001), "Already, tensions have developed among some groups, according to Anthony Gardner, who founded WTC United Family Group after his brother, Harvey Gardner III, a General Telecom employee, was lost at the World Trade Center." Concern about problems stemming from the money may well lead some people not to take any money, and that might set off still other family issues.

The Political Uses of the Deaths and the Grief

Many politicians talk about the 9/11 deaths in ways that support their political goals. That is how political rhetoric works—references to things that are heavily charged with feeling and meanings are used to persuade. That is how cultural attitudes toward grief work (Shapiro 2002)—they serve social and political purposes. As of the middle of 2003, if you check the White House website for speeches, news releases, and press conference statements related to 9/11, there will be several thousand hits. What might it do to grieving families to know that their losses and grief are being used by the president and other politicians to promote the silencing of political dissent (Chang 2002), drilling in the Arctic National Wildlife Reserve, or the killing of thousands of people in Afghanistan who might have had no demonstrable relationship with the 9/11 disaster? I imagine that the members of some families will differ strongly about being used in this way. Some will relish it while others resent it. So an added burden for some families grieving the deaths of 9/11 is family conflict over what politicians are saying.

This Could be Our Last Interaction

Any death, particularly a sudden death, can make one anxious about any family member going anywhere. One can feel that any interaction could be the last one. Such feelings can make for rich and profound family interaction. But they can also make for family interaction that feels smothering and controlling, and that restricts opportunities and activities that are considered by many in the United States to be normal and desirable. Thus, in some families grieving a 9/11 death there may be struggles over matters of freedom and opportunity versus control and safety. Imagine, for example, a widowed mother and a teenage son who struggle over whether the son should have the freedom to take a summer job in the Empire State Building or to be at a baseball game in Yankee Stadium on July 4.

The son may want the freedom and opportunity that his teenage peers have, while the mother may want to keep him out of what she perceives to be prime terrorist target zones. And if he does take the summer job or go to the ballgame, their goodbyes as he leaves the house may have a very intense emotional charge, partly because of the mother's experience of the loss of her husband and partly because of her sense that this could be the last goodbye.

The Horror of How the Death Happened

Many people have a sense of what a good death is (Leichtentritt and Rettig 2000). A good death is not untimely or mutilating, does not involve great pain or terror, is not preventable or undignified. A death that is far from "good" means that part of what is grieved is that the death was not "good." With a horrible death, there are more likely to be "what ifs" about how the death could have been prevented, more frequent painful ruminations about what the deceased might have experienced at the end of life, and a sense that something terribly wrong must be corrected but is also not correctable. In addition, an untimely death means that many people will lose someone they relied on. For example, elderly parents may lose a son or daughter whose support they counted on in old age (Moss, Lesher, and Moss 1986-87). As with other areas, family members may differ about what they do with their feelings about a death that was not "good," and that may be still another area of struggle among them and of dissatisfaction about their differences.

The Many Events That Memorialize and Honor the 9/11 Dead

The larger society recurrently memorializes and honors the 9/11 dead. It is a ceremony cycle not of the doing of the bereaved families, and yet they may be asked to participate. Even if they do not participate, the existence and perhaps even the details of these events will be in their awareness. For some, I think it will be reassuring to know that society still remembers and cares. For others, it means that whatever they are doing with the death and their grief will be recurrently rocked, intruded on, challenged, and undermined by events that define them and the death. At the family level there may be disagreement and conflict about what to make of these events and how to participate. For example, in New York, one group has formed "September's Mission" and plans to raise money for a park and memorial, a serene escape from the bustle of lower Manhattan, at the World Trade Center site. At the same time, in Belleville, New Jersey, the WTC United Family Group has already participated in a toy drive for victims' children. These are but two examples. The choice of some family members to participate or not to participate may be acts in family political struggles about who is counted as most bereaved, who has the primary role in meaning making, who hurts the most, and whose idea of how to grieve should take precedence.

Being a Symbol

The bereaved of 9/11, as individuals and families, are symbols. Being a symbol means that other people impute meanings to one that one might not share. It means that the family is on stage in ways that make it possible for others and for family members to connect everything they do or don't do to the symbolic level. Thus, for example, in Washington, DC's Virginia suburbs, a group calling itself "Families of September 11," with members in several states, wants to build on this symbolic power by becoming a national lobbying voice on family compensation and for issues such as aviation safety and terrorism.

This and other such developments raise an important question. Will the family be limited, criticized, or sucked into society symbolic values that take away abilities to act in different ways? For example, will they find themselves trapped in ways of behaving that block them from laughing in public, that make them feel that their interpersonal conflicts should be secret, that make it hard for a 9/11 widow to find a new partner, or in other ways?

What Do We Owe the 9/11 Bereaved?

Perhaps we owe any bereaved person that we will be there for them, to the extent we can be, if and when they want that. That means that we will give them their privacy to the extent that they want it, remember them and who they lost, and respect their sense of their own feelings, thoughts, and experiences.

For families bereaved by the events of 9/11, we should be careful not to fault them for being different from what we want them to be. We must not use them to deal with our issues. We need to understand them as complex, real humans, not saints, heroes and heroines, sages, or pillars of strength. We need to remember that much that has happened to them, even the collecting of money to compensate or help them, is not of their choosing. We need to hear their voices as they choose to speak out, and we need to remember that whatever voices we hear, there are other voices among the 9/11 bereaved that we are not hearing.

We also need to remember that the bereaved are in families. Helping a grieving individual may make an enormous difference in that person's life. It can even be lifesaving. But we must not assume that helping the individual will solve family problems. There are potentially many problems at the family level, of dealing with meaning making, individual differences, and so on. And these can only be resolved at the family level. At the very least that means that we must acknowledge that there is a family level, that family members may differ in many ways, and that family relationships can be quite difficult in bereavement.

References

Brabant, S. (1989-90), "Old pain or new pain: A social psychological approach to recurrent grief." *Omega* 20: 273-279.

Chang, N. (2002), *Silencing Political Dissent*. New York: Seven Stories Press.

Detmer, C. M. and Lamberti, J. W. (1991). "Family grief." *Death Studies* 15: 363-374.

Doka, K. J. (1989), "Disenfranchised grief," in K. J. Doka, ed., *Disenfranchised Grief*. Lexington, MA: Lexington Books, pp. 3-11.

Gilbert, K. R. (1996), "'We've had the same loss, why don't we have the same grief?' Loss and differential grief in families." *Death Studies* 20: 269-283.

Gottlieb, L. N., Lang, A., and Amsel, R. (1996), "The long-term effects of grief on marital intimacy following an infant's death." *Omega* 33: 1-19.

Gubrium, J. F. and Holstein, J. A. (1990), *What is Family?* Mountain View, CA: Mayfield.

Hagemeister, A. K. and Rosenblatt, P. C. (1997), "Grief and the sexual relationship of couples who have experienced a child's death." *Death Studies* 21(3): 231-252.

Johnson, P. A. and Rosenblatt, P. C. (1981), "Grief following childhood loss of parent." *American Journal of Psychotherapy* 35(3): 419425.

Kissane, David W. and Bloch, Sidney (1994), "Family grief." *British Journal of Psychiatry* 164: 728-740.

Klass, D., Silverman, P. R., and Nickman, S. L. (eds.) (1996), *Continuing Bonds: New Understandings of Grief*. Washington, DC: Taylor & Francis.

Leichtentritt, R. D. and Rettig, K. D. (2000), "The good death: Reaching an inductive understanding." *Omega* 41: 221-248.

Lofland, L. H. (1982), "Loss and human connection: An exploration into the nature of the social bond," in W. Ickes and E. S. Knowles, eds., *Personality, Roles, and Social Behavior*. New York: Springer, pp. 219-242.

Moss, M. S., Lesher, E. L., and Moss, S. Z. (1986-87), "Impact of the death of an adult child on elderly parents: Some observations." *Omega* 17: 209-218.

Nadeau, J. W. (1998), *Families Making Sense of Death*. Thousand Oaks, CA: Sage.

Peterson, M. R. (2000), "The search for Meaning in the Aftermath of Homicide: A Hermeneutic Phenomenological Study of Families of Homicide Victims." Unpublished doctoral dissertation, University of Minnesota.

Riches, G. and Dawson, P. (1996), "Making stories and taking stories: Methodological reflections on researching grief and marital tension following the death of a child." *British Journal of Guidance and Counseling* 24: 357-365.

Riches, G. and Dawson, P. (2000), *An Intimate Loneliness: Supporting Bereaved Parents and Siblings*. Philadelphia: Open University Press.

Rosenblatt, P. C. (1983), "Grief and involvement in wrongful death litigation." *Law and Human Behavior* 7(4): 351359.

Rosenblatt, P. C. (1993), "Grief: The social context of private feelings," in M. S. Stroebe, W. Stroebe, and R. O. Hansson, eds., *Handbook of Bereavement*. New York: Cambridge University Press, pp. 102-111.

Rosenblatt, P. C. (1996), "Grief that does not end," in D. Klass, P. R. Silverman, and S. L. Nickman, eds., *Continuing Bonds: New Understandings of Grief*. Washington, DC: Taylor & Francis, pp. 45-58.

Rosenblatt, P. C. (2000a), *Help Your Marriage Survive the Death of a Child*. Philadelphia: Temple University Press.

Rosenblatt, P. C. (2000b), *Parent Grief: Narratives of Loss and Relationship*. Philadelphia: Brunner/Mazel.

Rosenblatt, P. C. (2000c), "Protective parenting after the death of a child." *Journal of Personal and Interpersonal Loss* 5: 343-360.

Rosenblatt, P. C., de Mik, L., Anderson, R. M., and Johnson, P. A. (1985), *The Family in Business: Understanding and Dealing with the Challenges Entrepreneurial Families Face*. San Francisco: JosseyBass.

Rosenblatt, P. C. and Karis, T. A. (1993), "Economics and family bereavement following a fatal farm accident." *Journal of Rural Community Psychology* 12(2): 37-51.

Rosenblatt, P. C. and Karis, T. A. (1993-94), "Family distancing following a fatal farm accident." *Omega* 28: 183-200.

Rosenblatt, P. C., Spoentgen, P., Karis, T. A., Dahl, C., Kaiser, T., and Elde, C. (1991), "Difficulties in supporting the bereaved." *Omega* 23: 119-128.

Schwab, R. (1992), "Effects of a child's death on the marital relationship: A preliminary study." *Death Studies* 16: 141-154.

Shapiro, E. R. (1994), *Grief as a Family Process: A Developmental Approach to Clinical Practice*. New York: Guilford.

Shapiro, E. R. (2002), "Family bereavement after collective trauma: Private suffering, public meanings, and cultural contexts." *Journal of Systemic Therapies* 21(3): 81-92.

Sklar, F. and Hartley, S. F. (1990), "Close friends as survivors: Bereavement patterns in a 'hidden' population." *Omega* 21: 103-112.

Titus, S. L. (1978), "Friends, Comparison and Marriage Reality." Unpublished doctoral dissertation, University of Minnesota.

8

Traumatic Grief and Bereavement Resulting from Terrorism: Israeli and American Perspectives

Eliezer Witztum, Ruth Malkinson, and Simon Shimshon Rubin

Different Cultural Traditions of Grief and Mourning

Grief following loss through death is considered a universal, normal human reaction and a highly individual one, which always takes place within a sociocultural context. Cultural approaches to dealing with death are embedded in larger and well-articulated aspects of culture and society. Each culture has its own approach to dealing with loss. To understand a culture's way of dealing with loss and death will require extensive knowledge of its history, social structure, economy, politics, and much more. Beliefs and practices concerning death and mourning should not be thought of as a matter of taste but as connected vitally with much that exists in a person's life. In many non-western societies, death rituals are far more elaborate and protracted than those common in western societies (Parkes, Laungani, and Young 1997). They may require actions that to outsiders may seem pointless, destructive, or unpleasant (Rosenblatt 1997).

Cultures also vary in ways of dealing with death, such as who has the right or obligation to grieve, who is defined as the principal mourner, and who are the bereaved; what is the relationship between the bereaved and others; and who is seen as experiencing the most loss following the death. Cultures define death, what are the causes of death, and the purpose of life among major societal values. These understandings are filtered through the rituals. Failure to enact them in full may leave people confused and distressed. Sometimes there are barriers to performing the appropriate rituals. For example, immigrants from different cultures may lack institutional support for engaging in necessary rituals, particularly from the establishment, that deal with funeral ceremonies, employers, and school officials. Sometimes deliberate attempts may be made to stop practices that are seen as abhorrent (Rosenblatt 1997).

Thus understanding that, in spite of the common universal elements of grief and bereavement, there are many variations and forms that are specific to different societies requires a sensitivity to matters of culture as well as careful examination of these variations and their meaning and implications. Moreover, changes in the construction of the "culture of grief and bereavement" take place within each society. As an illustration, we would like to mention the changes in this culture that took place within Israeli society throughout the years.

Characteristically, in the first few decades after Israel's independence, bereavement patterns were constructed around collectivist ideas and myths of heroism. Those who lost their loved ones in wars defending Israel were referred to as "the family of the bereaved." Although bereavement and heroism were considered two sides of the same coin, grief was not publicly expressed. This was at least in part because there was a consensus within the "Israeli family" with regard to the idea of "necessary sacrifices," especially in light of the fact that six million Jewish victims had lost their lives during World War II, and building a homeland was crucial. In general, throughout the years since then, Israelis have witnessed a gradual shift from this collective perception and attitude to a more individualistic one. Some theoreticians call it "privatization" of grief. (This parallels a general tendency in Israel, which in many ways has been a society that has moved from a collective emphasis to an individualistic one—as seen in the decline of the *kibbutz*, for example, and the growth of private ownership.)

The main change is in the emergence of many voices expressing grief and pain over the loss of a soldier within the "family of the bereaved." Nowadays, in the contemporary cultural environment of Israel with its growing emphasis on individual life and pursuits, the losses of sons are no longer typically "justified" as essential for the Israel's existence. There are of course many variables involved in the changes that took place over the years, yet these changes are more prominent (Malkinson and Witztum 2000).

There have been other important changes going on in contemporary culture. Prominent among these is the realization that our world is becoming more dangerous, violent, and less secure. Moreover, in this modern era of highly developed electronic communications, there are no unaffected spectators. Each one has the capacity to become a passive participant in terrible events happening in real time. Yet as Janoff-Bulman (1989, 1992), who describes the concept of the assumptive worlds and shattered assumptions that operate on the basis of an illusion of invulnerability, explains, such spectators also hold a basic belief that it "cannot happen to me." She maintains that there are three main categories of such assumptions: Perceived benevolence of the world, meaningfulness of the world, and worthiness of the self. Those assumptions are, however, shattered in individuals following stressful negative events and in individuals who experience trauma and loss. This sort of shattering occurred in a particularly striking way in the events following the 9/11 disasters.

9/11 and Traumatic Grief

The attacks of September 11, 2001 on the World Trade Center (WTC) in New York, the Pentagon in Washington D.C., and in Pennsylvania represent the largest act of terrorism in U.S. history; 2,823 people were killed in New York City alone. In the wake of these attacks, there seems to have emerged, in different quarters, a global sense of vulnerability. In large measure this came out of the fact that millions of Americans watched the fall of the twin towers and were anxious about the final destination of the fourth plane before its final downing in a Pennsylvania field. Hence, large numbers of those who were aware of the events as they unfolded, although not directly involved, became "passive participants" in the disaster, and later would share no less in the sense of bereavement and loss.

There may be a parallel between the unique massive terrorist attack and the continuous stream of smaller terrorist events as is the case in Israel where during the outburst since September 2000 there were 833 Israeli victims killed and thousands more wounded (during the time that we worked on this paper we had to update this list nine times). Both the attacks on 9/11 and those during the current sequence of assaults on Israelis have increased the sense of vulnerability and uncertainty among survivors in both these societies, who sense exposure and a feeling of bereavement. Hence, these attacks have destroyed the sense of invulnerability in which the world was perceived as essentially a secure place. Instead, people in both these societies now believe that their wounds will never completely heal, and that it is more difficult to raise children in such a dangerous world. Likewise, grief feels as if it will never completely subside, even among those who are "passive participants" in the loss. Two recent research papers document this.

A recent Israeli study (with a participation rate of 57 percent) reported the results of a nationally representative telephone survey of 902 Israeli households, which included 742 residents aged eighteen years or older in April-May 2002. Most expressed a low sense of safety with respect to themselves (60.4 percent) and their relatives (67.9 percent). More than 16 percent of the respondents said they had been directly exposed to a terrorist attack, and 37 percent reported that a family member or friend had such exposure. Some 9.4 percent of the respondents met symptom criteria for PTSD (Post-traumatic Stress Disorder), a psychological impact the researchers termed "moderate" (Bleich et al. 2003).

In another, still unpublished Israeli study, researchers surveyed 1,028 adolescents, aged thirteen to eighteen years, who in June 2002 were attending a comprehensive junior high-high school in the Gilo area of Jerusalem and nearby in two high schools in Gush Etzion settlements. The study used a self-reporting questionnaire developed specifically for the Israeli context, as well as a standard validated PTSD questionnaire. A school counselor interviewed students whose responses suggested that they had PTSD individually. Five percent of the students were directly exposed to a terrorist attack; four students were injured. Additionally, 26 percent of the students reported a person close to them was killed in an attack, and 22 percent reported a person close to them was injured. Fifty-five adolescents, 5.4 percent of the sample, reported symptoms meeting criteria for PTSD, and 141 (14 percent) reported some PTSD symptoms (Lamberg 2003).

The experiences these studies document resonate with the feeling of "traumatic loss," an understanding of which becomes essential for an understanding of the psychological responses and process that follow such events as the prolonged Intifida in Israel and the attacks of 9/11 in the United States. There are variations on the concept of "traumatic loss," one of which is "traumatic bereavement" (Raphael and Martinek 1997), and another "traumatic grief" (Prigerson et al. 1995). Traumatic loss has been proposed to refer to circumstances in which in addition to the sense of loss there are elements of sudden, perhaps horrific, shocking encounters (Raphael and Martinek 1997). Examples of such circumstances include personal and community violence, catastrophes, war, and terrorist attacks. Prigerson and associates (1995) have suggested that traumatic grief may be further divided into two: traumatic distress and separation distress. Whereas the former includes traumatic symptoms such as avoidance of reminders of the dead person, the latter focuses on preoccupation with the deceased, such as yearning for them.

For the bereaved individual or family, sudden, unexpected bereavements that breach the normal expected life trajectory, particularly ones such as those effectuated by the events of 9/11 and the attacks in Israel, carry much the same psychological charge as a traumatic loss. Furthermore, the enormity of the losses and the traumatic nature of the events during which they occurred confront the field of thanatology with new challenges in assisting the bereaved in their experience of a multi-layered process of meaning-making in the wake of the loss. Under such circumstances the "normal" course of grieving is affected and its closure may at times be absent. Put differently, the grief in the face of a catastrophic and unexpected event is not simply grief that can resolve itself into mourning; it is trauma that abides or at least lasts longer.

On Loss and Trauma

The nature of the relationship between loss, bereavement, and trauma is of increasing interest to researchers and clinicians (Green 2000). There are varying opinions among these regarding the overlapping of the sub-fields. While there are those who emphasize the similarity between trauma and loss, there are others who emphasize that the phenomena of trauma and loss differ in important ways. Regretfully, experiencing trauma is part of human history and coping with trauma has become all too frequent. In medical terminology, trauma is synonymous with injury.

Loss is always an injury, and although the external wounds are not always apparent, the internal or psychosocial wounds and their healing have become a predominant focus in bereavement literature. One wonders whether these internal wounds can be compounded following the death of a loved one. The answer, which we are suggesting in light of what we have learned from the Intifida and the 9/11 disaster, would seem to be unequivocally yes—one can compound the trauma of loss under certain circumstances, and equally important, one can suffer the effects of trauma without suffering bereavement.

Especially in the psychiatric and psychological literature of today, trauma has taken on additional meanings in addition to that of injury. Trauma is often defined as the exposure of an individual to events out of the ordinary, so that a traumatic event is one that is beyond what could be expected to occur in the "normal" course of life. Perhaps even more importantly, the processes and mechanisms by which individuals deal with events of traumatic proportion have also become part of the hallmark of trauma.

The American psychiatric culture uses the DSM (*Diagnostic and Statistical Manual*) as kind of canonical text. According to the DSM's first version (1980) the diagnosis of PTSD expresses the clinical reality that after trauma, features such as the intrusion and avoidance of the traumatic event become synonymous with the trauma itself. The result is that trauma can be used to denote injury, it can be used to denote events of extreme proportion, and it can be used to characterize those experiences that institute the reparative (more or less successful) processes that are associated with PTSD.

Loss and bereavement have until now received only marginal consideration in the DSM in the category of "Other conditions that may be the focus of clinical attention," where bereavement is mentioned as a kind of complication that can lead to the development of a "Major Depressive Episode." While there is wide agreement that grief can become such a prolonged state of distress and impairment there has been reluctance in health fields to define when grief should be considered "pathological" (Shear and Smith-Caroff 2002). Recently in DSM–IV there appears the addition of "Bereavement-Related Major Depression," but the diagnosis is "generally not given unless the symptoms are still presented 2 months after the loss." (It is not clear on what basis two months was chosen as the critical time benchmark.) Also new in the DSM-IV is the statement that "learning about the death of a close relative or a friend from any cause (including natural cause) qualifies as stressor for PTSD as long as the death was sudden and unexpected." However, as there are no operationalized criteria for "sudden and unexpected," one is left to subjective criteria (Shear and Smith-Caroff 2002). Hence, some therefore have argued that inclusion of such loss in the PTSD category is questionable (Breslau and Kessler 2001). We can see from this brief discussion that the term "traumatic loss" is problematic.

To clarify and elaborate the relationship between trauma, loss, and the term "traumatic loss" we want to suggest the following table (Rubin, Malkinson, and Witztum 2000). In this table the mechanisms of the two processes, responding to loss and responding to trauma, are compared. In both processes re-experiencing and preoccupation are important psychological processes for dealing with the event. The differences are expressed, however, in the specific contents of each experience. While in traumatic reaction the dominant form of the aftermath is in *intrusion by and preoccupation with the traumatic content*; in bereavement the dominant content of the aftermath is *preoccupation with the lost person*. Thus, to use the case of 9/11 as an illustration, the traumatic element is expressed in a continuing fear of and worry about the way the people were attacked and killed while the expression of the bereavement is in the inability to let go of the attachment to the loved one lost in the disaster.

Other significant differences refer to the impact of the elements of arousal and avoidance. While in traumatic reaction these patterns of behavior are very important and are an essential part of the clinical picture, in bereavement reaction they are minor and less pronounced. Both processes have also the potential of developing into a chronic state; the differences are in the form of a final common pathway of the complication of each reaction. While the psychiatric sequelae of traumatic reactions may be PTSD, usually the sequelae of bereavement reaction centers on types of complicated grief and depression (Prigerson et al. 1995, 1996, 1997).

The major elements associated with characterizing trauma include intrusion of the scene of the trauma and/or its avoidance, anxiety and depression, and re-experiencing the traumatic event. The major elements of loss and bereavement include preoccupation, reliving, and yearning for the lost person, the profound sad and painful feelings following the loss, and sadness and anxiety. These reactions can coexist and vary—depending on the circumstances of the death and the response of the bereaved.

If one were to consider a situation where loss and trauma coexist, there is no need to look further than the reported research and clini-

Table 1

Traumatic Reactions	**Dimensions**	**Bereavement Reactions**
Intrusion of the scene of the trauma and the circumstances of the event; re-experiencing images and memories of the traumatic event and with trauma.	**Cognitions**	Reliving the images and memories of the deceased; preoccupation with the lost person.
Fear, anxiety, and a sense of threat and danger; sadness and a sense of irreversible change in life.	**Affects**	Anxiety—separation and death anxiety, sadness and depression.
Decrease in functioning during the acute phase.	**Functioning**	Decrease in functioning during the acute phase.
The complication of traumatic reaction is the development of PTSD.	**Consequences**	The complication of bereavement reaction is complicated (chronic) grief and depression.

cal data. Response to trauma and bereavement are like spokes emanating from a hub of the experiencing and coping with significant life events. In the case of traumatic loss, there will be an overlap of the two spokes. Loss under particularly traumatic circumstances can occur, and when it does, it will compound the recovery process. Witnessing the death of a loved one can be traumatic in many cases (illness, accident, violent deaths), as was the case in the WTC disaster, with family and friends witnessing it on TV, swaying between despair and hope, and when reality dawned with the finality of the loss, it turned out to be a loss with no bodies to mourn for.

A survey of a representative sample of adults living in Manhattan (Galea, Ahern, Resnick et al. 2002) was conducted five to eight weeks after the September 11 attacks. The researchers used random-digit dialing to contact a representative sample of adults living south of 110th Street in Manhattan. Participants were asked about demographic characteristics, exposure to the events of September 11, and psychological symptoms in the aftermath of the attacks.

The results were that seven and a half percent of the respondents reported symptoms consistent with the diagnosis of current PTSD, and nearly ten percent (9.7) reported symptoms consistent with the diagnosis of current depression. According to the researchers these findings suggest that at least in the area below 110th Street approximately 67,000 persons had PTSD and approximately 87,000 had depression during the time of the study. Although the estimated prevalence of current psychopathology varies according to the population studied, in a benchmark national study, the prevalence of PTSD within the previous year was 3.6 percent, and the prevalence of depression within the previous thirty days was 4.9 percent, suggesting that the prevalence in this survey was approximately twice the baseline values. This survey showed that the prevalence of PTSD was higher among the persons who were most directly exposed to the attacks or their consequences (e.g. those in the area closest to the attacks, and those who lost possessions) than among persons with less direct exposure. Factors associated with grief (e.g. loss of a family member) increased the likelihood of depression, a finding that is consistent with the results of previous studies (Galea, Ahern, Resnick et al. 2002). This was a very early survey and the researchers note that, "how long the psychological sequelae of the September 11 attacks will last remains to be seen, and it is possible that the prevalence of symptoms in this study reflects transient stress reactions to some degree."

Another report from May 2002 claims that public school children throughout New York City evinced a broad range of symptoms of mental illness at a higher than expected prevalence six months after the September 11, 2001 attacks on the World Trade Center. The researchers surveyed a representative sample of all NYC public school students (N = 8266) in grades four through twelve at ninety-four schools (selected randomly, proportional to size, excluding only the special education district). The researchers over-sampled schools in the WTC, or "Ground Zero," area, and areas such as Staten Island, home to many firefighters, police officers, and other rescue workers who had responded to the WTC attack. Final results were weighted to reflect the true population of all NYC public school students in grades four through twelve. The children completed a self-report questionnaire that assessed their own and family exposure to the WTC attack, exposure to news media reports, prior exposure to violence, loss and bereavement, impairment in day-to-day functioning, symptoms of psychiatric disorders, and other effects. The questionnaire, developed for the study by the research team, incorporates the *Diagnostic Interview Schedule for Children Predictive Scale*, a widely used psychiatric screening tool. Although the sample of approximately 2,000 children who attend school in the Ground Zero area had greater direct exposure than other students—most had to flee for safety after the attack and were exposed to smoke and dust—few children live in that area. Of NYC's 1.1 million public school students, 750,000 take public transportation every day. Using buses, subways, and boats, they pass through tunnels, and go over bridges to go to and from school. *About 15 percent of the children reported symptoms of agoraphobia, the most prevalent disorder, and 10 percent reported symptoms of generalized anxiety disorder. About 11 percent met symptom criteria for PTSD, 12 percent for separation anxiety, 8 percent for major depression, and 13 percent for conduct disorder.*

Overall survey findings suggest that approximately 200,000 (27 percent) of NYC public school children met criteria for one or more of eight psychiatric disorders. While no baseline prevalence rates exist for NYC students prior to the September 11 attack, the survey found elevated rates for each of the eight psychiatric disorders assessed in NYC students, especially among those exposed directly or indirectly. Those with minimal exposure had rates of symptomatology similar to rates in other communities before the WTC attack. Exposure to any prior trauma proved a major risk factor for symptoms. More than three-quarters of the students said they often thought about the attacks, and about half reported trying to avoid thinking, hearing, or talking about them, symptoms that are among criteria for PTSD (Initial Report to the New York City Board of Education 2002).

A Case History of Traumatic Grief

The following case history of traumatic grief provides a clinical description to illustrate the character of what we have described thus far.

> Mr. F, an Israeli in his fifties, lost his wife under very violent circumstances. After visiting friends in the territories, the couple was driving back home to Israel at night. After they had crossed into Israel proper, Palestinian gunmen attacked them. Mrs. F was killed immediately and seeing his wife was dead, her husband, only slightly wounded, ran for help. His wife's body was burned in the remains of the automobile, and he was later hospitalized.

A few months later, Mr. F arrived for therapy. He told his story in a very quiet, somewhat remote, way saying that the attack occurred following an argument they had as to whether or not it was safe to travel through the area after dark. Mrs. F, wary of the risks, had not wanted to do so, but her husband was for making the trip, and he prevailed. During the evening she was quiet but waited patiently for him to decide to return home. They were attacked on the way home.

He described his initial reaction of shock, pain in the chest, and inability to cry. Since the attack, he remained unable to sleep and lost his appetite. He gave up his work and stays at home, very restless and unable to concentrate. In addition, in a series of intrusive flashbacks, Mr. F repeatedly experiences the night of the attack. He also remains preoccupied with his dead wife and summons up his last moments with her. The trauma of that night has become inextricably bound up with his feelings of bereavement.

His world is shattered and he sees no reason why he should go on with life, which for him has, in his words, "lost its meaning." He feels depressed for most of the day. His heavy sense of grief expressed itself in his feelings of guilt and anger for convincing her to join him that night to visit his friends. He felt that had he not done so, she might still be living. Those feelings are blended with yearning for his wife to whom he was married for thirty years.

We can clearly identify elements of both trauma and grief, each of which need to be addressed in therapy. In the initial presentation of the narrative elements, the trauma is dominant whereas the feelings of bereavement and grief appear later.

Grief and a feeling of bereavement that emerge as a result of the trauma that comes from a continuous sense of being under attack or as a victim of "terrorism" such as is true for Israelis in the case of the Intifada and to some extent for Americans in the aftermath of 9/11 imposes additional difficulties for the bereaved, their families, and society at large (including therapists). The difficulty is that grief is inextricably bound up with trauma because much of the population feels itself to be in a situation similar to Mr. F. They continue to feel that they could have been victims too and are unable to get past their grief for those who have been lost. The continuing focus on memorials and revenge simply intensify this connection. These are also affected by an atmosphere of uncertainty, which increases feelings of vulnerability, issues that need to be addressed in therapy.

While Mr. F has already lost his world and needs to be given help to overcome his trauma and his grief, the populations in Israel and America at large remain anxious and vigilant, expecting at the next terror event to become victims like Mr. F.

The Problems of Ambiguous or Absent Loss

Another important aspect of the events in New York is that the bodies of the victims were unavailable and in such a case where there is no grave, the process of grief takes a unique course. It is not an absent grief; rather, it is a disrupted, incomplete grief, wherein the missing component is physical separation from the dead. Death is always an inconceivable term for conceptualization and at times even evokes cognitive and emotional resistance and denial. The actual separation from the body, as in the ritual of laying the dead in the earth, serves as a rite of passage, symbolizing the end of life and reminding us of "dust to dust, ashes to ashes." This sequence is important for the bereaved to assimilate the sad fact that their loved one is really dead. A disruption in this sequence can lead at times to a disturbance in the process of mourning. Incomplete or unresolved grief may develop in such cases.

The pertinence of the construction of mourning rituals and the use of linking objects adapted specifically to cases of incomplete grief may be illustrated when taking into consideration the individual needs and circumstances of each mourner (Malkinson 2002). It was common to view grief as pathological when time-wise there was no completion or resolution of the process and the grieving person was endlessly attached to an object connected with the deceased. This concept of "linking object" (Volkan 1981) has been used to refer to those objects that are associated with and used for dealing with cases of grief where an ambivalent relationship with the deceased prevents the bereaved from evolving the necessary and normal emotional detachment from the deceased or from an object representing them. We have learnt from bereaved people that a linking object may have a healing effect by helping them maintain a feeling of closeness to the deceased as they search for new meaning to life without him or her (Malkinson 2001; Niemeyer et al. 2000).

Wheeler's (1998-99) study on the role of linking objects in parental bereavement reports that contrary to Volkan's view of linking objects as indicators of pathological grief, linking objects were reported as meaningful in the process of shaping the memory of the dead child, a normal expression of a relationship with the deceased over time (Klass, Silverman, and Nickman 1966; Malkinson and Bar-Tur 2000; Witztum and Roman 2000). In the event of unavailability of the body, real or abstract objects can in fact facilitate the process of grieving, as they become a link between the cognitive knowledge of the loss and emotional refusal to accept it.

Additionally, the chosen object is a source for remembering, a kind of substitute for the missing grave, which is also a linking object. A grave symbolizes the finality and irreversibility of the death, while not having one creates an ambiguity (Boss 2002), and at times a vacillation between hope and despair.

Grief without a Grave

In her book *Night of Stone*, historian Catherine Merridale (2000) describes the uncovering of a mass grave in one of the villages in Russia and the gathering of relatives to commemorate the memory of their loved ones. The mass killing took place fifty years earlier. When the burial place was discovered only bones remained. A memorial service was held: "Just after the first speaker was preparing his text a woman in a black woolen shawl began to wail and wring her hands in the snow a few yards from the tribune. As she threw herself on the frozen ground, another joined her, and then more. The sound they were making was unearthly poetry and lament.... Karleia is remote, and there are women there who have never learned to behave like discrete Soviet mourners beside the family grave. They wept for their lost husbands; they described the life-long search that was about to end, the bitter years through which they longed to find the grave that soon they hope to share.... Eventually someone began to move the women away, and the crowd closed over the places they had claimed" (pp. 7-8).

What this case demonstrates is the importance of graves for providing closure to death. Although the bodies were still unavailable for each of the mourners, Merridale shows us how the very fact that the bones were retrieved provided a sense of completion and closure fifty years later with the uncovering of the burial place. Some of the same has taken place in the killing fields of Iraq, as those who lost loved ones find their remains after the fall of Saddam Hussein's murderous regime.

Concluding Remarks

The goal of this paper has been to describe the various psychological consequences of terror in its various forms on both the society and the individual. We have considered terror as a unique apocalyptic event, as occurred in the American case of the 9/11 disasters as well as a chain of continuing events as has gone on in Israel since September of 2000, the start of the latest round of violence with the Palestinians. One of the results of all this has been the phenomenon of "traumatic grief." This is a kind of intermediate situation between traumatic reaction and intense grieving in which aspects of both post-traumatic stress syndrome and intensive grief or mourning are expressed.

Our work has tried to describe the theoretical position that this traumatic grief fills in the clinical setting and the need to recognize its existence as a diagnostic and therapeutic category. On the personal level, traumatic grief emerges in the first wave of victims of terror and their families. These we have tried to exemplify with the tragic case of Mr. F. In the collective situation (divided into a second wave consisting of those who knew those who have died and those who share in the grief by virtue of being at the incident or a third wave of those who watched the death and its aftermath on television), the terror results in its various forms in a break in the sense of social equilibrium and a wound in the assumptive worlds and taken-for-granted assumptions of society that no matter what "life goes on." Instead an atmosphere of anxiety, confusion, and pessimism dominates collective life. An ongoing exposure to the effects of terror and bereavement, moreover, may even result in the destruction or at the very least the erosion of the defensive mechanisms of the individual to these traumas. In this connection, the results of the terror and bereavement in American society are exacerbated by the absence of bodies and the need to mourn without the normal funerary rituals or rites associated with the disposal of the remains and instead having to create an alternative social instrument for dealing with loss, mourning, and closure.

Based on empirical data we can see that the impact of loss supersedes cultural differences. In both American and Israeli societies short-term effects of terror events include tension, anxiety, and a decrease of a feeling of security, whereas long-term results may be expressed in demoralization and a loss of collective resilience.

References

American Psychiatric Association (1980), *Diagnostic and Statistical Manual of Mental Disorders*. 1st edition. Washington, DC: American Psychiatric Association.

American Psychiatric Association (1994), *Diagnostic and Statistical Manual of Mental Disorders*. 4th edition. Washington, DC: American Psychiatric Association.

Bleich, A., Gelkopf, M., and Solomon, Z. (2003), "Exposure to terrorism, stress-related mental health symptoms, and coping behaviors among a nationally representative sample in Israel." *Journal of American Medical Association* 290(5): 612-620.

Boss, P. G. (2002), "Ambiguous loss: Working with families of the missing." *Family Process* 41: 14-17.

Breslau, N. and Kessler, R. C. (2001), "The stressor criterion in DSM-IV Post Traumatic Stress Disorder: An empirical Investigation." *Biological Psychiatry* 50: 699-704.

Galea, S., Ahern, J., Resnick, H., et al. (2002), "Psychological sequelae of the September 11 terrorist attacks in New York City." *New England Journal of Medicine* 346(13): 982-987.

Green, B. (2000), "Traumatic loss: Conceptual and empirical links between trauma and bereavement." *Journal of Personal and Interpersonal Loss* 5: 1-17.

Initial Report to the New York City Board of Education (2002), "Effect of the Word Trade center attack on NYC Public School Students."

Janoff-Bulman, R. (1989), "Assumptive word and the stress of traumatic events: Application of the scheme construct." *Social Cognition* 7:113-138.

Janoff-Bulman, R. (1992), *Shattered Assumptions: Towards a New Psychology of Trauma*. New York: The Free Press.

Klass, D., Silverman, P. R., and Nickman, S. (1966), *Continuing Bonds*. Washington DC: Taylor & Francis.

Lamberg, L. (2003), "In the Wake of tragedy: Studies track psychological response to mass violence." *Journal of American Medical Association* 290: 587-589.

Malkinson, R. and Bar-Tur, L. (2000), "The aging of grief: Parents' grieving of Israeli soldiers." *Journal of Personal and Interpersonal Loss* 5(2-3): 247-262.

Malkinson, R. and Witztum, E. (2000), "Collective bereavement and commemoration: Cultural aspects of collective myth and the creation of national identity in Israel," in R. Malkinson, S. Rubin, and E. Witztum, eds., *Traumatic and Nontraumatic Loss and Bereavement: Clinical Theory and Practice*. Madison, CT: Psychosocial Press.

Malkinson, R. (2001), "Cognitive behavioral therapy of grief: A review and application." *Research on Social Work Practice* 11: 671-698.

Malkinson, R. (2002), "Battling the Black Sea despair: Cross-cultural consultation following an air disaster." *Journal of Trauma and Loss*. Accepted for publication.

Merridale, C. (2000), *Night of Stone: Death and Memory in Russia*. London: Granta Books.

Niemeyer, R. A., Keese, N.J., and Fortner, B. V. (2000), "Loss and meaning reconstruction: Proposition and procedures," in R. Malkinson, S. Rubin, and E. Witztum, eds., *Traumatic and Nontraumatic Loss and Bereavement: Clinical Theory and Practice*. Madison, CT: Psychosocial Press.

Parkes, C. M., Laungani, P., and Young, B. (1997), *Death and Bereavement across Cultures*. New York: Routledge.

Prigerson, H. G., Frank, E., Kasel, S. V., Reynolds, C. F. et al. (1995), "Complicated grief and bereavement-related depression as distinct disorders: Preliminary empirical validation in elderly bereaved spouses." *American Journal of Psychiatry* 152: 22-30.

Prigerson, H. G., Bierhals, A. J., Kasel, S. V. et al. (1996), "Complicated grief and distinct disorders from bereavement-related depression and anxiety: A replication study." *American Journal of Psychiatry* 153: 1484-1486.

Prigerson, H. G., Bierhals, A. J., Kasel S. V. et al (1997), "Traumatic grief as a risk factor for mental and physical morbidity." *American Journal of Psychiatry* 154: 616-623.

Raphael, B. and Martinek, N. (1997), "Assessing traumatic bereavement and posttraumatic stress disorder," in J. P. Wilson and T. M. Keane, eds., *Assessing Psychological Trauma and PTSD*. New York: Guilford Press.

Rosenblatt, P. C. (1997), "Grief in small scale societies," in C. M. Parkes, P. Laungani, and B. Young, eds., *Death and Bereavement Across Cultures*. New York: Routledge.

Rubin, S., Malkinson, R., and Witztum, E. (2000), "Loss bereavement and trauma: An overview," in R. Malkinson, S. Rubin, and E. Witztum, eds., *Traumatic and Nontraumatic Loss and Bereavement: Clinical Theory and Practice*. Madison, CT: Psychosocial Press.

Shear, M. K. and Smith-Caroff, B. S. (2002), "Traumatic loss and the syndrome of complicated grief." *PTSD Research Quarterly* 13: 1-4.

Volkan, V. D. (1981), *Linking Objects and Linking Phenomena*. New York: International Universities Press.

Wheeler, I. (1998-99), "The Role of linking object in parental bereavement." *Omega* 38: 289-296.

Witztum, E. and Roman, I. (2000), "Psychotherapeutic intervention with complicated grief: Metaphor and leave-taking rituals with the bereaved," in R. Malkinson, S. Rubin, and E. Witztum, eds., *Traumatic and Nontraumatic Loss and Bereavement: Clinical Theory and Practice*. Madison, CT: Psychosocial Press.

9

Tragedy and Transformation: Meaning Reconstruction in the Wake of Traumatic Loss

Robert A. Neimeyer

When Sara interrupted her morning routine of readying her two daughters for school to answer the telephone, she was unprepared for the voice on the other end of the line, and even less prepared for the immersion into the horrific events into which it called her. The call was from her brother, David, half a continent away in New York City, a brother from whom she seldom heard except on important family occasions or during dutiful periodic calls that one or the other would make to stay in touch. But today, the sharp edge of anxiety in David's voice as he intoned "Sara?" strongly contrasted with his usually controlled, businessman's demeanor, and Sara felt her heart leap in her chest, imagining that something had happened to their mother, who lived only blocks from David's home. The next panicked question banished that thought, but introduced only bewilderment and confusion, as she heard him ask desperately, "Are you watching television?" Sara stammered out a "no," and then, following his instructions, dashed from the kitchen to the living room to turn it on. The images and experiences that followed magnified her growing sense of the surreal, and introduced a rupture into her morning, and her life, with which she continued to struggle some eighteen months later.

Every television station on that morning of September 11, 2001 carried the same images, and wrestled with the same questions. What happened to cause two commercial airliners to crash into the twin towers of the World Trade Center, and what did this imply for the loss of life of those aboard, as well as those thousands of people just reporting for work in this icon of American finance on a bustling weekday morning? For Sara, these questions had a stark and immediate urgency, as she simultaneously watched the coverage and spoke with her frantic brother on his mobile phone, some ten floors below the point of impact. Cut off from information on what was happening in his city and in his building from the shuddering explosion above him only minutes before, David had first called his wife, and then, unable to reach her, his sister, in a distant Midwestern city to help him understand what was happening, and what he should do. Sara found herself screaming her response to "Get out!" into the receiver, urging her brother to head for the nearest staircase. Pausing only once to collect an officemate who was hysterically frozen at her seat, David did as he was bidden, and dashed toward the clogged, narrow staircase that was beginning to fill with smoke from the floors above, and with the high-heeled shoes of women employees who could not negotiate the steep, crowded corridor in footwear that clearly was not designed for a life-saving race toward light and safety. Over the next twenty-two minutes, Sara stayed on the phone with David, conveying as best she could what was happening on the television before her eyes, and giving him encouragement through her tears and sobs. She was still on the phone with him when the horror ratcheted up to still higher levels, and she watched the collapse of the structure that held her brother, just as he had reached the 11th floor. As her ear pressing against the receiver registered only screams, a terrible rumble, and then silence, Sara felt something collapse in her as well.

* * *

My goal in the present chapter is to draw on Sara's story, relayed to me poignantly in our earliest psychotherapy sessions, to open a window on the experience of traumatic loss and its impact on human life. Drawing on a contemporary conceptualization of grieving as a process of reconstructing a world of meaning that has been challenged by loss (Neimeyer 1998), I will try to convey some of the unique features of Sara's response to the tragic murder of her brother and thousands of others in an act of terrorism, and use them to illustrate the more general category of complicated grief (Jacobs, Mazure, and Prigerson 2000). In so doing, I will concentrate especially on those factors within and around Sara that complicated her bereavement, as well as those that promoted her germinal transformation in the aftermath of tragedy. While resisting the urge to be overly sanguine about the prospect for "recovery" from so devastating an experience, I believe that Sara's story demonstrates that traumatically bereaved persons can integrate the losses they sustain, and in many cases move from a position of horror and helplessness to one of hope and healing.

Narrative Processes in the Construction of Self

To understand the impact of tragic loss on people's lives, it is helpful to begin with an understanding of the structure of those lives, a structure that a good deal of contemporary scholarship suggests can be understood in *narrative* terms (Bruner 1990). The architecture of stories, with their canonically sequential *plots* organized around beginnings, middles, and ends, seems to function as a prototypically human way of organizing experience over time (Neimeyer 2000)—so much so that cognitive scientists have documented people's tendency to "massage" the data of experience to make it conform to the requirements of a "good story" (Mancuso, Yellich, and Sarbin 2002). At a deeper level, the plot structure of the story is organized around an implicit *theme*, the latent "gist" or "take-home message" of the account, which gives the narrative its deeper significance. Perhaps the most overarching of these thematic structures is the *fictional goal* toward which the story moves, the larger "moral" that it instantiates. Thus, if the surface plot of the narrative describes "what" happens, the theme addresses "why" the story unfolds as it does, and the fictional goal hints at the ultimate "wherefore" or teleological meaning toward which the story points (Neimeyer 2000).

What does this excursion into literary theory have to do with the structure of human lives, and the nature of the self? In a word, everything. If, following existential and postmodern philosophy, we concede that human existence has no essential, predetermined meaning, then we are led to consider the processes by which a sense of self or personal identity is constructed, maintained, and modified across time, processes that can be understood in terms of the "authorship" and revision of a *self-narrative* (Neimeyer and Stewart 2000). Viewed in this perspective, the events of life make sense only when they are integrated into a "master story" of who we have been, who we are now, and who we are becoming.

Indeed, the narrative impulse gives rise to our seemingly endless immersion in a sea of stories, from those we read in books, to those we watch on television, in the movies, or on stage, and from those we tell about the mundane events of our day to our loved ones, to the problematic episodes of our lives on which we focus with our therapists. Nor are stories merely told, heard, or read—as, at a still more active level, they are "performed" in the selves we project onto the social stage (Newman and Holzman 1999). Thus, narrative structures assist in the integration of disparate experiences by prompting us to "emplot" and thematize them in significant ways, and to enact a reasonably consistent self-narrative in the presence of others, who serve as a potentially validating audience for our performance (Neimeyer 2000).

Trauma, Loss, and the Disruption of the Self-Narrative

Viewed in this perspective, traumatic life events can be defined as those that are so radically incoherent with the master narrative of our lives that they cannot be emplotted or integrated into the framework of meaning that it confers (Stewart and Neimeyer 2001). Such traumatic experiences therefore resist assimilation into volitional declarative memory, instead persisting as isolated, fragmented perceptions (the sound of an explosion, the sight of blood, or the smell of burning flesh) and associated feelings (e.g., of horror, helplessness, rage, fear, or despair) that can continue to intrude into conscious attention for months, years, or even decades after the event (van der Kolk and van der Hart 1991). Because of their painful, horrific, or even incomprehensible quality, such intrusions often alternate with avoidance of the traumatic memory (Horowitz 1997), further compounding the difficulty of integrating it into the survivor's self-narrative.

But trauma in general, and traumatic loss in particular, disrupts the survivor's life story at levels far beyond the level of emplotment noted above. Still more perniciously, it often shatters those abiding themes—perhaps of human or divine benevolence, justice, safety, and trust—that jointly constitute the "assumptive world" (Janoff-Bulman and Berg 1998) that once underpinned the master narrative of the individual's life. Even the basic "wherefore" of living, its ultimate goal or purpose, can be cruelly invalidated by traumatic loss. Thus, the survivor is left in the tenuous position of confronting a radically threatening, incomprehensible event, with only the resources of a decimated system of meaning to provide orientation.

When the traumatic event involves the loss of loved ones, still other disruptions uniquely undermine the survivor's sense of autobiographical continuity. Because our very fabric of selfhood is threaded through with those others to whom we are intimately attached (Bowlby 1980), the death or loss of the other can threaten both our sense of self and our basic bonds of connection to others in general. Especially when our existing attachment styles tend toward insecurity (as expressed, for example, in a highly dependent style of pursuing close relationships), the loss of a security-enhancing relationship can have devastating consequences for the coherence and consistency of the survivor's identity (Neimeyer, Prigerson, and Davies 2002).

Recently, the diagnosis of "complicated grief" has been sharpened to refer to those cases of bereavement in which, six or more months following the death of a loved one, an individual continues to experience pervasive problems in functioning in social or occupational spheres, accompanied by intense daily yearning or "searching" for the deceased, intrusive thoughts about him or her, and extreme loneliness (Prigerson and Jacobs 2001). This diagnosis also requires that the bereaved person report several additional specific "symptoms" of distress, including an inability to acknowledge the death, a decimated sense of purpose, a feeling that a part of oneself had died, a shattered worldview, and a sense that life is meaningless. Significantly, each of these responses can be viewed as a reflection of the profound challenge that loss poses to the individual's master narrative, which can struggle to assimilate it into the plot, themes, and goal structure of his or her familiar life story (Neimeyer, Prigerson, and Davies 2002). Mounting research evidence suggests a difficult prognosis for bereaved persons whose grief is complicated in this sense, insofar as the diagnosis has been linked to elevated risk of a host of psychological and physical disorders in the months and years that follow (Prigerson and Jacobs 2001).

Finally, it is important to emphasize that meaning making is as much a social as it is a personal process, insofar as grieving individuals seek validation of their experience from others in their family and community. Such affirmation of private pain in a public sphere can be complicated when the grief is "disenfranchised" or construed as in some sense illegitimate by the individual's social world (Doka 2002). The more non-normative the death, the more likely it is that the bereaved person's unique responses will meet with such "empathic failure" (Neimeyer and Jordan 2002), further compounding his or her problem in reconstructing a viable life narrative that integrates the loss in a meaningful way.

Sara's Struggle

Clearly, the events of the 9/11 disasters, as they unfolded not only in New York, but also in Washington, DC, and rural Pennsylvania, qualified as traumatic losses by any conceivable scale of human tragedy. At a collective level, they presented immediate witnesses and television viewers with images so incoherent and at odds with Americans' optimistic cultural self-narrative that they seemed impossible to assimilate, as evidenced by TV anchor Dan Rather's inability to realize what was happening before his eyes during the obvious physical collapse of the first of the World Trade Towers. Perhaps more insidiously, the attacks also decimated the assumptive world of millions of people, whose sense of relative safety, invulnerability, and justice were shattered in a few short hours.

As incomprehension gave way to recognition of the enormity of the events, the outpouring of rage and grief was palpable, as was a lingering diminution of the perceived value of everyday pursuits. Concurrently with societal responses of shock, disbelief, and outrage, there occurred efforts to reconstruct some framework of meaning in terms of *comprehensibility* (reflected in the preoccupation with what had happened, and why), *existential significance* (signs of renewed spirituality or reordering of values), and *cultural identification* (the upwelling of patriotism that typically accompanies mortality salience) (Solomon, Greenberg, and Pyszczynski 1991). Each of these responses might be viewed as having a darker side, as people's attempts to reconstruct a comprehensible worldview or find spiritual significance might sometimes have had a wishful, or illusory aspect, and the identification with core cultural norms sometimes degenerated to bigotry, threats, or violence against anyone viewed as "Arabic." But in general, across the months that followed the terrorist actions, there was evidence that many people had begun to restore their assumptive world, core values, and relational bonds in ways that suggested growth through grief. One powerful contributor to this process was the great number of spontaneous shrines and planned public ceremonies in the months that followed, most of which honored the victims of the atrocities, recognized the changed status of first-degree survivors, and reaffirmed a broader sense of national identity and community (Romanoff and Terenzio 1998). Thus, such events harnessed the considerable symbolic power of ritual to assist most Americans with the integration of the attacks into a partially retained, partially revised cultural narrative that helped relocate the eulogized dead in collective memory (Kunkel and Dennis 2003). Equally important, such public displays of mourning also validated goals consistent with most Americans' cultural identity, and evoked familiar themes of justice and beneficence associated with a narrative of Judeo-Christian religiosity.

In contrast, Sara's grief took a rather different course. She, like millions of others, was haunted by images of the burning and collapsing towers, but for her, these same sequences were suffused with the immediate knowledge that her brother was fighting for life in one of those very buildings. Indeed, her recurrent nightmares built more on the "soundtrack" of the disaster, as fragments of emotionally wrought dialogue from their panicked phone call were "fleshed out" by dreamed and imagined scenes on the inside of the smoking structures. With these intrusive memories she was frequently reintroduced in an unbidden way to a tumultuous world of pain, horror, and helplessness—both her own and David's—after which she found herself almost consciously trying to reconstruct what David's life must have been like in its final moments. Thus, at the level of emplotment of the traumatic event, Sara's struggle reflected the assault on coherence that the terrorism represented, as well as the "effort after meaning" entailed in her persistent attempt to construct a fuller narrative sequencing of the closing chapter of her brother's life.

If anything, the thematic disruption of Sara's life narrative was still more profound and problematic. In contrast to the traditional optimism and trust that characterized the larger American cultural narrative, Sara's basic life themes from early childhood were more pessimistic and mistrustful, as a function of her experience of early and sustained sexual abuse. In her words, she "had fought all [her] adult life" against the dark subtext that this introduced into close relationships, centering on a yearning for a sense of safety and beneficence in human intentions. Now, in a single traumatic moment, the efforts of a lifetime to build a secure foundation for a more hopeful assumptive world were decimated, reactivating an old and compelling theme of her powerlessness in the face of unspeakable evil. As a consequence, Sara found herself thrown back into the threatening outline of an older, all-too-familiar narrative as she painfully attempted to give meaning to the terrorism and her brother's death.

Caught at the intersection of trauma and bereavement (Malkinson, Rubin, and Witztum 2000), Sara clearly exemplified the diagnosis of complicated grief. In the earliest days following the attacks, she found herself alternating between numbing and disbelief on the one hand, and intrusive re-immersion on the other. The latter was particularly sharp and crippling when, as soon as the four-day ban on commercial air travel lifted, Sara dashed to the deserted airport to fly to her distraught mother in New York, who awaited news of the discovery of her son's body—news that was never to come. Flying in a commercial jetliner toward the looming skyscrapers of her home city powerfully reactivated the trauma for Sara, who dissolved in hysterical tears and fear as the plane began a descent reminiscent of the one so graphically and compulsively replayed in telecasts of the tragedy.

In addition to severely compromised work and home functioning in the months following her brother's death, Sara experienced disconcerting fantasies that David had not actually died, but was trying to reach her, thoughts that in the next moment she recognized as wildly unrealistic. She also reported or evidenced nearly every additional symptom of a complicated grief diagnosis, from a decimated worldview, through a sense that she had died, at least emotionally, with her brother. Session after session was filled with tears and plaintive sobs as she expressed her inability to see any purpose in continuing to live in a world filled with such unpredictability, evil, and human malevolence. Though Sara was never actively suicidal, it was clear that her traumatic loss had cruelly fractured her world of meaning, contributing to an anguishing and seemingly unlivable grief that was complicated in nearly every imaginable respect.

A deep-going exploration of these issues in the context of our therapy led to her articulation of the encompassing goal of her life story: to find salvation from the unpredictable anguish of the world through securing the love and commitment of at least one other person. For the past several years, this quest had found expression in her relationship to her husband, Michael, on whom she concentrated her needs for reassurance and constancy in the wake of her loss. To a remarkable extent, Michael initially rose to the occasion, accompanying her on her flights home, and providing a safe "holding environment" for her early grief. Gradually, however, the demands of his own life—including their children's heightened need for care taking in the aftermath of the national and family disaster—limited his availability and sensitivity to a wife whose well of grief seemed to have no bottom. This sharp "empathic failure" (Neimeyer and Jordan 2002), evidenced in escalating conflict about Michael's inability to accept her overwhelming needs, introduced a dynamic of social disenfranchisement of Sara's grief. The resulting sense of invalidation compounded her internal struggle to construct a meaningful narrative of the loss, by depriving her of the intimate affirmation of her suffering that she craved from the one person she still fully trusted.

Ironically, the growing feeling of empathic failure she experienced at other levels in her internal and external world exacerbated Sara's increasingly stormy patterns of engagement with and disengagement from Michael. These included her own tendency to deny, reject, or criticize herself for her emotional desolation out of the sense that she did not "deserve" to grieve so deeply, given the "far greater burden" that David's widow and children were being required to bear. Likewise, President Bush's announcement some weeks after the terrorism that "the time for grief is over, the time for action has come," only confirmed for her that something was terribly wrong with her for continuing to harbor horrific images of her loss, which easily dissolved her into helpless tears. These broad cultural messages were reinforced at community levels, as the inhabitants of the city in which Sara now lived, a thousand miles from Ground Zero, began to resume "life as normal" as the calendar turned to 2002, even as Sara herself continued to grieve as if it were still October of 2001. Sara's sense of the empathic failure of others even had its transcendent features, as she came to question whether God or the universe, if it had intentionality, was fundamentally cruel or merely indifferent to the suffering of victims of great tragedy. Thus, not only did Sara find few consistent coauthors for the new and more adequate life narrative that she was attempting to construct, but she also felt deprived of the patient and caring audience for her efforts that she desperately craved.

The Therapy

A narrative conceptualization of loss and a corollary emphasis on the struggle to reconstruct a shattered world of meaning informed my therapy with Sara, and in the several sessions he was invited to attend, her husband Michael. Our first session focused largely on inviting her story, prompting a telling in a less severely "edited," summarized, and sanitized form than she had told previously, even to her accompanying husband. By inviting the disclosure of details, sounds, images, and even feared fantasies of what she had experienced in the final call from her brother, I conveyed a willingness to hear the whole story, including its most distressing features. Asking her husband's "permission" to interview her further in his attentive presence, I then encouraged a still fuller telling of the experience, focusing on Sara's "internal" narrative of her feelings and reactions (Neimeyer and Anderson 2002), her "landscape of consciousness," complementing the more "external" or journalistic narrative of the traumatic "landscape of action." This elaboration of the story was useful in not only helping Sara formulate previously unarticulated aspects of her reaction—such as making the link to the assault on human trust that the attacks represented—but also in indirectly legitimizing her "storying" the loss, while modeling for Michael a way to empathically hear and invite it.

Of course, the horrific reality of the loss could not be assimilated quickly, and new and disturbing aspects of the trauma continued to emerge for Sara in the early weeks of our contact, often prompted by further media reports on the rescue and recovery efforts. We therefore focused on helping her find means of "titrating the dose" of these hard realities, alternating between safeguarded opportunities for private conversations with Michael, and structured activities that she could pursue to disengage from the trauma (Sewell 1997). Under this regimen, Sara's attention gradually shifted from attempting to emplot the traumatic events associated with the terrorism to its thematic significance for her life. Central to this stage of the therapy was what it revealed about her relationship with Michael, who alternated between sympathetic connection and radical distancing when he became overwhelmed. Just as the traumatic loss had reopened the fault lines of her fractured trust resulting from her history of sexual abuse, so too it placed in starker relief some of the longstanding deficiencies in the marital relationship. Contemplating several recent and past stories of their relational conflicts and disappointments, Sara began to recognize their consistent subtext, centering on Michael's withdrawal in the presence of her need and her concentrated dependency on him to somehow give her the total, unconditional love she had desperately needed. She also began to realize how she had given up nearly all her dreams—to become an artist, to live in a cosmopolitan center of diversity, to work as a social activist—all to follow a basic teleological script that emphasized finding and submerging herself in an all-satisfying, caring relationship, the antithesis of her childhood experience. As nearly a year of biweekly sessions reached an end, Sara began to consolidate these insights in a series of hard-hitting free verse poems, which poignantly captured both the internal and external dynamics of her relationship with Michael. This opened the door to more explicit use of personal journaling as a means not only to integrate her losses and explore her grief (Neimeyer 1995), but also to experiment with artistic forms of self-expression that coalesced into reordered vocational priorities. Ultimately, she took tangible steps to relinquish occupational commitments that left her feeling estranged from herself, and made time for activities that moved her closer to being the sort of person she had wanted to be, before sacrificing her independence and goals to seek a kind of "healing" immersion in her husband. As therapy ended, she had instituted fundamental changes in her relationship with Michael, and despite the pain involved, felt that she had restored a kind of forward momentum to the story of their lives. In narrative terms, a life story that had been shattered by the events of 9/11 had been "deconstructed," opened to deep scrutiny in the process of rebuilding a "progressive narrative" to integrate the losses of her life and move her closer to valued goals. As she recruited a new and more empathically responsive audience for the self-narrative she was beginning to enact (consisting of other living family members and friends, as well as her children), Sara was able to find a place for her ongoing grief without allowing it to become the dominant story of her life. As a result, she felt like a sadder but wiser person at the conclusion of our fifteen months of contact, and felt a sense of control and guarded optimism as she found new orientation and meaning in the life she was now beginning to lead.

Coda

Events on the scale of the 9/11 terrorism prompt fundamental questions about their causes and effects, the nature of conflict and suffering in human life, and what might be done to alleviate the latter. Going beyond the constraints of older stage theories of grieving outlining purportedly predicable psychological sequelae of bereavement, I have tried to suggest the relevance of viewing the activity of grieving as a *quest for narrative coherence*. Among other things, this quest typically entails both the construction of an emotionally resonant, elaborated understanding of the loss itself, and its place in the broader narrative of the survivor's life. This insertion of the account of loss into the survivor's life story invites attention to problematic themes evoked by the trauma that challenge his or her assumptive world, as well as those that are sometimes reactivated from his or her prior self-narrative. As the individual elaborates a more adequate telling of the trauma and its implications for who he or she now is, there often emerges a natural penchant to harvest the lessons of the loss, and consider horizons of future possibility in new ways. Sara's story further suggests that this effort after meaning on a personal level is typically tethered to a concern for more public response, as the survivor not only searches for significance through the construction of a more coherent account of the experience, but also seeks an affirming audience for the self-narrative she or he is beginning to perform.

What might be learned from Sara's struggle about our collective vulnerability to trauma and tragedy, and our response to it? Families, communities, and whole societies, no less than individuals, can experience losses that rend their sense of continuity and challenge the assumptive structures on which they rely. The events of 9/11 transformed not only the vista of New York, but also the vision of a nation that could no longer sustain a sense of invincibility and relative insularity from conflicts seemingly taking place a world away. Like the broadcasts of the Pearl Harbor bombing a generation before, media reports of the unfolding terrorism on that September morning literally and figuratively awakened a nation from its slumbers, and introduced its citizens—and those of a broader international community—to a world that had changed in essential respects, and whose historical course may be altered in directions that will only be clear in retrospect.

Also like individuals, the human collectives shaken by the tragedies of that day show signs of both regressive and progressive revision of their narrative sense of identity. On the darker side, the corrosive anxieties engendered by the attacks contributed to a regrettable, if understandable sense of pervasive insecurity, which gave rise to a xenophobic paranoia and erosion of civil rights, accompanied by a legitimation of a belligerent foreign policy unfettered by world opinion. Equally evident, however, was an outpouring of altruism, and a profound, if perhaps temporary, suspension of the self-interest and materialism that can often characterize a capitalist culture. Thus, in their ambivalent reaction to the massive disruption of a cultural narrative predicated on the assumptions of "life, liberty, and the pursuit of happiness," Americans in general as well those most intimately bereaved by the events of 9/11 continue to seek the reconstruction of a world of meaning that had been devastated on that day, with at least some signs of practical and philosophical re-orientation in hopeful directions. Viewed in this light, grief can lead to growth, and tragedy can set the stage for transformation.

References

Bowlby, J. (1980), *Attachment and Loss* (vol. 3). New York: Basic Books.

Bruner, J. (1990), *Actual Minds, Possible Worlds*. New York: Cambridge University Press.

Doka, K. (ed.) (2002), *Disenfranchised Grief*. Champaign, IL: Research Press.

Horowitz, M. J. (1997), *Stress Response Syndromes*, 3rd ed. Northvale, NJ: Jason Aronson.

Jacobs, D., Mazure, C., and Prigerson, H. (2000), "Diagnostic criteria for traumatic grief." *Death Studies* 24: 185-199.

Janoff-Bulman, R. and Berg, M. (1998), "Disillusionment and the creation of values," in J. H. Harvey, ed., *Perspectives on Loss: A Sourcebook*. Philadelphia: Brunner/Mazel, pp. 35-47.

Kunkel, A. and Dennis, R. (2003), "Grief consolation in eulogy rhetoric: An integrative framework." *Death Studies* 27: 1-38.

Malkinson, R., Rubin, S., and Witztum, E. (eds.) (2000), *Traumatic and Nontraumatic Loss and Bereavement*. Madison, CT: Psychosocial Press.

Mancuso, J. C., Yelich, G. A., and Sarbin, T. R. (2002), "The poetic construction of AD/HD," in R. A. Neimeyer and G. J. Neimeyer, eds., *Advances in Personal Construct Psychology*. Westport, CN: Praeger, pp. 233-258.

Neimeyer, R. A. (1995), "Client -generated narratives in psychotherapy," in R. A. Neimeyer and M. J. Mahoney, eds., *Constructivism in Psychotherapy*. Washington: American Psychological Association, pp. 231-245.

Neimeyer, R. A. (1998), *Lessons of Loss: A Guide to Coping*. New York: McGraw Hill.

Neimeyer, R. A. (2000), "Narrative disruptions in the construction of self," In R. A. Neimeyer and J. Raskin, eds., *Constructions of Disorder*. Washington: American Psychological Association, pp. 207-242.

Neimeyer, R. A. and Anderson, A. (2002), "Meaning reconstruction theory," in N. Thompson, ed., *Loss and Grief: A Guide for Human Service Practitioners*. Basingstoke (UK) and New York: Palgrave, pp. 45-64.

Neimeyer, R. A. and Jordan, J. R. (2002), "Disenfranchisement as empathic failure: Grief therapy and the co-construction of meaning," in K. Doka, ed., *Disenfranchised Grief*. Champaign, IL: Research Press, pp. 95-117.

Neimeyer, R. A., Prigerson, H., and Davies, B. (2002), "Mourning and meaning." *American Behavioral Scientist* 46: 235-251.

Neimeyer, R .A. and Stewart, A. E. (2000), "Constructivist and narrative psychotherapies," In C. R. Snyder and R. E. Ingram, eds., *Handbook of Psychotherapy*. New York: Wiley, pp. 337-357.

Newman, F. and Holzman, L. (1999), "Beyond narrative to performed conversation." *Journal of Constructivist Psychology* 12: 23-40.

Prigerson, H. G. and Jacobs, S. C. (2001), "Traumatic grief as a distinct disorder: A rationale, consensus criteria, and a preliminary empirical test," In. M. S. Stroebe, R. O. Hansson, W. Stroebe, and H. Schut, eds., *Handbook of Bereavement Research: Consequences, Coping, and Care.* Washington DC: American Psychological Association.

Romanoff, B. and Terenzio, M. (1998), "Rituals and the grieving process." *Death Studies* 22: 697-711.

Sewell, K. (1997), "Post-traumatic stress: Towards a constructivist model of psychotherapy," in G. J. Neimeyer and R. A. Neimeyer, eds., *Advances in Personal Construct Psychology* (vol. 4). Greenwich, CT: JAI Press, pp. 307-335.

Solomon, S., Greenberg, J., and Pyszczynski, T. (1991), "A terror management theory of social behavior: The psychological functions of self-esteem and cultural worldviews," in M. P. Zanna, ed., *Advances in Experimental Social Psychology* (vol. 24). New York: Academic Press, pp. 93-159.

Stewart, A. E. and Neimeyer, R. A. (2001), "Emplotting the traumatic self: Narrative revision and the construction of coherence." *The Humanistic Psychologist* 29: 8-39.

van der Kolk, B. and van der Hart, O. (1991), "The intrusive past: The flexibility of memory and the engraving of trauma." *American Imago* 48: 425-454.

10

Coping with Chaos: Jewish Theological and Ritual Resources

Neil Gillman

In the four decades in which I have been engaged in teaching and writing on Jewish theology, the challenge to faith posed by apparently unjustifiable and irremediable human suffering has become increasingly central to my work. The issue was always present in my course syllabi and in my personal wrestling with God, but it is no longer simply one of a series of issues assigned more or less equal standing. It has become the core issue, the issue that threatens to upset the entire system.

I have tried, without significant success, to account for this change. After all, I did begin to teach in the wake of the Holocaust. I have long been aware that innocent children die from disease. And I know that, each year, thousands of equally innocent human beings perish in a variety of natural disasters. None of that is new. What is decidedly new is the weight I have come to assign to these realities in reaching some considered judgment on the role that the God, whom I worship daily, plays in history, nature, and the human experience. What is also new, I confess at the outset, is my increasing despair at the very possibility of dealing with this issue in purely theological terms.

In retrospect, on some level, I had begun to be aware of that gradual shift in my theological agenda even prior to the events of September 11, 2001. But the events of that day served to bring it into much sharper focus. I recall standing among a group of students and colleagues, transfixed before the television screen, as the towers crumbled, when a student turned to me and remarked, "So what does our professor of theology have to say about this?" Totally intuitively, I responded, "Right now, your professor of theology feels that we should declare a moratorium on doing theology for at least a full year." "So," he remarked, "our professor of theology's theology works for sunny days only!" I could not summon up an answer, hence the subtitle of my paper.

Theology is only one of the resources an ancient and respected religious tradition can bring to bear on coping with human experience. Religion is much more than theology. Religion also involves a sense of community, liturgy, ritual, and a wide range of institutions. What role these other resources can play in helping us cope with life, and their relationship to the more cerebral role that is played by theology are the issues I would like to address. I need not add that I can only work from within my own religious tradition, which is Judaism.

The Function of Religion: Cosmos and Chaos

I begin then with a definition of religion that I have found to be useful in all of my work. The anthropologist, Clifford Geertz, in his seminal paper, "Religion as a Cultural System," proposes this definition.[1] I should add that I came across Geertz's paper relatively late in my career but it served to help me concretize a significant transformation in my personal theological approach. I was then in the process of moving toward the theological naturalism of Paul Tillich and of my late teacher, Mordecai Menachem Kaplan, which is doubtless why the social science study of religion and the work of an anthropologist such as Geertz proved to be so useful at that stage of my thinking.

"A religion is," Geertz suggests, "a system of symbols which acts to establish powerful, pervasive, and long-lasting moods and motivations in men by formulating conceptions of a general order of existence and clothing these conceptions with such an aura of factuality that the moods and motivations seem uniquely realistic."[2]

The nub of Geertz's definition is the notion of order. Religion is an ordering device. This sense of an ordered world is conveyed through "a system of symbols." My own preferred term for this symbolic system is "myth," understood, not in its popular sense as synonymous with "fiction" and contrasted with "the facts," but rather in its academic sense as an imaginative pattern of meaning imposed upon a complex set of data. In the course of this paper, I will use both "myth" and "symbol" interchangeably, for I understand a myth to be a set of symbols extended and interconnected.[3]

In this definition, we encounter Geertz, the "outsider," the observer, speaking. For the "insider," the believer, functioning "within" the system, this sense of an ordered world and the moods and motivations that it inspires are not at all symbolic but rather utterly factual, as the closing phrase of the definition indicates. For Geertz, the outsider, the sense of order conveyed by the symbolic system conveys not "factuality" pure and simple but rather an "aura of factuality." To use the terminology of Paul Tillich, for this writer (a post-critical believer), who remains aware of the symbolic nature of religion, the myth is both "broken" and "living."

If Geertz is correct, then, the core issue with which any religion must cope is the tension between order and chaos. In this, he acknowledges his debt to Susanne Langer and to Salvador de Madariaga, who reduce the definition to "the relatively modest dogma that God is not mad."[4]

The Multiple Challenges of Chaos

The bulk of Geertz's essay proceeds to unpack his definition, phrase by phrase. For our purposes here, the most significant section of Geertz's analysis deals with the challenge posed to any religion when chaos, which he defines as "a tumult of events which lack not just interpretations but *interpretability*," erupts into our experience.[5] This challenge, Geertz suggests, is threefold: testing the limits of our analytic capacities, of our powers of endurance, and of our moral insight. "Bafflement, suffering and a sense of intractable ethical paradox," he writes, "are all...radical challenges to the proposition that life is comprehensible and that we can...orient ourselves effectively within it—challenges with which any religion, however 'primitive,' which hopes to persist must attempt somehow to cope." [6]

My own formulation of these three challenges is to define them as, respectively, an intellectual challenge, an emotional challenge, and a moral challenge. The first stretches our intuitive need simply to account for the eruption of the chaotic, to explain how it fits into our developed sense of how the world works or is supposed to work. The second stretches our equally intuitive need to believe that we should be able to cope with, to endure whatever it is that our experience delivers. The third stretches our again equally intuitive sense that the world and human life are or should be fundamentally fair, that our conceptions of right and wrong make sense, and that they cohere with our experience. This last challenge is the impetus for the part of theology that we call theodicy, literally, vindicating or justifying God's judgment.

The Classic Jewish Explanation: Suffering as Divine Punishment

One example of how these three challenges were met in Judaism is the biblical understanding of human suffering as God's punishment for Israel's sin. According to this doctrine, articulated, for example, in Deuteronomy 11:13-21 that is recited twice daily by the worshiping Jew, or in a more detailed form, in the sixty-eight verses of Deuteronomy 28, and which permeates all of prophetic historiography, obedience to God's command as embodied in the covenant will bring all manner of blessing, and disobedience, all manner of suffering, including pestilence, famine, drought, exile, military defeat, and exile.

This doctrine can be shown to meet all three of Geertz's challenges. It explains why the suffering has come upon the community—because despite God's admonitions, Israel disobeyed God's command. It gives the community a liturgical and ritual vocabulary for coping with the suffering that ensued—a vocabulary that centers on repentance, ritual sacrifice (in biblical times), confession of sin, return to God, and renewed obedience to the covenant. Finally, it vindicates God's justice—sin is punished and obedience is rewarded. In prophetic historiography, this doctrine is invoked, first to predict, and then to justify the destruction of the Jerusalem Temple in 586 BCE, and in rabbinic historiography, to justify the destruction of the Second Temple in 70 CE. It has in fact enjoyed a singular tenacity: to this day, in certain Orthodox Jewish circles, it is invoked as a response to the Holocaust. God punished European Jewry for its "sins," including the "sins" of Zionism, emancipation, enlightenment, assimilation, and the rest.[7]

That doctrine works as long as one accepts all of its theological underpinnings, which require, first, that the believer recognizes God's hand in history, and understands the Torah, God's covenant and the system of Jewish law, to have been explicitly revealed by God. Equally important, the doctrine must be perceived to cohere with the community's perception of its historical experience.

But What About Job?

The Bible itself, however, provides at least one instance where the doctrine is repudiated, precisely because it seemed to be contradicted by experience. The Book of Job portrays a totally righteous man who suffers terribly as a result of God's wager with the Satan. The bulk of the book has Job's consolers articulating classical biblical theodicy: Job has suffered because he must have sinned. Throughout, in Job's responses to his consolers, he disagrees; he has *not* sinned, or sinned sufficiently to merit his suffering. At the very end of the book (chapters 38-41), in God's communication out of the whirlwind, God challenges Job's attempts to account for his suffering. Finally, in the concluding chapter of the book (42), God repudiates the consolers and vindicates Job's own judgment that—at least in this instance, if not in principle—suffering was not the result of Job's putative sin and had nothing to do with divine punishment. The author of Job, then, perceived the weakness at the heart of the traditional doctrine; sometimes, it simply is not true to the facts. More subversively, in this book that idea was accepted into the canon, for the book has God explicitly repudiating traditional theodicies.

To put all this in more modern terms, the data of experience are never perceived in a totally objective way; we see what we want to see, what we are prepared to see, what we have been educated to see, what we already believe we are going to see. Job's consolers wanted or needed to uphold the traditional doctrine so they "saw" Job's sinfulness as a necessary cause for his suffering. But the author of the book perceived no such need. He saw a different Job, and when he pitted his picture against the doctrine, not only did the doctrine yield, but God did as well. Job himself, in 42:5-6, seems to find a measure of closure:

> I had heard You with my ears, But now I see You with my eyes.
> Therefore, I recant and relent, being but dust and ashes.[8]

He seems to have achieved a deeper understanding of God's complex and not altogether humanly understandable dealings with humanity.

Job may have found a measure of closure, but can we? After denying the traditional doctrine, all that the author can offer as an alternative is the message of God's concluding speeches that affirm human suffering to be an inescapably mysterious dimension of God's complex dealings with creation. But this reader, at least, is left in a state of bewilderment. What has happened to Geertz's three challenges? In the world according to Job, chaos now triumphs over cosmos, anarchy over order. All that God can offer Job is the assurance that the world is incredibly complex, that God is in control, that there is order beyond the apparent anarchy, but that Job, as a mere human, cannot hope to understand it.

The problem with this conclusion is that it is precisely we humans who need to understand it, who must have a way of coping with the chaos—not God. We also need to find answers that will satisfy us today, in the wake of the Holocaust and the events of September 11. In terms of Geertz's definition of religion, therefore, the Book of Job is the most anti-religious book in the Bible, for it leaves the task of bringing order out of the chaos completely up to him. Indeed, some traditional Jewish commentators argue that Job was a Gentile, as if to say his religion is not *Jewish* religion. That may be why citations from this book appear almost nowhere in the later liturgy of rabbinic Judaism, which is the way we measure the impact of biblical texts on the post-biblical Jewish consciousness.

The most prominent exception is the oft-quoted verse in 1:21, "the Lord has given, and the Lord has taken away; blessed be the name of the Lord," which appears in the Jewish burial service, but which is perhaps more a cry of human impotence than any form of explanation.

In the Wake of Job

From a strictly theological perspective, where then does the Book of Job leave us? It leaves us, I believe, with four options. First is the notion that suffering is the ultimate mystery. That response is echoed most frequently in the face of a premature or particularly horrifying death—the death, for example, of a young person from a dreaded disease. This is the conventional interpretation of God's response to Job at the end of the book and it is omnipresent in our eulogies. God's message to Job seems to be, "You are a mere human being and I am God; you cannot hope to understand my complex dealings with creation. You must simply accept the fact that I am here, that I am in control of creation, and that I continue to be in a relationship with you."

But note that the one thing God does not tell Job is the real reason why he suffered, namely, that God wagered with the Satan that Job would retain his faith, even in the face of his suffering. What would

Job have made of this revelation? What can we? There are no easy answers to these questions.

As a second option, we may believe that certain instances of suffering are the inevitable result of human freedom. God created human beings free. In the exercise of that freedom, we can inflict terrible suffering on other human beings. Indeed, the more power we wield, the greater the suffering we can and often do inflict. God must simply accept that as the inevitable tradeoff for the way God created us, as must we. True. But first, this does not justify the kind of suffering caused by nature, which was also created by God and that seems to operate randomly. Even for the kind of massive suffering inflicted by human beings on other human beings—the events of 9/11, for example—can we let God off the hook so easily? At the very least, does this image of a God who tolerates historical evil not compromise our readiness to credit God for those moments when human beings manifest astonishing charity to other human beings, for example, in the case of the numerous incidents when people sacrificed themselves to save others as the towers fell on 9/11, or in the fourth plane that day that was crashed in a Pennsylvania field by passengers halting its progress toward sabotage? If the latter is an example of God's intervention in history, as some have maintained, how do we account for those moments when God chooses not to intervene? Or to use an example that is closer to home for the Jewish community, can we praise God for bringing the State of Israel into existence, as some liturgical traditions do, and not condemn God for having tolerated the Holocaust? Can we have it both ways?[9]

A third option that we can elect after Job is the eschatological response. In this world, in this eon, there simply is no equitable distribution of justice, no accounting for the suffering of the righteous and the flourishing of the evildoer. But if we broaden the frame to include an eschatological age, God's power and justice will assert themselves; the righteous will receive their ultimate reward, and the evildoers, their ultimate punishment.

It is worth noting that in the very large part of the Bible, death is terminal; it marks the total end of a human being's relation to God. God's power over my destiny ends with my death. Only toward the very end of the biblical era does the notion of life after death enter into biblical thinking—most notably in the concluding chapter of the Book of Daniel, in a passage composed in the middle of the second century BCE—after which it becomes a centerpiece of rabbinic theology. It may well be that one of the impulses behind the reversal of the biblical notion that death limits God's power over the destiny of the individual human being to life on earth, was precisely the impasse left in the wake of Job. Eschatology answers the community's demand for theodicy.

Finally, there is the option that chaos is simply an inherent and persistent dimension of God's creation. There are two versions of this response. One has received a great deal of attention with the popularity of Harold Kushner's *When Bad Things Happen to Good People*, arguably the most widely-read book written by a rabbi in centuries.[10] Kushner's book is primarily a pastoral response to human suffering but there is a theology at its core, a theology that posits a limited God. "Residual chaos, chance, mischance, things happening for no reason will continue to be with us," Kushner writes. "We will simply have to learn to live with it, sustained and comforted by the knowledge that the earthquake and the accident...are not the will of God, but represent that aspect of reality which stands independent of His will, and which angers and saddens God even as it angers and saddens us."[11]

A significantly different and more scholarly version of this notion is the thesis of Harvard theologian Jon D. Levenson's *Creation and the Persistence of Evil*.[12] Levenson suggests that in contrast to Genesis 1 where God's creation of the world is unopposed, the Bible preserves vestiges of alternative creation myths where God's creation is achieved after a primordial combat against the forces of chaos, and where God's mastery of these chaotic forces remains fragile and perpetually imperiled. Levenson cites passages such as Job 38 in which God is portrayed as barricading the surging waters, setting up bars and doors, ordering them to stop and proceed no further, or, in Psalm 74, where God is portrayed as "driving back" the sea, "smashing" the heads of the monsters of the deep, "crushing" the head of Leviathan. Here, God's creation is triumphant despite the opposition of natural forces that constantly threaten to erupt once again.

In that same psalm, God's victory over the chaotic forces of nature is contrasted with God's failure to control the equally chaotic forces of history as manifested in the apparent victory of Israel's enemies over God's people. The most vivid portrayal of God's failure to control the chaotic forces of history is Psalm 44. Here, the psalmist contrasts God's victories in the past with a current, unspecified situation where God seems to have abandoned Israel:

> You let them devour us like sheep,
> You disperse us among the nations.
> You sell Your people for no fortune...
> You make us a byword among the nations...
> a laughing stock among the peoples (12, 13, 15).

Yet none of this can be accounted for as divine punishment for Israel's sin.

> All this has come upon us, yet we have not forgotten You,
> or been false to your covenant. (18)

Indeed, the very opposite is the case, in one of the most painful passages in the entire Bible:

> It is for Your sake that we are slain all day long,
> that we are regarded as sheep for the slaughter. (23)

Job could not have said it more clearly. It is that passage that makes this psalm the most appropriate response to the Holocaust. In this Job-like repudiation of the traditional doctrine, the psalmist claims that Israel is suffering precisely because of its loyalty to God.

What is most striking here is that in confronting God's abandonment of Israel, God's apparent absence, God's impotence in the face of historical chaos, the psalmist does not abandon the covenant. Rather, he turns his despair, indeed his rage, into a challenge to God from within the covenant. In the concluding verses of the psalm, he exclaims:

> Rouse yourself, why do you sleep O Lord?
> Awaken! Do not cast us off forever! (24)

In contrast to Kushner, the psalmist is not suggesting that the prevalence of chaos in history testifies to a limited God. The very opposite is the case. God's power is not limited. It is assumed. That is precisely why the psalmist despairs, why he cries out for God to manifest His power once again, as in the past. The point is that chaos seems to be an intrinsic dimension of God's creation, an echo of Isaiah 45:7's claim that God has created both light and darkness, *shalom*—cosmos, harmony, order—and *ra*—the bad, or chaos. Or, of the sixteenth-century kabbalistic myth of Isaac Luria, where the notion that the chaotic forces in nature and history are the result of some primordial fault inherent in God's creation, what Luria called "the breaking of the vessels."[13] This response projects God's ultimate conquest of chaos into the eschatological future. In historical time, we can only wait and hope, and live with the tension.

All of this is speaking theologically, to which I add one final note on this aspect of our inquiry.[14] In a peculiar way, the image of God in Job 1, however disturbing it may be, is also liberating. In fact the classical texts of Judaism are populated by a plethora of images of God, many positive, nurturing and comforting, but others quite disturbing. The very richness of the imagery reminds us that no human being has a fix on God, simply because God is God and we are humans. That those responsible for editing the canon felt free to include all of these images permits us, their heirs, to select those images that speak to our own experience at any point in our lives. The failure of any one of these images to address our own needs does not, then, preclude the success of others, even the God of Job and of Psalm 44.

In a more extended sense, the unraveling of one corner of the Jewish religious myth does not forecast the undoing of the myth as a whole. Another way of making that claim is to say that myths enjoy a degree of plasticity. They too evolve in time; portions die and disappear; others continue to live; still others are reformulated. This element of plasticity accounts for the singular tenacity that ancient religious myths exhibit. To this believing Jew, then, the substance of the classic Jewish religious myth, however broken, remains palpably alive, despite the death of the doctrine of suffering as punishment, and maybe even because of Job.

Beyond Theology

But as we noted at the outset, religion is much more than theology. The theological impasse opens the way for other religious resources to assert themselves. Of Geertz's three challenges—the intellectual, the emotional, and the moral—theology deals with the first and the third. The second remains, and it is here that these other resources may be of help.

This is what Geertz has to say about ritual:

> ...[I]t is in ritual—that is to say consecrated behavior—that this conviction that religious conceptions are veridical and that religious directives are sound is somehow generated. It is in some sort of ceremonial form...—the recitation of a myth, the consultation of an oracle, or the decoration of a grave—that the moods and motivations which sacred symbols induce in men and the general conceptions of the order of existence which they formulate...meet and reinforce one another. In a ritual, the world as lived and the world as imagined, fused under the agency of a single set of symbolic forms, turn out to be the same world.[15]

Our religious symbols, our myths, are frequently implicit, buried in our unconscious. The dramatic effect of ritual is to make us aware, to bring the myth into the forefront of our consciousness. The late Barbara Myerhoff, in her remarkable *Number Our Days*, tells us how ritual accomplishes these tasks:

> Ritual may be likened to a vessel into which anything may be poured: an order-endowing device, it gives shape to its contents. This ordering function is furthered by the morphological characteristics of a ritual—precision, accuracy, predictability, formality, and repetition. Thus the characteristics of ritual as a medium suggest that its contents...are enduring and orderly. By virtue of these traits, ritual always delivers a message about continuity....[16]

Similarly, the second of Geertz' three challenges that is posed by the eruption of chaos into our ordered world—what we named the emotional challenge, the challenge to our ability to suffer and to cope—to the extent that it is effective, is anchored in a religion that provides "symbolic resources for expressing emotions—moods, sentiments, passions affections, feelings...." And Geertz concludes, "for those able to embrace them, and for so long as they are able to embrace them, religious symbols provide a cosmic guarantee not only for their ability to comprehend the world, but also, comprehending it, to give a precision to their feeling, a definition to their emotions which enables them, morosely or joyfully, grimly or cavalierly, to endure it."[17] These symbols are all a central component of ritual.

Ritual thus defines our feelings; it lends precision to our emotions. It helps us identify what we feel. It gives us a vocabulary—both verbal and behavioral—to articulate our feelings by placing human suffering "in a meaningful context, providing a mode of action through which it can be expressed, being expressed understood, and being understood endured."[18] That progression—from expression to understanding to enduring—strikes me as a remarkably insightful formulation of what we might call the therapeutic effect of ritual behavior. If, on this issue of human suffering, Judaism leaves us at a theological impasse, it more than compensates by encircling the experience of mourning with a ritual pageantry that does everything that Geertz and Myerhoff attribute to great ritual.

Jewish Mourning Rituals

My illustrations are taken from Jewish mourning rituals because for most of us, the death of a member of the immediate family constitutes our most familiar encounter with chaos. Judaism structures the act of mourning from the moment of death to burial, from burial through the initial seven days (*shivah*) of mourning, then the thirty days (*shloshim*) of less intensive mourning, then through the eleven months and a day during which the mourner recites the mourner's *kaddish* (for the death of a parent, thirty days for the death of a spouse, child, or sibling), then through the annual observance of the anniversary of the death (*yahrzeit*), then on the five occasions during the year when the memorial prayers (*yizkor*) are recited. It provides the mourner with a vocabulary of words and behaviors that lend precision to feelings, and formality and predictability to behavior. And all of this fuses Judaism's myth with the life experience of the believer so that they become one. The net effect of the entire experience is that the sense of the chaotic, now at its most acute, is immersed in the sense of an ordered world. Once again, the world becomes ordered.

An exhaustive illustration of this claim would require a full-fledged description of the Jewish laws of mourning;[19] I will restrict myself to a few.

Those present at the moment of death are commanded to recite a blessing, which reads: *Barukh dayyan emet.* [20] I have long struggled to find an accurate English translation of these three Hebrew words. The conventional translation is "Blessed is the true Judge." More accurately, "...the Judge whose judgment is true," or "...is accurate," or more colloquially "...whose judgment is right on!"

Is this theodicy? Not at all, for it justifies nothing, least of all God. It is not a vindication of God's judgment. It is, rather, pure ritual, a verbal throwing-up-of-the-hands in despair, an affirmation of God's justice, a case of "doing things with words." If anything, it is the repudiation of the very possibility of theodicy.

The blessing is recited again at the funeral or burial, and this time it is accompanied by the ritual of the tearing of a garment, on the left side above the heart for the death of a parent, and on the right for the death of a spouse, child, or sibling. That ritual gesture is a choreographed scream. Job tears his garment after hearing of the death of his children (1:20), as does Jacob when he is informed of Joseph's death (Genesis 37:34). The tear symbolizes the tear in my life, in my family, in the community. It is pure feeling, an externalization of what is inside me. It lends precision to my feelings. Again, none of this has anything to do with theology.

Then, the mourner's kaddish, literally the prayer of "sanctification" of God's name. It is conventional to claim that these words say nothing whatsoever about death—which is correct. In fact, in its origins, it was a prayer recited after the study of Torah, and since it was customary to study Torah in memory of the departed, it subsequently became a mourner's prayer even when it is not preceded by study.

The liturgical content of the prayer sanctifies God and God's name, asks God to establish God's kingship on earth, and asks that as God established *shalom*—literally order, harmony, cosmos—in heaven, so may God establish shalom on earth.[21] Again there is a minimum of theology here. But anyone who has recited the kaddish for the prescribed period is well aware that after a few weeks of doing this, three times daily, the words become irrelevant. Here, it is primarily the medium that conveys the message. The very fact that one joins a community of Jews—for one needs a *minyan*, a quorum of ten Jews, to recite the kaddish—and recites an ancient and sanctified text in a formalized, totally predictable manner, is the entire story. I recall that when I was reciting kaddish upon the death of my parents, I lay in bed early in the morning and planned my day around the two moments in the morning and the evening when I would have to find a minyan in order to fulfill my obligation. The kaddish is an act of ordering. It lends structure to the day, to the week, to the year, and—on the anniversary of the death—to one's entire lifetime. It is pure ritual.

There is one occasion when the kaddish also includes formidable theological content. That is in the form of the kaddish recited at the graveside, immediately following the burial. At that moment, the following text is added:

> May God's name be sanctified and exalted in the world which will be renewed, where God will resurrect the dead and raise them to eternal life, and rebuild the city of Jerusalem, and establish the Temple in its midst, and uproot alien worship from the earth and establish the worship of heaven in its place, and when the Holy Blessed One will reign in sovereignty and splendor, in your lifetimes, in your days, and in the lifetime of all of Israel....[22]

This complex theological statement is in effect a one-paragraph summary of classic Jewish eschatology.

Ritual and Theology

It may be useful, in this context, to note that the distinction between ritual and theology may not be as sharp as I have suggested.

Clearly, ritual always nurses from the myth and, at least in Judaism, liturgy carries a formidable theological content. It is equally clear that Geertz's three challenges work together. But they seem to address different human needs: theology addresses our intellectual need while ritual addresses our emotional needs.

One further point: the entire pageantry of mourning demands community. The Jew is forbidden to mourn alone. From the moment of death, the entire funeral process is arranged by a *hevra kadisha*, literally, a "sacred society," a burial society. The mourner does not go the synagogue during the week of shiva—the community comes to him, to worship with the mourner and the family in their home. The door of the house of mourning is never locked; the assumption is that the community will come in and out, and the mourner should not have to open or close the door. Upon leaving the mourner, one recites a formal, liturgical formula: "May God console you, among the other mourners of Zion and Jerusalem." There is a community of perpetual mourners in the Jewish community.

Great rituals are rarely created by committee. They evolve, in time, as a community searches for ways to express feelings, to recall transforming events, and even more complicated, to determine what the event means, how it fits into the community's way of ordering the world, how it affects the community's classic myth.

In regard to the events of 9/11, that process has already begun, as we have witnessed in the year following the catastrophe: the visit to Ground Zero, the recitation of the names of the deceased, the tolling of bells, the singing of "God Bless America," the moment of silence, the erection of mini-shrines throughout the city, the assemblage of photographs of the deceased, the recitation of Lincoln's Gettysburg address—these are all ritual expressions. Some will survive, some will pass, and new ones will be forged. It will probably take a generation.

I have a strikingly informal test for judging the power of a ritual. I call it the "goose bump effect." A ritual that leaves me with goose bumps on my flesh is one that has genuinely moved me; that effect testifies to great ritual. As these lines were being written, I re-experienced the drama of President John F. Kennedy's funeral on the fortieth anniversary of his assassination. Like most of my generation, I have vivid memories of the four-day period from his death to his burial. For that entire period, I sat transfixed and could barely leave my spot in front of the television screen. To my amazement, watching the video of the military funeral this year—the drumbeat, the riderless horse, the folding of the flag, the music—the formality, the precision, and the drama of the entire pageant produced the same goose bumps they did forty years ago. My sense is that forty years from now, we will watch a video of the events of 9/11 and of the rituals of remembrance that will have evolved just as transfixed as we were that day.

But recall that it took centuries for the Passover seder—arguably, the single most impressive ritual pageant in the life of the Jewish community—to assume the shape that it has for Jews today, and that even after a half-century, the Jewish community has yet to create vivid new rituals to commemorate the two transforming Jewish events of the past century: the Holocaust and Israel Independence Day. My sense is that this failure to create new rituals for these events reflects our continuing struggle to integrate them into our classic religious myth. We are still not clear, in our minds, what the events mean, and therefore, we have not as yet achieved a consensus regarding what the rituals should say. The more immediate challenge, then, is to achieve a similar consensus on the meaning of the events of September 11, 2001. Once we have achieved that consensus, the rituals will follow by themselves.

Notes

1. Clifford Geertz, *The Interpretation of Cultures* (New York: Basic Books, 1973), chapter 4.
2. Ibid., p. 90.
3. Paul Tillich, *Dynamics of Faith* (New York: Harper & Row, 1957), chapter 3.
4. Geertz, p. 99.
5. Ibid., 100ff. (italics in the original).
6. Ibid.
7. For a clear statement of prophetic historiography, see Isaiah 1. The rabbinic model is captured in the liturgical passage, "Because of our sins, we were exiled from our land..." in the *Musaf Amidah* for festivals. See *The Complete ArtScroll Siddur* (Brooklyn, NY: Mesorah Publications, Inc., 1984), pp. 678-681. The contemporary invocation of the doctrine is discussed (and vigorously repudiated) by David Weiss Halivni, "Prayer in the Shoah," *Judaism*, Vol. 50, No. 3, Summer 2001, pp. 268-291.
8. This is the conventional translation of these two verses as it appears in The Jewish Publication Society of America translation of *Tanakh* (Philadelphia, 1985). For a more cynical translation, see Jack Miles, *God: A Biography* (New York: Vintage Books, 1996), pp. 323ff: "Word of you had reached my ears, but now that my eyes have seen you, I shudder with sorrow for mortal clay." If this translation is correct, Job has hardly achieved closure. The very opposite is the case.
9. See, e.g., the version of the *Al HaNissim* ("For the miracles...") prayer, commonly recited on the festivals of Hanukkah and Purim, now newly composed for Israel

Independence Day, in *Siddur Sim Shalom* (New York: The Rabbinical Assembly and The United Synagogue of America, 1985), pp. 118-119.

10. New York: Schocken Books, 1981.
11. Ibid., p. 55.
12. Princeton, NJ: Princeton University Press, 1988. What follows is my summary of Levenson's thesis in Part I of his book, "The Mastery of God and the Vulnerability of Order."
13. The classic summary of Lurianic mysticism remains Gershom G. Scholem, *Major Trends in Jewish Mysticism* (New York: Schocken Books, 1941), Seventh Lecture, pp. 244-286.
14. These four broad theological options are by no means exclusive. They do, however, seem to this author, at least, to be the most theologically significant ones, the most thoroughly explored in the literature, and the most challenging. Other options refer, for example, to the numerous biblical references to God's momentary hiding of the divine face, to interpretations of Isaiah's suffering servant, or to the rabbinic notion of human suffering as an expression of divine affection (based on interpretations of Prov. 3:12, and Ps. 94:12). Understandably, the most interesting exploration of these and other responses deal with the Holocaust. For two notable surveys of these and other options, see Steven T. Katz, *Post-Holocaust Dialogues: Critical Studies in Modern Jewish Thought* (New York: New York University Press, 1983), and Irving Greenberg, "Cloud of Smoke, Pillar of Fire: Judaism, Christianity and Modernity After the Holocaust," in Eva Fleischner (ed.), *Auschwitz: Beginning of a New Era? Reflections on the Holocaust* (Ktav Publishing House, Inc., 1977), pp. 7-55.
15. Geertz, p. 112.
16. New York: Simon and Schuster, 1978, p. 86.
17. Geertz, p. 104.
18. Ibid., p. 105.
19. See "The Laws of Mourning" in Isaac Klein, *A Guide to Jewish Religious Practice* (New York: The Jewish Theological Seminary of America, 1979), chapters 19-20.
20. Based on M. Berakhot, 9:5: "One is bound to bless God for the evil even as he blesses God for the good." More conventionally, both the blessing and the tearing are done before the funeral or the burial.
21. For the full text of the Mourner's Kaddish, see *ArtScroll Siddur*, pp. 56-57.
22. *ArtScroll Siddur*, pp. 800-801.

11

From Ground Zero: Thoughts on Apocalyptic Violence and the New Terrorism[1]

Charles B. Strozier

The World Trade Center Disaster

It is altogether appropriate to place the World Trade Center disaster at the center of any inquiry into the meaning of collective trauma in the contemporary age. The disaster symbolizes the new violence of the twenty-first century. Some mutter snidely that it is hype to say the WTC disaster changed everything. They are wrong, in part because of the scale of the death that occurred, in part due to the form of the dying, and in part due to the psychological shock of the experience.

The scale of the death is gripping. 2,792 people died in the towers in New York (not counting ten hijackers), 179 at the Pentagon (not including five hijackers), and forty in the plane in Pennsylvania (not including four hijackers). We live with that horror, though the accurate counting of victims was for many months a moving target with confusing consequences. On 9/11 itself the media assumed the death toll would reach 20,000, given the number of those who might have been expected to be in the towers. That number quickly dropped to about 6,000, where it remained for nearly a month, because in the chaos of the rescue and recovery operations at Ground Zero and the general confusion in the city (Strozier and Gentile 2004), no one was comparing overlapping lists. During the next few months, thousands of names were removed from the lists of victims. It was nearly six months before what seemed to be a final figure for the number of those who perished was reached, though even that number was decreased by three as late as December 13, 2002 (Kugler 2002). That radical process of decline in the number of victims during the first half a year, and the more gradual falling off after that, was wrenching for family members, and for the culture. The dread, mostly unexpressed, was that at some completely unknown point the number would become psychologically insignificant. It is fair to say that such a point was never reached, but something happened to our grasp of the event when it became no longer bloodier than Pearl Harbor (2,403 killed in action but 640 never accounted for) and a good deal less so than Antietam (3,650 killed and 17,300 wounded).

The form of the dying, however, never altered and remained psychologically confusing and painful. Here the issue was the radical dismemberment and disfigurement of bodies that occurred in the disaster, even though images of the hundreds of people jumping and the scene on the ground that was out of the book of Revelation was leeched from what appeared on television. On Thursday, September 13, the *New York Times* on its cover showed a man who had jumped from one of the towers falling head first. That picture prompted a coordination among media executives to curtail showing any more images of people jumping (Blakemore 2002). The first documentary to break this self-imposed taboo was that by the Naudet Brothers, Jules and Gedeon, shown on CBS March 10, 2002. Others followed, and it seems such images are gradually entering the culture.

The dying was not natural. It left us all bereft. For no group was this more important than for the observant Jewish community. A tenet of Judaism is that when someone dies the body must be accompanied from the moment of death to burial (the ritual of the *shmira*). Psalms are customarily chanted during this process. A corollary of this ritual is that the entire body must be together upon burial. In the event of amputations prior to death, these must be buried in the same plot where the dead will later be interred. Terrorism in Israel has profoundly disrupted the ability to gather the body together, which is why after any attack one sees a volunteer task force, organized by fervently Orthodox Jews, called ZAKA, combing the streets for even the smallest body parts of victims. ZAKA, which was founded in 1995, is an acronym for *Zihui Korbanot Ason*, Hebrew for Identification of Disaster Victims. Its volunteers, who are easily identifiable by their bright yellow vests, are often the first rescue workers to appear at the scene of a terrorist bombing or shooting—and the last to leave. At the WTC there was at best a vast number of often minute body parts. But those were precious. After the disaster, a Jewish group in the city emerged very quickly to do the best that was humanly possible under the circumstances to carry out the familiar ritual. They called themselves the Shomrim, or guardians, conducting the shmira. From very soon after the disaster volunteers gathered at the city morgue on 30th Street and First Avenue next to Bellevue Hospital for four hour shifts of prayer as the vans with body parts arrived from Ground Zero, on the rationale that whatever was being recovered had to include substantial parts of Jewish bodies. Because Jewish practice requires expeditious burial, normally the shmira lasts twenty-four to forty-eight hours until a funeral. But since in this case a quick burial was not possible, this shmira lasted seven months. At least one member of the Shomrim remained at the morgue to pray every minute of the day until May of 2002, as Uriel Heilman did on September 21, 2001:

> The site where the dead were kept was bustling with activity when I arrived, even in the pouring rain at four in the morning. New York police officers and state troopers stood guard as police, firemen, FBI agents, federal investigators, and other officials made their way in and out of the cordoned off area. I picked up my clergy tags from the previous volunteer and entered the scene.
>
> Eight or so simple white trucks, each draped with the American flag, each containing bags filled with countless body parts of the unidentified dead—victims of being in the wrong place at the fatally wrong time. A small American flag bound to the pole of the tent in which forensic investigators waited for the next truck to come in was drenched by the lashing rain, and even the flags adorning the trucks were curled up inside themselves (Uriel Heilman 2002a, 2002b, and 2001).

But the lack of whole bodies of the victims, or anything resembling whole bodies, affected everyone. Even the few firemen, among the 343 who perished who were recovered more or less intact in their protective suits, were crushed beyond recognition. For the rest a body part was recovered, a hand here, part of a leg there, a piece of a spleen, sometimes little more than a fingernail. With DNA analysis these fragments that eventually numbered in the thousands were carefully assembled for detailed forensic investigation that as of the end of 2002 had led to the identification of 1,439 victims (Kugler 2002). The other way of framing that fact is that approximately 1,000 people disappeared into nothingness in the fiery inferno. They left only the smell of death, of singed hair, as one respondent in an interview study I am conducting put it.[2]

The form of the dying radically impaired mourning. I had a very personal reaction to this dimension of the disaster. The trauma of my childhood was when my father died suddenly just after I turned sixteen. We had him cremated, and along with my brother, I picked up the ashes the next day at the funeral home. I was handed an innocuous tin can filled with white and gray ashes that were partly in clumps. It looked like the ashes that covered lower Manhattan on 9/11. Later that day, I stood in ocean water up to my knees near a cottage off the coast of Florida that our family had treasured, pried open the top of the can, peered for a long time at the clumps of ashes, and then tossed them out into the water where they sank slowly and disappeared.

In a similar way, many respondents in my study commented on their weird, desiccated, and fragmented death encounters. Henry T. was walking to work south of the World Trade Center that exquisitely beautiful Tuesday morning.

> Henry T.: I work on the corner of Rector Street and West. Ahm, and I walked all the way down and I was right in front of my office kind of getting ready to turn into the doors to go in my building, and heard an explosion, really loud explosion, and almost simultaneously saw a, ahm—about a six-feet-long piece of lamppost fly kind of onto Rector Street in front about 10-12 feet in front of me. And a couple of other large pieces of metal, ahm, landed like in front of me, too, and so I didn't—I kind of didn't know what was goin' on, obviously, and I smelled a little...
>
> Strozier: At that point you're on the southwest corner of the [WTC] complex?
>
> Henry T.: Yes, but I'm not—I'm still a few blocks away, right. As I started walking up West Street towards the World Trade Center, I walked up West Street a little bit, I could see that there were pieces of debris and there were, ahm, pieces of bodies on West Street. And this is still a couple hundred yards away [from the towers themselves]. So either—I initially felt that those people had got hit by the flying debris and it killed them, but, ahm, now I'm thinking maybe that somehow they—they could have got...like thrown out of the building that far or something. So I saw essentially what was like a torso, like the torso of somebody laying there, ahm, a head, and then one other large like piece of flesh.

Henry T.'s astonishing encounter with such body parts left him quite confused because his experience was so completely out of context. Miranda M., in turn, began to exit from her office on the 67th floor of the south tower the minute she saw the fire in the other building. She did not understand what was happening but had been hyperalert to the threat of terrorism at the WTC since 1993, the time of the first attack on the building complex. As she descended the crowded staircase, she had no idea what was happening outside, only that it was bad. Her fear became panic when the second plane hit her building while she was halfway down. The entire 100-floor structure wavered and rumbled, and then smoke was everywhere.

She finally made it to the bottom of the stairs only to discover the door was locked. At that point she seems to have dissociated in ways that left her filled with trauma and Post Traumatic Stress Disorder (PTSD) symptoms six months later when I interviewed her. Somehow, she stumbled back up two flights of stairs and, rather miraculously, found an open door and walked out onto a plaza, unsure where she was or what was going on.

> Miranda M.: I saw all chunks of metal and paper. There was a lot of paper. And then for a little way of running, like for one second I'm looking and I said, "This is weird. It's so stupid. This is weird. Stuff is"—I don't even know how I had time to think of it. "Is there a butcher that stuff's blowing out of?"
>
> Strozier: A butcher?
>
> Miranda M.: Yeah. I know I said that to myself and then like a couple of feet later, I was like, "Holy heavens, it was pieces of people." But like the first ones, like I guess the small stuff I saw, 'cause it looked like from a butcher like. And I'm like—'cause like you don't know what you do when you're running and then you see that and like you're stepping and I'm like, "Is there stuff blowin' out of a butcher?" And then that's when I knew—then like I saw stuff, then I knew what it was. And then like then you knew like—and we still—I—like by then, I was alone and then I got to a street...
>
> Strozier: Was there a lot of it, a lot of body parts?
>
> Miranda M.: Yeah. I mean I ran—I don't know if I had the bad luck of being in a—yeah. I mean I—there was like...like if you looked down, you'd see a chunk there, a chunk—like, to me, I thought it was meat, which I'm not saying that to be cruel. Like I just couldn't figure out—like I'm like...
>
> Strozier: You still didn't know what had happened.
>
> Miranda M.: No. No. By then, I still thought it was a bomb, 'cause—no, I didn't know... Oh, yeah. No, I didn't look up, but that's right. I saw—yeah. Oh, God. I saw stuff falling, so I was runnin' like this and that's why I had to see everything down. I never looked up, but you could see in front of you stuff falling.

Miranda M.'s confusion when she first escaped from the WTC was so great that she thought a butcher shop had been bombed. In her terror she is even afraid to look up and get herself oriented. Some respondents did look up, but it was only to watch helplessly as people jumped. Deirdre L. had a day job catering meetings with a business in 7 World Trade Center just to the north of the towers (that would itself collapse at 5:20 p.m. that day). She was in a room on the 39th floor (of fifty) when the first plane hit the north tower but had almost no idea of the magnitude of what was happening. In a few minutes, however, she and the others were told to evacuate the building. The long walk down the stairs without windows or knowledge of the terror outside was eerie, though mostly peaceful. The one moment of dread came when the second plane hit the south tower and the whole building she was in shook. No one knew what was happening but there was collective terror. When Deirdre finally reached the street and relative safety, she stood for a few minutes to watch the burning buildings. A man hung from a sheet or tablecloth outside a window some ninety stories up, then gave up the struggle and fell back with his arms outstretched. He seemed to fall in slow motion. Crying now, Deirdre sensed the terrible danger of the scene and felt she had to escape. With a friend she walked quickly up West Broadway to Greenwich Street, fleeing north. On the way crowds going toward the burning buildings, including three women with babies, two in strollers and one with an infant so young it was in her arms, slowed her progress. Deirdre shook that woman by the shoulders and said she shouldn't be going that way, that it was dangerous and she was going the wrong direction, and that she should turn around. The woman ignored her and pushed on. For weeks afterwards Deirdre had nightmares of these women with their children getting buried by the collapsing buildings.

These complex reactions to the form of the dying took shape within "zones of sadness," a term first used by my colleague, Michael Flynn, and one I have written about extensively, that radiated out from Ground Zero (Strozier 2002). The issues of trauma and impairment of mourning depended in large part on one's proximity to the actual scene of the destruction and as such constitute areas of consciousness in the moral topography of the disaster. Many factors influenced the reaction of the witness, the pain suffered, even the trauma endured, but it did matter enormously how far one was from the epicenter of death. The zones, despite the fact that they are dimensions of experience, can even be mapped, and include, first, those between the Hudson River and the Brooklyn Bridge, and below Chambers Street as far as Battery Park, who directly witnessed the death; second, those in Greenwich Village below 14th Street who saw the disaster directly but could not see people jumping; third, those in metropolitan New York but without a clear line of vision of what was happening (or from such a great distance as to make the image of the buildings burning surreal); and, fourth, those outside New York and in the world who watched the disaster on television.

The difference between zones three and four is worth some comment. To observe the disaster through the medium of television had the contradictory psychological effect of intensifying the experience of horror through the endless repetition while simultaneously numbing the viewer to its real meaning, in part because of the repetition but also because it was watched in protected spaces, there was commentary to contextualize what one saw, and the direct experience of death was leeched out of the images. The New York experience of the disaster, even outside the radius of death, was full of confusion and chaos, with people being evacuated from tall buildings and a mass exodus across the bridges, and much general fear. There was also the smell and taste of death, for in that cloud of incinerated computers and rugs and drapes and tons of cement were all the people whom we breathed into our lungs, into our souls.

Finally, there was the shock of what was experienced in the World Trade Center disaster. History had not prepared us for such a disaster. We were much too convinced of what has been called the American sense of exceptionalism that blessed, or cursed, us with a sense of entitlement and special security. We never feared attacks from foreign shores. The most important document in our political history about the danger of tyranny, Lincoln's "Young Man Lyceum Speech" in 1838, argues that because we face no threat of foreign invasion the danger is that domestic unrest (the mobocratic spirit) will loosen our attachment to our democratic institutions and cause the emergence of a dictator.[3] There are other aspects of American exceptionalism. Ours was the first and greatest democratic republic. We had the richest soil and best institutions. Our military became the strongest. That sense of invincibility reached its zenith in our history, I would say, in the 1990s. America then had reached a pinnacle of absolute power and confidence. There was serious talk the new economy would never collapse and we would simply continue to get richer. American culture completely suffocated global heterogeneity. And American power after our so-called victory in the Cold War left us with absolute dominance and what Robert Jay Lifton (2001) has called a "superpower syndrome." Our arrogance was supreme, and nowhere was that sense of invincibility more supremely centered than New York, and no single image more concretely symbolized American power and authority and dominance than those giant towers reaching into the heavens.

To attack and actually crumble those towers was to demolish in a heartbeat all that security. It literally rocked the ground of our being. We could not have been less prepared psychologically. It is fair to say that before 9/11 we lacked an appropriate level of fear of the apocalyptic. Now we are in a state of panic and hysteria. Perhaps the issue, touching as it does collective death, only invites extremes.

Apocalyptic Context

The twin towers were still burning but standing when commentators began to draw the parallel between the WTC and Pearl Harbor. Both shook the ground of our being and undermined our sense of invincibility. Both led to war. Both are etched in historical memory. And yet what distinguishes these two dramatic events is that Pearl Harbor occurred in a world without nuclear weapons. In that difference lies the main conceptual point I want to make.

People have probably thought about the end of the world since its beginning. Such imaginings have stirred much creativity in religion and the arts and been an essential ingredient in the making of culture. But images of the end of human life itself also involve great violence and collective death. The apocalyptic is not benign. It is seductive, because in many traditions such narratives involve the death of all evil and redemption for the saved.

One might say there are three dimensions of the apocalyptic. First, there is the ontological. Because we all die, we know of collective death, and that knowledge may, in fact, be what separates us from the higher primates. Second, there is the cultural and religious dimension to the apocalyptic. Images of our collective end lie very deeply imbedded and their protean expressions in culture and religion are carried forward by mystics, artists, and psychotics. These three marginal groups played a critical role in keeping alive for everyone that image of an apocalyptic future that makes an ethical present more necessary. But finally there is a historical or psychohistorical dimension to the apocalyptic. Something shifted in our consciousness in the middle of the twentieth century that was directly associated with the presence of nuclear weapons in the world. We don't need God any longer to end it all. The power is entirely within us and in our arsenals. We alone possess it.

Nuclear Weapons and the New Terrorism

This new psychology of weapons of mass destruction (and of course one now has to include biological and chemical weapons in what is an ever-more fearsome expansion of ultimate weapons in human hands) was not that apparent for the first few decades of the nuclear age because it seemed only states could possess the weapons. Technology has altered that limitation, and in retrospect it seems the 1990s was the hugely significant turning point in that historical process. One can't quite make a nuclear bomb in one's bathtub yet, but nor does one need the mobilization of resources such as those represented by, say, the Manhattan Project to imagine having the ability to kill not just hundreds, or thousands, but millions.

There is no question it is a huge threat to us all that apocalyptic groups may well very soon, if they don't already, have access to weapons of mass destruction. The respondents in my study report the generalized dread that if Osama bin Laden had had access to nuclear weapons he would have placed them on the planes flying into the towers on 9/11. But I want to turn this question around and stress its more general and psychological aspects, namely that the mere existence of the weapons themselves play what is perhaps the central role in evoking the new violence of the contemporary age.

Why?

(1) Nuclear weapons totalize politics, religion, indeed the self. They make possible the most extreme reach of violence and stir the worst devils, rather than what Abraham Lincoln called the better angels, of our nature. Richard Falk in this regard has written extensively about the way the weapons "deform" our politics (Lifton and Falk 1982).

(2) Nuclear weapons totalize death itself, and change what Kurt Vonnegut called plain old ordinary death into absurd death (Vonnegut 1969).[4] Robert Jay Lifton has said that nuclear weapons bring about a "pointless apocalypse" (Lifton 1979). Millennialists of all kinds have long imagined that God must destroy the world as the necessary precursor to the arrival of a messiah (or his return). At the fanatical border of such thinking, people take it upon themselves to help God along by doing things that they imagine will hasten the destruction and thus bring the messiah sooner rather than later. Some form of such thinking exists in all religions. Fundamentalists who toy with ideas of world destruction, in other words, at least believe

they get something wonderful out of the violence. Nuclear weapons bring back nothing and are utterly and completely pointless.

(3) Nuclear weapons open up new possibilities for violence, because the new power of God in human hands makes possible, and therefore affirms, the sinister workings of the paranoid mindset.

Paranoia and Terrorism

Paranoia may be the heart of the matter. There is a psychological synergy between the survivor's sense of endangerment and the more extreme imagery of victimization for the paranoid. The experience of suffering can ennoble and expand empathy. But victimization is not always or even mostly ennobling. It stirs rage and fury and the call for revenge (Kohut 1972). The trauma gets imbedded (Caruth 1995; Herman 1992; van der Kolk 1987 and 1996; Strozier and Flynn 1996a, 1996b, and 1997). All is false and counterfeit in the world. No one can be trusted. Evil is everywhere and the world a malevolent, threatening, dangerous place. In time such collective feelings get institutionalized and built into politics and culture. A paranoid style (Hofstadter 1964) takes shape that merges self and world.

Because paranoia is essentially at the border of psychosis, when it enters politics its forms can be sometimes quite amusing. The John Birchers of the 1950s, for example, were terribly worried about communism but their most immediate policy issue in the country was the eminently sensible public health move to fluoridate the water. The movie *Dr. Strangelove*, from the late 1960s, makes funny parody of this fear in the obsessions of the mad Brigadier General Jack D. Ripper, who rants about the Commies trying to get at our precious bodily fluids.

Then there is Osama bin Laden, the malevolent and mysterious figure who has wreaked such havoc in our city and made our world such an unsafe place. At some level we understood completely the apocalyptic dangers he represented.

But who is this Osama bin Laden? And what does he want? On the personal side, he is all the more dangerous because he is not as schizoid as someone like Timothy McVeigh or as openly psychotic as Shoko Asaharo, the leader of the Japanese cult, Aum Shinrikyo, that actively tried to bring about Armageddon. Bin Laden does warmly embrace the apocalyptic. As it has been said, he is like the president of a terrorism university, a charismatic figure with money who can inspire others to act. He does not lead a cult but rather a movement. He is not a cleric but arranges to wrap himself in religious sanctity by having a coterie of radical imams issue fatwas that legitimate his actions.

Bin Laden is a curious blend of political and religious leader and plays an important role vitalizing Islamists who see the downfall of their faith and their lands the result of outside western corrupting influences. Bin Laden has wrapped himself around the Palestinian cause, mainly for pragmatic reasons in his effort to gain support in Arab lands and unify the struggle, but he hardly cares about the PLO or Israel. What he does care about is the presence of U.S. troops in Saudi Arabia during and after the Gulf War, which he sees as a desecration, an affront to his faith, the presence of the evil other in holy land. Here I would note that the difference between his pragmatic appropriation of PLO goals and his real feelings about American infidels in Saudi Arabia is exactly the difference between the old and new terrorism. Bin Laden was moving toward radical action in the late 1980s, but his Al Qaeda organization came in the wake of the Gulf War and was its direct consequence.

So what does he want? He wants to destroy America and its culture, and out of such a victory make a purified Islam. It seems the attack on our majestic towers in his eyes was both real and symbolic *and* succeeded beyond his wildest dreams. He also fits snugly into the paranoid style. He has made his fight a jihad, or holy war, which puts God on his side. There is an urgency to the struggle and it has to happen now, as time is running out. The end is at hand, which is fateful but offers the powerful appeal of transformation and redemption. Furthermore, the malice Americans create in the world is the motivating force in history. He has special knowledge of that evil and must act to oppose it. That led him to organize terrorist training camps that have carried out actions ranging from the first bombing of the WTC (which he seems to have had some relation to), to the Embassy bombings in 1998, to the Cole, and of course the attacks on 9/11.

Disaster and Psychoanalysis

We live in a state of chronic fear and paranoia. It is not altogether inappropriate. There are those in the world with a grim determination to destroy us, and increasingly these new terrorists have access to means of annihilation that can realize their most extravagant dreams. Such threats, and a keen awareness of the dangers, have long been a part of our psyches. In my WTC interviews, for example, I have been struck by how many people imposed preexisting nuclear ideas onto their experience of the disaster. Many saw the plume of smoke from the burning buildings as a mushroom cloud. Miranda M., after her escape when the dark cloud from the collapsed tower entrapped her, jumped into a bush and passed out for she was sure it was nuclear and meant the end of the world. This sequence suggests the heart of my argument. We are all unsteady in the nuclear age. Something profound shifted when humans came to possess weapons with the destructive power of God. The new terrorists embrace that power with alacrity and seek to employ it. To fend off such dangers we first need to recognize its centrality in our souls and then find concrete ways to mitigate the threat.

These are issues psychoanalysts can think about, and in the process make a genuine contribution to a deeper understanding of the threats to our existence in the world. We can begin that process in our consulting rooms—if we are open to the psychological significance of nuclear weapons. In a seminar some years ago, a psychoanalytic colleague gave a clinical example to disprove my thesis about the centrality of nuclear weapons in our souls. He reported the dream of an eleven-year-old boy whose parents were in the middle of an angry divorce. In the dream the boy woke in terror to the image of a mushroom cloud as a bomb exploded. Obviously, my colleague said, the boy had borrowed a powerful metaphor to convey his inner sense of the chaos and violence he felt about his exploding family. That was the sequence, he said, and the way to understand the dream. I responded that, of course, the dream has that meaning, and it probably would make the most sense in a clinical setting at least to begin the analysis of the boy's feelings about the divorce from within the image of the mushroom cloud. But the dream is incompletely interpreted if we stay only in its personal context. As I told my colleague, what this troubled but insightful boy has done from within his misery over his fragmenting family is to open himself to the meaning of totalized death in the world that we face with nuclear weapons. In that process the boy grew and deepened. The most significant level of the dream, I feel, is the way it suggests the workings of history in the boy's psyche, not the other way around. This precocious boy took in the existential reality of our lives that we ignore at our own peril. It is entirely false to live as if there is a secure human future. What we can do is move through the doubt and fear and dread into cautious hope. In a dark time the eye begins to see.

Notes

1. An earlier version of this paper appeared in Dialogues and Terror: Patients and Their Psychoanalysts, Special Issue, Psychoanalysis and Psychotherapy, Fall 2003, Volume 20, Number 2.
2. I head a study of the World Trade Center disaster that has been underway since the beginning of the second week at my Center on Terrorism and Public Safety at John Jay College. The method used is that of my friend and colleague, Robert Jay Lifton (who is consulting on the team) in his five major empirical investigations of extreme situations (1961, 1968, 1974, 1985, and 1999). Other members of the research team include Michael Flynn, Cindy Ness, Katie Gentile, and Paula Glickman, all skilled therapists familiar with the method and concepts of the study. As of December 2002, we conducted nearly 100 interviews with fifty-four respondents and had approximately 140 hours of interview data. Each respondent, where possible, is interviewed two times for about 1 and ½ hours.
3. "All the armies of Europe, Asia and Africa combined, with all the treasures of this earth (our own excepted) in their military chest; with a Buonarparte for a commander, could not by force, take a drink from the Ohio, or make a track on the Blue Ridge, in a trial of a thousand years," he says, 1953, I: 109.
4. Robert Jay Lifton has shared this idea of the weapons totalizing death with me in many conversations over the years but most especially in connection with my study of Christian fundamentalists (1994).

References

Blakemore, B. (2002), Personal communication, July 18 (Blakemore is a high-level ABC correspondent).

Caruth, C. (1995), *Trauma: Explorations in Memory*. Baltimore: Johns Hopkins University Press.

Erikson, K. (1995), *A New Species of Trouble: The Human Experience of Modern Disaster*. New York: Norton.

Heilman, U. (2001), Personal and unpublished statement, September 21.

Heilman, U. (2002a), Interview, December 19.

Heilman, U. (2002b), Dept. of Remembrance, Praying for the Dead, Personal and unpublished statement.

Herman, J. (1992), *Trauma and Recovery*. New York: Basic Books.

Hofstadter, R. (1964), "The paranoid style in American politics," in *The Paranoid Style in American Politics and Other Essays*. Chicago: The University of Chicago Press.

Kohut, H. (1972), "Thoughts on narcissism and narcissistic rage," in Paul Ornstein, ed., *The Search for the Self: Selected Writings of Heinz Kohut: 1950-1978*. New York: International Universities Press.

Kolk, B. van der, (1987), *Psychological Trauma*. Washington, DC: American Psychiatric Press.

Kolk, B. van der, McFarlane, A., and Weisaeth, L. (eds.) (1996), *Traumatic Stress: The Effects of Overwhelming Experience on Mind, Body, and Society*. New York: Guilford.

Kugler, S. (2002), SFG.com, December 13.

Lifton, R. (1961), *Thought Reform and the Psychology of Totalism: A Study of "Brainwashing" in China*. New York: Norton.

Lifton, R. (1968), *Death in Life: Survivors of Hiroshima*. New York: Random House.

Lifton, R. (1973), *Home From the War: Vietnam Veterans, Neither Victims nor Executioners*. New York: Simon and Schuster.

Lifton, R. (1979), *The Broken Connection: On Death and the Continuity of Life*. New York: Basic Books.

Lifton, R. (1999), *Destroying the World to Save It: Aum Shinrikyo, Apocalyptic Violence, and the New Terrorism*. New York: Metropolitan Books.

Lifton, R. (1985), *The Nazi Doctors: Medical Killing and the Psychology of Genocide*. New York: Basic Books.

Lifton, R. (2001), Presentation at conference, "The Second Nuclear Age and the Academy," sponsored by the Center on Violence and Human Survival, John Jay College.

Lifton, R. and Falk, R. (1982), *Indefensible Weapons*. New York: Basic Books.

Lincoln, A. (1953), *The Collected Works of Abraham Lincoln*, Roy Basler et al., eds. Volumes 1 and 5. New Brunswick, NJ: Rutgers University Press.

Macdonald, A. [William Pierce] (1978), *The Turner Diaries*. Hillsboro, WV: National Vanguard Books.

Macdonald, A. [William Pierce] (1989), *Hunter*. Hillsboro, WV: National Vanguard Books.

Miller, M. (1995), "The intellectual origins of modern terrorism in Europe," in Martha Crenshaw, ed., *Terrorism in Context*. University Park, PA: The Pennsylvania State University Press.

New York Times (September 13, 2002).

Strozier, C. (1994), *Apocalypse: On the Psychology of Fundamentalism in America*. Boston: Beacon Press.

Strozier, C. (1995), "The new violence." *The Journal of Psychohistory*, 23: 168-193.

Strozier, C. (2002), "The World Trade Center disaster and the apocalyptic." *Psychoanalytic Dialogues* 12: 361-380.

Strozier, C. and Flynn, M. (eds.) (1996a), *Trauma and Self*. Lanham, MD: Rowman & Littlefield.

Strozier, C. and Flynn, M. (eds.) (1996b), *Genocide, War, and Human Survival*. Lanham, MD: Rowman & Littlefield.

Strozier, C. and Flynn, M. (eds.) (1997), *The Year 2000: Essays on the End*. New York: New York University Press.

Strozier, C. and Gentile, K. (2004), "The mental health response to the World Trade Center disaster," in Danielle Knafo, ed., *Living With Terror, Working With Trauma: A Clinician's Handbook*. Northvale: Jason Aronson, 2004.

Vonnegut, K. (1969), *Slaughterhouse Five*. New York: Delacourt.

12

The Apocalyptic Face-Off: The Culture of Death after 9/11

Robert Jay Lifton

The culture of death and apocalypticism has infected the thinking of the contemporary world, and certainly the events of September 11, 2001 and their aftermath demonstrate this unequivocally. This infection has come in the form of an apocalyptic imagination that has spawned a new and particularly deadly kind of violence at the beginning of the twenty-first century. So much is this so that one can now speak of a worldwide epidemic of violence aimed at massive destruction in the service of various visions of purification and renewal, of which the attacks of 9/11 were among the most spectacular but by no means the last. In particular, we are experiencing what could be called an apocalyptic face-off between Islamist forces, overtly visionary in their willingness to kill and die for their religion, and American forces, claiming to be restrained and reasonable but no less visionary in their projection of a cleansing war-making and military power. Both sides are energized by versions of intense idealism; both see themselves as embarked on a sacred mission of combating evil in order to redeem and renew the world; and both are ready to release untold levels of violence to achieve that purpose. These "holy wars" are part of the aftershocks and echoes that remain in the air since the 9/11 disasters.

The religious fanaticism of Osama bin Laden and other Islamist zealots has by now a certain familiarity to us as to others elsewhere, for their violent demands for spiritual purification are aimed as much at fellow Islamics as at American "infidels." Their fierce attacks on the defilement that they believe they see everywhere in contemporary life resemble those of past movements and sects from all parts of the world; such sects, with end-of-the-world prophecies and programmatic violence in the service of bringing those prophecies about, flourished in Europe from the eleventh through the sixteenth centuries. Similar sects like the fanatical Japanese cult, Aum Shinrikyo, which released sarin gas into the Tokyo subways in 1995, have existed, even proliferated, in our own time.

The American apocalyptic entity is in contrast less familiar to us. Even if its urges to power and domination seem historically recognizable, it nonetheless represents a new constellation of forces bound up with what I have come to think of as "superpower syndrome." By that term I mean a national mindset—put forward strongly by a tight-knit leadership group—which takes on a sense of omnipotence, of unique standing in the world that grants it the right to hold sway over all other nations. The American superpower status derives from our emergence after World War II as uniquely powerful in every respect, still more so as the only superpower—both economic and military—since the end of the Cold War in the early 1990s. But only in the early years of the twentieth-first century did the full superpower syndrome develop.

More than merely to dominate, the American superpower seeks to control history. Such cosmic ambition is accompanied by an equally vast sense of entitlement—of special dispensation to pursue its aims. That entitlement stems partly from historic claims to special democratic virtue, but has much to do with an embrace of technological power translated into military terms. That is, a superpower—the world's only superpower—is entitled to dominate and control precisely because it is a superpower.

The murderous events of 9/11 hardened that sense of entitlement as nothing else could have. Superpower syndrome did not require 9/11, but the attacks on the twin towers and the Pentagon rendered us an *aggrieved superpower*, a giant violated and made vulnerable, which no superpower can permit. The American encounter with death and the mourning it engendered, in the minds of many and certainly of those in authority, provided a justification for striking at perceived enemies with unlimited power. Indeed, at the core of superpower syndrome lies a powerful fear of vulnerability. A superpower's encounter with death and destruction and its sense of victimization bring on both intolerable humiliation and an angry determination to restore, or even extend, the boundaries of a superpower-dominated world.

The war on Iraq, a country with longstanding aspirations toward weapons of mass destruction but with no apparent connection to the assaults of September 11, was a manifestation of that American visionary projection—an expression of a prior policy of American world domination that could now be implemented. As Secretary of Defense Donald Rumsfeld made clear on the day after, the broad definition of the "war on terrorism" required us to invade Iraq. One can say that Iraq rose to the surface from the deeper dreams and ambitions of our leaders at that moment, even when our attackers came from elsewhere. This readiness to go to war was a manifestation of the superpower syndrome and its post-9/11 immersion in a culture of death.

Integral to superpower syndrome and the expansion of the culture of death are the existence of menacing nuclear stockpiles and their world-destroying capacity. Over the decades of the Cold War, America and the Soviet Union both lived with a godlike nuclear capacity to obliterate the cosmos—along with a fear of being annihilated by the other. Now America alone possesses that world-destroying capacity, and post-Soviet Russia no longer looms as a nuclear superpower adversary. We have yet to comprehend the full impact of this exclusive capacity to blow up anyone or everything. But its reverberations are never absent in any part of the world.

The confrontation between Islamist and American versions of planetary excess has unfortunately tended to define a world in which the vast majority of people embrace neither. But the apocalyptic vision needs no majority to dominate a landscape. All the more so when, in their mutual zealotry, Islamist and American leaders seem to act in concert. That is, each in its excess evokes the apocalypticism of the other, resulting in a malignant synergy.

As a psychiatrist concerned with history, I have in my past work explored the destructive excesses of our times—Nazi genocide, the atomic bombings of Hiroshima and Nagasaki, Chinese Communist "thought reform," the Vietnam War, and the apocalyptic forays of Aum Shinrikyo and other cults of the late-twentieth century. In each of these events there was a powerful impulse to destroy the existing world so that it might be purified and renewed.

The Nazis had a vision of renewing their world biologically by ridding it of "defiling" races and bad genes. In dropping atomic bombs on Hiroshima and Nagasaki, the United States sought to end a bloody war but also to display its awesome power and so to alter and reshape the postwar world to come. Chinese thought reform aimed at rooting out bad thoughts and ill-formed minds associated with an old and corrupt regime and way of life in order to purify, politically and ethically, a vast society. In Vietnam, villages, towns, and parts of cities had to be sacrificed and destroyed in order to be "saved" from communism. And Shoko Asahara, the guru who formed the Aum Shinrikyo cult, dedicated his group to achieving a biblical Armageddon in order to bring on a world of spiritual perfection.

These extreme twentieth-century dreams and expressions of totalistic control and mass killing were bound to reverberate in the twenty-first century. On September 11, some of those reverberations became all too cruelly evident. My past work suddenly became current. Indeed, my last book of the twentieth century had been entitled *Destroying the World to Save It*, an image that could be readily applied to the Islamist-American encounter in the twenty-first.

Psychology and History

The "psychohistorical approach" that I have used in all of my studies is no more than the application of psychological methods to historical questions. While I have been much influenced by the psychoanalytic tradition, and especially by the work of Erik Erikson, I have found it necessary to modify that tradition considerably in order to address some of the historical convulsions of our time. In the classical Freudian model, our energies are derived from our instincts, or "drives" (sexual and aggressive), and from the psychological defenses (such as repression) that we call forth to cope with these drives. But the cataclysmic events I have studied required a different emphasis: a focus on death and the continuity of life, or the symbolization of life and death. That kind of model or paradigm is, I believe, appropriate for any study of collective behavior, especially for the apocalyptic currents of our contemporary world.

To look at people's behavior in the midst and aftermath of these upheavals has also required me to supplement their ordinary nitty-gritty level of function—their everyday struggles with love, family, bereavement, work, and overall self-esteem—with an ultimate level, that of larger human connectedness, or what I call symbolic immortality. Here I mean combining the knowledge that we die with a quest to be part of something larger than the self: the sense of living on in children and grandchildren (biological or family mode), in religious expressions of an immortal soul, in one's "works" or influences on other human beings, in what most cultures describe as "eternal nature," or in experiences of transcendence ("high states" so intense that within them time and death disappear). This quest for symbolic immortality is of great importance for all of us, but becomes particularly crucial for grasping the experience of people undergoing historical convulsions.

In my work I have explored such convulsions through face-to-face encounters, individual interviews, with twentieth-century victims and victimizers: with death-haunted Hiroshima survivors, with Nazi doctors who participated in medical killing and with their victims who survived the death camps, with Chinese and Westerners subjected to "thought reform," with American Vietnam veterans who turned against their own war but had difficulty extricating themselves from it, and with former members of Aum Shinrikyo still longing for their lost guru and his mystical visions. I sought out all of these people as having acted upon (or themselves been acted upon by) history. Throughout, I have looked for what I call "shared themes" in such people in order to shed light not only on their own experience but also on that of their—and our—larger historical era.

Looking now at the intricate maneuvers taking place between Islamist apocalyptics and our political leaders, I find much that is unnervingly familiar from my past studies. History, as the events of 9/11 and its aftermath have demonstrated, is not something just "out there" in the larger cosmos—but part of the inner self of each of us and of our shared intellectual and emotional life.

9/11 Continues

More than that, 9/11 is not over. We are still in it. I have become aware of the ways in which I, too, am a survivor of 9/11—not in the sense of having been directly victimized by the attacks but rather, because like all Americans, I was exposed to the intense death-related imagery of a suicidal assault on my country. Those televised images had a near-apocalyptic aura for almost everyone, and they remain indelible in the collective memory no less than the personal recollections of each of us. They are at the epicenter of our most recent brush with death.

Hence, the immediate reference to the space where the two towers collapsed as "ground zero," a term previously reserved for the hypocenter of a nuclear explosion. The 9/11 experience has become a continuing disaster that remains with us. It is impossible as yet to look at 9/11 in retrospect. Its active reverberations are everywhere. We remain in thralldom to what happened on that day. The dynamic of 9/11 dominates American thought and our national life.

We have responded apocalyptically to an apocalyptic challenge. We have embarked on a series of wars—first in Afghanistan, then in Iraq, with suggestions of additional targeted countries in the offing—because we view the amorphous terrorist enemy as evil, dangerous, and ubiquitous. But our own amorphously extreme response feeds a larger dynamic of apocalyptic violence, even as it constructs a twenty-first-century version of American empire. We press toward mobile forays of military subjugation. Crucial to this kind of *fluid world control* is our dominating war machine, backed by our still dominant nuclear stockpiles. Such an arrangement can lend itself to efforts at the remote control of history. Any such project, however, becomes enmeshed in fantasy; in dreams of imposing an omnipotent will on others, and in that way of conquering death itself. Driven by superpower syndrome, the imagined project, the visions of domination and control can prove catastrophic when, as they must, they come up against the irredeemable stubbornness of reality.

9/11 has been a vast trauma to Americans on many levels. But there is danger in absolutizing our sense of victimization. Hiroshima survivors some years ago told me of their concerns about this "victim consciousness" as a psychological and social impediment to progress and change. And Islamist extremists are importantly motivated by their own sense of historical victimization. We can extricate ourselves from this vicious circle of victimization and violence only by extricating ourselves from our own superpower syndrome. We could then regain our moral compass and respond to a dangerous world with measure and restraint. To do so we must confront our own totalism and instead embrace what Albert Camus called "thought which recognizes limits." In that way we would replace our post-9/11 amorphous violence with genuine survivor wisdom.

13

The Aftermath of Death: Collective Reintegration and Dealing with Chaos in Light of the Disaster of September 11

Samuel Heilman

Introduction

The great anthropologist of death, Robert Hertz, once noted that because society "feels itself immortal and wants to be so; it cannot normally believe that its members...should be fated to die."[1] Death, which carries off the leaders as easily as the led and the so-called "important" as much as the putatively marginal, throws a challenge at the very heart of that belief. Mass death does so even more powerfully. In addition, the natural sense of chaos that predominates in the immediate aftermath of death becomes even more acute when the numbers of dead are great. Moreover, when such mass death is sudden and unexpected, coming "out of the clear blue sky," such as happened, literally, on September 11, 2001, the threat to society's sense of immortality, order, and confidence is felt in particularly compelling fashion. Such death strikes society "in the very principle of its life, in the faith it has in itself."[2]

However difficult the encounter with death is, for those who are left behind the journey back toward life requires even more prodigious efforts. While Jews, out of whose traditions my thoughts emerge, have endeavored no less than others to find answers to the question of death's ultimate meaning or to the more personal one of *why* it has made its particular appointment with them, as the remarks by Neil Gilman elsewhere in this volume make clear, in practice Jewish tradition is more immediately concerned with answering the question that follows hard upon death: What do we do now? In the answers to *what* should be done, Jewish traditions and supporting rituals sustain the idea that whatever is done, it is never done unaided. Jews, who following the encounter with death have taken the prescribed steps of the tradition and custom, are meant to emerge bit-by-bit from its chaos neither beaten nor depressed but instead assured that, though bereft, they are not without help or alone. That sense of solidarity, of finding a place in a consoling community, offers the emerging mourner precisely what Emile Durkheim has suggested is the key contribution of collective experience: "confidence and…a feeling of an increased energy."[3] Nothing is a more powerful antidote to the anxiety and being at loss in chaos that an encounter with death may engender.

While all this comes into play in the case of individual death and the loss of a loved one, the occasion of violent mass death—the result of an attack of one group of human beings against another—makes this process far more challenging. While the survivors feel the company of misery, they are—both as individuals and as a group—also far more shaken and torn from their moorings than might otherwise be the case. The sense of chaos may be more powerfully overwhelming. When the consolers are as shaken as those who need consoling, the intensification of the collective experience, even in the wake of traditional ritual responses, may not as easily offer comfort, closure, and new beginnings. Additionally, when the dead leave few or no remains behind, the sense of closure is far more tenuous, perhaps impossible to attain. Jews have experienced this most vividly in the aftermath of the Holocaust. The situation following the 9/11 disasters, although of a different order of magnitude, also resonates with this truth. Yet if the Jews got past the Holocaust and before that revived themselves after repeated mass attacks against them, their way of life, and their people by emphasizing their collective consciousness as a people—as they have always done when encountering death—perhaps this offers guidance for Americans no less.

These thoughts were originally collected on the first anniversary of the 9/11 disasters, a day the Jews call the *yahrzeit*. In Jewish tradition, a yahrzeit is an occasion for reflection, when the initial sense of loss comes back with an echoed intensity but in a different tone. This is not just a time to recall the past on the pretext of excising its pain, for to do that, as the Talmudic sage Rabbi Meir put it, would be like a physician offering one who has fractured a leg that has since healed to "come to me and I shall break your leg again and heal it so that you may see how well I can heal the wounded."[4] The first yahrzeit is rather an occasion to at last put an end to mourning and a beginning to a new life, when the wisdom that comes from experience of loss is integrated into one's understanding of how to go on living. It is in this spirit that I turn back to 9/11 in order to draw on lessons that I believe the aftermath of that day provide.

If the moment and reality of death demonstrate the limits of the human ability to master the riddle of existence and our ultimate failure to prevent mortality, much of its aftermath is driven by a repeated display of how much we the living (particularly if we are not alone) can still do, how in spite of the death life is not vanquished, how the living can still take charge and can escape from the clutches of mortality. What could be a more essential element of civilization?

Congregation and collective action, from which there emerges a more powerful sense of collective consciousness, is the Jewish antidote to the sense of anxiety, abandonment, and chaos that death initially engenders. In a sense some of this collective experience, so familiar to those anchored in Jewish tradition, is an essential part of the legacy of the events of September 11 and their aftermath. It is there in the heightened sense of American solidarity that was a primary element in the bereavement as it was experienced especially in New York and Washington, but in some measure throughout the country. The gatherings throughout the America, the prominent displays of the flag, the streams of people who came and continue to come to what became called Ground Zero, the collective concern with the retrieval of bodies and memorialization are all expressions of this renewed and revitalized collective consciousness.

In the initial aftermath, these feelings of collective solidarity were not limited to Americans. The outpouring of world sympathy in the days and weeks after the attacks—a remarkable turn from the anti-Americanism so often dominant in the world—underscored the national sense of collective solidarity.[5] When the world reached out to Americans, this in turn enhanced the sense of their shared circumstances. As those abroad at the time of the attacks and in the days and weeks afterward discovered, any American could stand for all Americans; all those who survived were considered to be and treated as if they were among the bereaved. To be sure, a part of the collective consciousness was a shared sense of anxiety, grief, shock, and even a feeling of powerlessness about the inability to prevent or foresee the disaster and to save those who died. But in these common feelings was the overarching sense of not being alone that largely mitigated these negative feelings.

After Death: What is to be Done?

Death plunges us into a state of limbo, the dead not fully gone and the bereft not knowing what is to become of them. For Jews, this liminal period on the threshold between death and the funeral is called *aninut.* This is a time when reality seems somehow suspended over a breach: what happens next? It is a period when both the newly bereaved and the newly dead must be moved beyond the rupture in the normal fabric of existence that death has engendered. For Jewish tradition, which seeks to offer the bridge from chaos to order, this must come swiftly, for aninut is too hard to sustain very long. Liminality, as students of this betwixt-and-between state have noted, is an extraordinary state of being, fraught with both danger and potential.[6]

The dead and the bereaved need to move on, each in their own way, and it is the role of the consoling community to help bring this about. That is why we find the tradition pushing for a swift resolution of this in-between state. The shock, the grief can overwhelm. The proximity of death can frighten one to death. Death almost seems contagious. To free one from its defiling grasp, to end the danger, Judaism makes this stage as brief as possible and moves toward purification and a swift burial.

But if Americans would have wanted to follow this Jewish model, the circumstances since September 11 have made such a pace unachievable. Too many bodies are missing; too many remains remain unclaimed, threats of death continue. In a sense, all this has led to a situation in which much of America remains in aninut. This has led, perhaps, to an intensification of the feelings among Americans in general and New Yorkers in particular that we are living in a time fraught both with danger and potential. The former comes not only from the inability to lay all the dead to rest and move on to mourning and re-knitting life's order but also in the form of the increasing national "alerts" that warn us that the threat out of which the death of 9/11 came remains real. For many of the survivors who want to get beyond 9/11, the blue sky no longer seems emotionally cloudless and people stay tensely vigilant, expressing all sorts of ad hoc alarms and feelings of stress.[7] The sense of potential, such as it is, has been articulated in the assertion by some Americans that this moment, however grim, offers an opportunity to wipe out the threat of terror and assure a future life undisturbed by this sort of death attack. In the meantime, of course, many Americans remain in limbo, sharing a sense of the limits of the human capacity to deal with death.

While in the aftermath of 9/11, the bereaved looked for help from the community as well as from those who could share in their grief and assist them in getting beyond it, many of the living could not offer that final consolation that the dead were at peace. The general condition was, as already noted, one of shared powerlessness, anxiety, vulnerability, and a common feeling of a failure to reach a resolution along with the lingering feelings of chaos. Hence, the collective consciousness, which would otherwise be a consoling source of strength and regeneration, became paradoxically often a source of stress.

In Jewish tradition, what ends the vigil is normally the preparation of the corpse, a ritual that begins with ablutions. Water, the source of life, is poured over the corpse or alternately the dead body is immersed in the waters of the *mikveh*. These immersions lead directly to the funeral and much of what follows symbolizes the desire of Jewish tradition to transform death into its opposite, into an encounter with life and rebirth as symbolized by water and the "journey of the now purified soul freed from its earthly remains to a spiritual high ground." *Life has been reversed by death, and now death will be reversed by life*. That end will be accomplished by the living, and in this they will begin the human mastery over death's dominion.

Funerals are often cathartic moments when the sense of chaos recedes and the first steps of mourning and resolution occur, when the liminality ends as survivors step over the threshold of their anxieties. They seek to satisfy: "the deepest human yearnings for order, meaning, and structure in what would otherwise be utter chaos."[8] But, while there were many funerals and memorials, the outstanding element of the collective experience of this aftermath has been keeping vigil. Among Jews, the vigil—*shmirah*—is a key feature of the liminal period of aninut and indeed there was an organized shmirah over the remains, carried out from almost as soon as the dust settled until the cleanup of Ground Zero had been completed.[9] Throughout

New York, however, there was as well another kind of vigil. This was in the posters and pictures put up asking people to be on watch for the missing who had been in the twin towers, a vigil documented and considered by Ilana Harlow elsewhere in this volume. It was in the search mission by firefighters and citizen volunteers who tried to retrieve the dead.

Vigils, however, are among the most difficult aspects of the aftermath of death. The intensity of the watch, the suspension of all else that it requires, the waiting—all wear down the bereaved. Moreover, they prevent the end of liminality, the funeral, and the onset of mourning and the healing consolations they can engender. That is why in Jewish tradition the vigil must normally be limited. But for all of the bereaved since September 11, and likewise for those who witnessed the imminence of death as the twin towers burned and fell (and who among us has not seen these images), the vigil seems to go on and on. Indeed, the rebroadcast of images of destruction as well as the ongoing watch at Ground Zero reinforce the sense of that ongoing watching. It is as if we are, as a people, frozen into re-viewing the moment before and of the mass death again and again, until the scar at the twin towers is repaired and the sources of the terror neutralized.

Funerals and Memorials

"The death of every person must be followed by a reaffirmation of the social character of human existence."[10] While the funeral and the memorial service are on their face a ritual of leave-taking for those who have died, much of these rites speak to the troubling collective reality that the living, now bereaved, confront. That reality is the uncomfortable reminder of death's capacity to tear anyone and everyone away. That is why death is never just the concern of the immediately bereaved nor is it only the affliction of those who have died. This is even more intensely the case when the death is collective, the result of an attack against an entire population as was the event we recall on September 11.

Moreover, when the bereaved, stricken by pain and diminished by a sense of loss, might be moved to withdraw into themselves, to be alone with their sorrow, and tear themselves away from the fabric of the living—no less than has the dead person—or, in extreme cases, even to follow those who have died, society forces them instead to plan a funeral, a ceremony of departure and memorialization for the dead at which everyone who knew the deceased or who has a relationship with those who have been bereaved must be assembled.[11] All this is as if to say, we have lost someone; we are attacked in life, but though we have thereby been diminished we are still here. This attitude of course is part of the emotional drive behind much of the bluster that followed the 9/11 attacks—but it is also part of the motive behind the expressed desire for attending the many funerals and creating occasions of memorialization.

The people who worked in the American defense establishment at the Pentagon, those who labored in the financial capital at the World Trade Center, the fire and police personnel sent to save the endangered, and even the "heroes" on the downed plane in Pennsylvania were among the "mightiest" of American society. Their demise in the 9/11 attacks served as a particularly vivid reminder of the limits on our might as a people. While the bereaved always feel vulnerable, when those lost have been particularly powerful in life or figures of collective or symbolic significance, the sense of vulnerability among the bereaved is especially acute. The need then for the memorials or funerals to resolve these feelings of helplessness becomes magnified. But if there are at the same time factors that hamper the carrying out of these ritual resolutions—as has been the case because of the many still missing—the bereavement cannot be resolved into mourning and recovery.

The mass memorial held at Yankee Stadium a month after the disaster, led by clergy and celebrities from across the American spectrum, the numerous gatherings at police and firefighters' funerals, the solemn assembly and dramatized procession on the occasion of the final cleanup of the Ground Zero area in New York, or the rededication of the repaired wing of the Pentagon were all expressions of this reaffirmation. So too were the many ad hoc memorials mounted around the New York area and the mini-obituaries published in the *New York Times*.[12] And of course, the many commemorations and gatherings on the first anniversary of 9/11 served as this kind of renewed affirmation of the continuity of collective life in the face of death.

A Time to Mourn

While the Jewish funeral is overwhelmingly a death-defying gathering of the living, in its ceremonial and ritual ordering of experience, it also manages to separate the realm of death irrevocably from that of the living.[13] At its successful conclusion, the dead must be buried completely before the eyes of all, while the bereaved are ushered away between two rows of consolers, to begin their mourning with an enhanced sense of solidarity. Mourning is in fact the first and crucial step in the return from the breach of death.

Mourning represents the key task that lies before all of those who feel bereaved by the events of 9/11. Yet while many individuals who have been bereaved have been able to get to the mourning stage once they have had the funerals of their dead, the collectivity, America, has not yet really been able as a people to enter this stage. Looking at the gaping hole in lower Manhattan at Ground Zero, so symbolic of the open wound that a funeral seeks to begin to close, together with the countless body parts awaiting positive identification, one sees physical evidence that the breach is not yet repaired. The hole cannot yet be closed and the body parts cannot be properly disposed of, and accordingly the mourning cannot be fully engaged. As a result, death will not be defied, and the living will not separate themselves from those they have lost. "The living" of course includes not just the immediately bereaved, but all those Americans who identify with the sense of loss.

Although there have been formal periods of mourning, it is clear that as a group, Americans, and even more so New Yorkers, have not yet made the transition into and out of mourning. They are still trying to fight back against death, caught in its chaotic aftermath, and have not found the proper tools of mourning. They have not yet found a way to turn the exclamation point into a period.

Of course when we speak of a single mourner, the step-by-step process by which mourning is meant to lead the bereaved back to life can run its course steadily. However, when the mourning is collective the pace of the progression is not always smooth, particularly if there is no common consent as to when the mourning can begin, as in the case of 9/11. Hence, the entire collectivity cannot move forward in the mourning process because there are elements of the community who are fixated at the chaotic moment of the bereavement, still waiting for the funeral. To move forward without these people is to undermine the sense of solidarity of the bereaved, the whole point of collective mourning. That would be at odds with the goals of restoring order, which propels the process.

The Community

As has been noted, Jewish custom and tradition recognize that in addition to the dead and the immediately bereaved, the community also suffers the aftereffects of death. Accordingly, even as the bereaved have needed to find a way to ease the pain of their loss, the group has needed to feel no less that it still has the capacity to heal and to provide order to those shaken by the chaos of death. That is why the community is ready and even eager to cooperate in the *shivah*, essentially taking care of all the mourners' spiritual and physical needs during these initial days of mourning following the funeral. The assumptions here are that by helping to mend and renew the bereaved, the group could in the process mend and renew its collective self. As such it asserts that in spite of death's entry into our lives, as a community we can still offer the benefits of solidarity. Moreover, the group feels whole again because those who have been torn away by death and grief are now moving past that breach: the dead into memory and the bereaved into the healing of mourning.

For all this to happen, expressions of hostility and conflict within the community have to be inhibited, and cooperation becomes essential. This is part of the process by which the community heals itself while it consoles the bereft. Thus shivah and the early days of mourning become a time when social antagonisms temporarily disappear as people commingle as one in the house of the mourner, often in an unending stream for much of the seven days. Everyone takes care of the mourners' every need, and public displays of anger and conflict are banished. Many who have dealt with the remains of 9/11 have articulated these sentiments, some even going so far as to suggest that they have not done enough.[14]

In the early months of the aftermath of 9/11 one did get the feeling that America in general and New York in particular was a gentler place and those who felt bereaved shared feelings of tenderness for one another. The inter-religious service at Yankee Stadium—a kind of collective residence of New Yorkers—in which diversity was celebrated in an atmosphere of acceptance and tolerance, in which the antagonisms of religious ideology and race as well as social class and ethnicity seemed to momentarily evaporate, symbolically expressed this.[15]

One cannot regard this period of intense sociation and communion, of benevolent and compassionate cooperation that marks the early stages of mourning, without also realizing how ephemeral it must be. With all its rivalries and antagonisms, the human community cannot long sustain this kind of purely solicitous relationship. Thus, shivah—the time when these are suspended—lasts no more than seven days, and sometimes less. One senses likewise that the feelings of mutual solicitude that characterized the initial response to September 11 have receded into increasingly hazy memory. Yet, there continue to be residues of them, perhaps a legacy of the open wound that remains at Ground Zero.[16]

We Are Not Alone

As the Jewish people has in its collective life found the imperative to survive and create ritual order as the best defense against the abiding anxiety of extinction that is so much a part of its collective historical consciousness, so it has in ritual response to death also created a series of practices meant to counteract the anxiety of Jewish precariousness, to repair morale, to reestablish order, and to insure the continuity of life, collective life in particular.[17] A Jew has died, but the Jews come together, grieve for the loss, support the bereaved, and remind one another that they and the rest of the Jews have survived. "The snare is broken but we have escaped," as the Psalmist writes and as Jewish tradition has the mourners repeat at the close of the funeral. And we have escaped with the help of the other Jews who live.

As a people, Americans do not have the same familiarity with and anxiety about death and persecution. Our most significant encounter with national mortality came as a result of our own doing in the Civil War. Nor have we known persecution and exile; we are not a people who have very often felt ensnared. Rather the American experience is one of triumph and power, and as a nation of immigrants, of new beginnings. Yet when we *have* felt ensnared—at Pearl Harbor, in Vietnam, and most recently on September 11—that feeling has engendered within us the need to stress our collective being. What made Vietnam so traumatic and difficult was the nation's inability to reach a collective consensus and feeling of solidarity so that we could "escape" the snare. But following 9/11, as we did after Pearl Harbor, the American people have once again been able to build upon the commemorations and feelings that assure us that "we are not alone." Indeed, in the immediate aftermath of the attacks in 2001, not only did Americans express solidarity, but, as earlier noted, most of the nations of the world expressed solidarity with America.[18] These feelings of solidarity remain essential for the collective emergence from the anxieties stimulated by 9/11 and its aftermath.

Jews do not simply bury the dead and forget them. While the dead are given their due, treated with the utmost respect, and eased into an otherworldly order, much more time and effort is expended among Jews in demonstrating that there is "a continuing community of the living and the dead."[19] *Kaddish*, the mantra-like memorial prayer recited by mourners, *yahrzeit*, the annual commemoration, *Yizkor*, the recollection of the dead at the holidays, and a variety of other practices extend the ties between the living and those they mourn in a series of continuing commemorations. Furthermore, in this continuing relationship, the dead are able to exert influence over the religious and social life of the living.

In what may be one of the great ironies of life, a Jew's death often brings about in the community of the bereaved a Jewish cultural, social, and religious renaissance and communal integration greater than he or she could ever accomplish during his or her lifetime. Out of the concern with the dead come Jewish assembly, study, prayer, and sometimes even a greater fidelity to Jewish goals. Never more powerfully are they are bonded together. On the individual level, even those who normally eschew or ignore religion, ritual, tradition, and Jewish custom often find themselves turning toward Judaism and the Jewish community in the face of death and in the desire to deal with it. And in collective life, Jewish behavior is intensified by the encounter with and effort to overcome death. In a sense, what the group does for the mourner and itself is an extension of what they wish they could also do for the one being mourned: *bring about repair*.

Much the same holds true for Americans following September 11. The continuing commemorations, concern with memorials, and expressions of mourning have, at least so far, contributed to a religious or spiritual renaissance (some have called this the a "Second Great Awakening," a religious revival to rival the so-called Great Awakening of 1735-4) and communal integration greater than we have seen in this country for many years—although the unilateralist actions by the Bush-Cheney administration and partisan politics have threatened this solidarity ands spirituality. If these divisions do not grow destructively malevolent, this integration and solidarity could turn out to be the national repair Americans seem to feel they so desperately need.

Sacred Ground and the Continuity of Life

Just as religions have sacred sites, so for the bereaved the final resting place of their dead becomes a special sacred place, somewhere to go to visit their dead. And on the eve of holy days, or around the time of yahrzeit, the anniversary of the death is the traditional time for a visit. The visit is of course a kind of worshipful personal pilgrimage, an opportunity to encounter the presence of the dead in a palpable way. In their sanctified places, the dead are, however, no longer a malevolent presence among the living. Visiting them is a way to demonstrate that while life goes on, they are not forgotten. Indeed, in some ways those memorial places give them a life greater than they had when they were still among the living. As Henry David Thoreau long ago noted: "Who is most dead—a hero by whose monument you stand, or his descendants of whom you have never heard?"

But the trip to these grounds is not just an occasion for worship, pilgrimage, or to somehow inform the spirits of the dead that they are not forgotten; it is also an opportunity for the living to celebrate their own escape from death. I am suggesting that those who survive death return to the dead not just to recall them but in a sense to recall that they are still alive, they and their memories of the deceased. In so doing they may come to understand the double truth of that verse repeated at the funeral: "The snare is broken, and we have escaped." We are not dead or deadened; nor our dead buried and forgotten; we are human beings, still alive to one another.

Perhaps this too is behind the unending trips that many have made and continue to make to Ground Zero. But the hole is still there, and with it the anxiety that perhaps we have not yet escaped the snare of death nor have those we have lost been properly mourned. Perhaps the great concern that so many have expressed about how best to rebuild this site and how to mark what happened here is what still holds us all in thrall. As a people, we await that memorial when at last we hope we shall be able to re-knit the fabric of who we are, when at last our mourning will have run its course, and we will have a new birth of life.

Notes

1. Robert Hertz, *A Contribution to the Study of the Collective Representation of Death*, trans. Rodney and Claudia Needham (Glencoe: Free Press, 1960), p. 77.
2. Ibid., p. 78.
3. Emile Durkheim, *The Elementary Forms of the Religious Life*, trans. J. W. Swain (New York: Free Press, 1965), p. 240.
4. B.T. *Moed Katan* 21b
5. The decline (to some the "squandering") of that international sympathy in the months

and years following 9/11/2001 has undoubtedly diminished the collective feelings among some Americans.

6. On "liminality," the state of being of being betwixt and between, no longer what one once was and not yet what one shall ultimately become, see Arnold van Gennep, *The Rites of Passage*, trans. Monika Vizedom and Gabrielle Caffee (Chicago: University of Chicago Press, 1960). Also Victor Turner, *Dramas, Fields and Metaphors* (Ithaca: Cornell University Press, 1974).
7. See the article by Charles Strozier elsewhere in this volume.
8. Lawrence Hoffman, *The Art of Public Prayer* (Washington, DC: The Pastoral Press, 1988), p. 107.
9. See Strozier.
10. Raymond Firth, *Elements of Social Organization* (London: Henry E. Walter Ltd, 1951), p. 64. See also David G. Mandelbaum "Social Uses of Funeral Rites," in Herman Feifel, ed., *The Meaning of Death* (New York: McGraw Hill, 1959), p. 189.
11. That there is a common impulse to follow a beloved who has died is amply illustrated in the literature on bereavement. See Howard Becker, "The Sorrow of Bereavement," in Hendrik M. Ruitenbeek, ed., *Death: Interpretations* (New York: Dell, 1969), pp. 195-216, esp. p. 204.
12. See the article by Ilana Harlow elsewhere in this volume.
13. S-A. Goldberg, *Crossing the Jabbok: Illness and Death in Ashkenazi Judiasm in 16th-19th Century Prague*, trans. C. Cosman (Berkeley: University of California Press, 1996), p. 134.
14. See Warren Spielberg, elsewhere in this volume.
15. Yet unlike the later service for the victims of the Columbia Space Shuttle disaster, when much of same happened, albeit on a national stage, the service for the 9/11 victims did not provide the collective closure that was possible after the shuttle service. In the case of the shuttle, by the time of the service all the victims had been identified and laid to rest, while at the 9/11 Yankee Stadium gathering that process remained unresolved.
16. The victims of the Pentagon do not figure in as prominently here because that gaping wound was swiftly and successfully repaired, while the site of the twin towers and the question of what will rise there remain open.
17. "Death represents a threat to the existence of the society and that is why every society has laws of mourning whose objective is not simply to offer support to the bereaved but as well to set the general order and organization of mourning." Eliezer Witztum and Ruth Malkinson, "Bereavement and Commemoration in Israel: The Dual Face of the National Myth," Ruth Malkinson, Simon Rubin, and Eliezer Witztum, eds., *Loss and Bereavement in Jewish Society in Israel* (Tel Aviv: Jerusalem: Ministry of Defense, 1993), p. 237.
18. There have been some who have argued that the unilateralism of the war in Iraq has squandered these feelings, while others have said that it was the residue of powerful collective feelings that enabled the nation to undertake this war even in the absence of worldwide support.
19. Thomas Laqueur, "The Sound of Voices Intoning Names." *London Review of Books* 19.11 (1996), p. xi.

Contributors

Henry Abramovitch is a psychologist and anthropologist living and working in Jerusalem who is on the faculty of the medical school of Tel Aviv University. He is also the author of *The First Father Abraham.*

Neil Gillman is a rabbi and theologian on the faculty of the Jewish Theological Seminary of America. He is the author of *The Way into Encountering God in Judaism*, *The Death of Death: Resurrection and Immortality in Jewish Thought*, and *Sacred Fragments: Recovering Theology for the Modern Jew*, among others, and a regular contributor to the *New York Jewish Week.*

Ilana Harlow, a folklorist, is coauthor with Steve Zeitlin of *Giving a Voice to Sorrow: Personal Responses to Death and Mourning*. She works as a folk life specialist at the Library of Congress. She has served as folk arts program director on the Queens Council on the Arts. She has presented a program on "Personal Responses to Death and Mourning" on the American Psychological Foundation radio series *Recovering America*.

Samuel Heilman, Distinguished Professor of Sociology at Queens College and holder of the Harold M. Proshansky Chair of Jewish Studies at the City University of New York is author of, among others, *When a Jew Dies*, winner of the National Jewish Book Award and the Koret Prize for Literature, *Defenders of the Faith*, *The Gate Behind the Wall*, winner of a Present Tense Jewish Book Award, *A Walker in Jerusalem*, winner of a National Jewish Book Award, and *Portrait of American Jews*, winner of the Gratz College Tuttleman Library Centennial Award.

Robert Jay Lifton, Distinguished Professor Emeritus at John Jay College City University of New York and Harvard University, is the author of *Living and Dying*, *Thought Reform and the Psychology of Totalism*, *Death in Life: Survivors of Hiroshima*, *History and Human Survival*, and many more.

Thomas Lynch is an undertaker and poet who is the author of three collections of poetry: *Skating with Heather Grace*, *Grimalkin & Other Poems*, and *Still Life in Milford*. His collection of essays, *The Undertaking—Life Studies from the Dismal Trade*, won the Heartland Prize for non-fiction, the American Book Award, and was a finalist for the National Book Award. It has been translated into seven languages. A second collection of essays, *Bodies in Motion and at Rest*, won the Great Lakes Book Award. His work has appeared in the *New Yorker*, *Poetry*, the *Paris Review*, *Harper's*, *Esquire*, *Newsweek*, the *Washington Post*, the *New York Times*, the *L.A. Times*, the *Irish Times*, and the *Times* of London.

Ruth Malkinson is at the School of Social Work of Tel Aviv University.

Peter Metcalf, professor of anthropology at the University of Virginia, is author (with Richard Huntington) of *Celebrations of Death: The Anthropology of Mortuary Ritual*, and of *They Lie, We Lie: Getting on with Anthropology*, *A Borneo Journey into Death: Berawan Eschatology from its Rituals*, as well as numerous articles and reviews.

Robert A. Neimeyer holds a Dunavant University Professorship in the Department of Psychology, University of Memphis, in Memphis, Tennessee, where he also maintains an active private practice. He is the author of seventeen books, including *Constructions of Disorder*, *Meaning Reconstruction and the Experience of Loss*, and *Constructivism in Psychotherapy* (all with the American Psychological Association), and *Lessons of Loss: A Guide to Coping*. He is editor of both the *Journal of Constructivist Psychology* and *Death Studies*.

Paul C. Rosenblatt, professor in the Department of Family Social Science, University of Minnesota, is author most recently of *Help Your Marriage Survive the Death of a Child*, *Parent Grief: Narra-*

tives of Loss and Relationship, and "Bereavement in Cross-Cultural Perspective," in C. D. Bryant, ed., *Handbook of Thanatology: Essays on the Social Study of Death.*

Simon Shimshon Rubin is on the faculty of the Department of Psychology of the University of Haifa.

Warren Spielberg, a psychologist in private practice in New York City, also teaches at the New School University. He has served as an adjunct clinical supervisor at Ferkauf Graduate School of Yeshiva University. He is author of "A Cultural Critique of Current Practices of Male Adolescent Identity Formation," in Arthur M. Horne and Mark S. Kiselica, eds., *Handbook of Counseling Boys and Adolescent Males: A Practitioner's Guide.*

Charles B. Strozier is professor of history, John Jay College and the Graduate Center, City University of New York, co-director, Center on Violence and Human Survival, John Jay College of Criminal Justice, City University of New York, and training and supervising psychoanalyst (with a practice) and senior faculty member, Training and Research Institute in Self Psychology, New York City. He is author of *Apocalypse: On the Psychology of Fundamentalism in America, Lincoln's Quest for Union: Public and Private Meanings*, and *Heinz Kohut and the Self: Psychoanalysis at the Millennium.*

Eliezer Witztum is a practicing psychiatrist at the Beer-Sheva Mental Health Center and professor at the Faculty of Health Sciences, Ben Gurion University of the Negev, Beer-Sheva, Israel.